GRE
高频真词表
便携版

北京新东方研发中心
韩 冰 潘晨光 编著

浙江教育出版社·杭州

图书在版编目(CIP)数据

GRE高频真词表便携版 / 北京新东方研发中心，韩冰，潘晨光编著. -- 杭州：浙江教育出版社，2017.8（2017.11重印）
ISBN 978-7-5536-5112-5

Ⅰ. ①G… Ⅱ. ①北… ②韩… ③潘… Ⅲ. ①GRE-词汇-自学参考资料 Ⅳ. ①H313

中国版本图书馆CIP数据核字(2016)第279259号

GRE高频真词表便携版
GRE GAOPIN ZHENCIBIAO BIANXIEBAN

北京新东方研发中心　韩　冰　潘晨光　编著

责任编辑	刘文芳
美术编辑	韩　波
封面设计	大愚设计
责任校对	罗　曼
责任印务	时小娟
出版发行	浙江教育出版社
	地址：杭州市天目山路40号
	邮编：310013
	电话：（0571）85170300－80928
	邮箱：dywh@xdf.cn
	网址：www.zjeph.com
印　刷	三河市良远印务有限公司
开　本	787mm×1096mm　1/32
成品尺寸	125mm×185mm
印　张	10.75
字　数	250 000
版　次	2017年8月第1版
印　次	2017年11月第2次印刷
标准书号	ISBN 978-7-5536-5112-5
定　价	25.00元

前　言

很多同学在备考 GRE 期间，最头疼的问题往往就是复杂繁多的词汇。2013 年，韩老师和我在实际教学过程中发现，同学们经常反映手里词汇资料词条多则七千有余，记忆负担沉重；少则在实际考试中复现率低，背诵性价比不高。我们在想，为何不基于每场考试的真实考情，整理一份真正针对现行 GRE 考试的词汇书呢？于是《GRE 高频真词表》（以下简称"佛脚词汇"）计划应运而生。

相信刚走出考场的同学，对于本次考试里那些晦涩难懂的词汇一定记忆犹新，佛脚词汇表希望能够展示那些真正在考试中有价值的词汇。经过 2013~2014 年的积累，佛脚词汇初版词表共整理全年难词 1163 个，并有针对性地给出了同义词词对 274 对，让大家在解答相关题目时更加游刃有余。我们将初版词汇表汇总成 PDF，于网上免费公开，当时的定位是同学们考前两个月必备的高性价比词汇材料。与此同时，恰逢北京新东方学校的圣诞班与寒假班，经过线下与线上成百上千名同学的集体试用，大家在肯定之余，也给出了诸多宝贵的改进意见，这坚定了我们打磨完善佛脚词汇表的信心。

2013~2017 年收集记录难词从未间断，我们于每个季度分别免费推出了 2.0~6.0 版本，词汇数目增加 1700 个，同义词词对增加至 550 对。此时，我们已经发现，每次有效收集整理的难词数明显减少；从同学们的实际反馈也看出，佛脚词汇相较于手中其它资料，词汇复现率更高。为了使词汇书针对性更强，我们决定在原有的佛脚词库基础上，整理加入常考短语与阅读题目中的难词，最终收录主词 2400 余个，同义词词对 850 余对。

这是一本经历了多个网络公开版才得以浓缩出来的词汇材料。至此，我们不妨总结一下本书都有哪些优势：

- 从 GRE 改革以来积累至今，选择真正意义上可能的 GRE 重点词汇，剔除无意义的词汇，切实反映词汇考点动向。
- 特别添加常考"六选二"同义词词对，使背诵有的放矢，所背即所考。
- 英文释义参考韦氏词典与美国传统词典，中文释义力图忠实于语境。

佛脚词汇包含着一种和 GRE 战斗的精神，代表着我们竭尽全力减轻大家考试负担的同时，又保证和考试高度统一的不懈追求，也是我们六年多来教学与实战经验的浓缩。我们当然不会就此满足，GRE 佛脚词汇将继续不断地迭代更新下去。在此，诚挚感谢读者们的积极反馈，以及北京新东方程黛苑老师与武汉新东方冷楠老师的诸多宝贵意见与建议。

语言是活的，由于每个人对于词汇的理解仁者见仁，又限于实际教学与考试经验，所以在实际使用过程中难免会遇到中文翻译上的一些分歧。如果读者朋友有更好的理解方式，望不吝赐教，共同进步。《GRE 高频真词表》读者意见反馈邮箱：fojiaocihui@163.com。

韩冰　潘晨光
于北京新东方大厦

使用说明

便携版设计本着极简与方便携带的原则，删除了完整版中例句、派生词、反义词等总结，只保留了词汇的中英文释义与六选二词对整理，这两部分是全书的精华。为此，我们也专门给出了便携版的记忆方案，如下表格所示：

GRE 高频真词表：便携版记忆方案

	当日背诵	当日复习1	当日复习2	当日复习3	当日复习4
DAY-1	List 1~2	List 1~2			
DAY-2	List 3~4	List 1~2	List 3~4		
DAY-3	List 5~6	List 3~4	List 5~6		
DAY-4	List 7~8	List 1~2	List 5~6	List 7~8	
DAY-5	List 9~10	List 3~4	List 7~8	List 9~10	
DAY-6	List 11~12	List 5~6	List 9~10	List 11~12	
DAY-7	List 13~14	List 7~8	List 11~12	List 13~14	
DAY-8	List 15~16	List 1~2	List 9~10	List 13~14	List 15~16
DAY-9	List 17~18	List 3~4	List 11~12	List 15~16	List 17~18
DAY-10	List 19~20	List 5~6	List 13~14	List 17~18	List 19~20
DAY-11	List 21~22	List 7~8	List 15~16	List 19~20	List 21~22
DAY-12	List 23~24	List 9~10	List 17~18	List 21~22	List 23~24

《GRE 高频真词表》就是风靡网络的
"GRE 佛脚词汇表"正式版
扫码关注 GRE 佛脚词汇官方平台，获取最新资料
读者意见与建议反馈：fojiaocihui@163.com

目 录

Word List 1

音 频

divulge /dɪˈvʌldʒ/	中 *v.* 泄露
	英 to make known (something private or secret)
inadvertent /ˌɪnədˈvɜːrtənt/	中 *adj.* 粗心的，不留意的
	英 marked by or resulting from carelessness; negligent
	中 *adj.* 无意的
	英 not deliberate or considered; unintentional
panegyric /ˌpænəˈdʒɪrɪk/	中 *n.* 赞文，赞美
	英 a formal eulogistic composition intended as a public compliment
draconian /drəˈkoʊniən/	中 *adj.* 极其严苛的
	英 exceedingly harsh or very severe
hodgepodge /ˈhɑːdʒpɑːdʒ/	中 *n.* 混杂物，混合物
	英 a mixture of different things
incontrovertible /ˌɪnkɑːntrəˈvɜːrtəbl/	中 *adj.* 不容置疑的
	英 impossible to dispute
impartial /ɪmˈpɑːrʃl/	中 *adj.* 公正的，不偏不倚的
	英 not partial or biased
endemic /enˈdemɪk/	中 *adj.* 地方性的，流行的
	英 prevalent in or limited to a particular locality, region or people
	中 *adj.* 常见的（问题、情形）
	英 common in or inherent to an enterprise or situation
minuscule /ˈmɪnəskjuːl/	中 *adj.* 微小的
	英 very small and tiny

| lucrative /'luːkrətɪv/ | 中 adj. 盈利的，赚钱的 |
| | 英 producing wealth |

compensate /'kɑːmpenseɪt/	中 v. 弥补
	英 to offset an error, defect or undesired effect
	中 v. 抵消
	英 to serve as or provide a substitute or counter balance

discursive /dɪs'kɜːrsɪv/	中 adj. 杂乱无章的
	英 moving from topic to topic without order; rambling
	中 adj. 理性的
	英 marked by analytical reasoning

| presuppose /ˌpriːsə'pouz/ | 中 v. 假定 |
| | 英 to require as an antecedent in logic or fact |

| intermediary /ˌɪntər'miːdieri/ | 中 n. / adj.（作为）中间人（的） |
| | 英 adj. acting as a mediator |

| derogate /'derəgeɪt/ | 中 v. 贬低 |
| | 英 to cause to seem inferior |

| overbearing /ˌouvər'berɪŋ/ | 中 adj. 专横的，压倒性的 |
| | 英 often trying to control the behavior of other people in an annoying or unwanted way |

| zealous /'zeləs/ | 中 adj. 对（某人或偶像）狂热的 |
| | 英 marked by fervent partisanship for a person, a cause or an ideal |

extraneous /ɪk'streɪniəs/	中 adj. 不重要的，不相关的
	英 not important
	中 adj. 外部的
	英 coming from the outside

rehash /ˈriːhæʃ/	中 v. （没有实质改变地）重提 英 to bring forth again in another form without significant alteration
perfunctory /pərˈfʌŋktəri/	中 adj. 不走心的 英 acting with indifference, showing little interest or care
compound /ˈkɑːmpaʊnd/	中 v. 混合，合成 英 to form by combining separate things 中 v. 使…变糟糕 英 to make worse
envy /ˈenvi/	中 v. 嫉妒 英 to feel a desire to have what someone else has
defensive /dɪˈfensɪv/	中 adj. 被动防守的，防御的 英 in a situation which you are forced to defend or protect someone or something
unbounded /ʌnˈbaʊndɪd/	中 adj. 不受限制的，无限的 英 not limited in any way
specious /ˈspiːʃəs/	中 adj. 似是而非的 英 falsely appearing to be right
aimless /ˈeɪmləs/	中 adj. 漫无目的的 英 not having a goal or purpose
ingenuous /ɪnˈdʒenjuəs/	中 adj. 纯朴的，真诚的 英 having or showing the innocence, trust and honesty that young people often have
intrinsic /ɪnˈtrɪnsɪk/	中 adj. 核心的，内在的 英 belonging to the essential nature of a thing

inevitable
/ɪnˈevɪtəbl/
中 *adj.* 不可避免的，必然的
英 sure to happen

intransigent
/ɪnˈtrænzɪdʒənt/
中 *adj.* 不妥协的，固执的
英 completely unwilling to change

detached
/dɪˈtætʃt/
中 *adj.* 不受感情影响的，公正的
英 not influenced by emotions or personal interest
中 *adj.* 脱离的
英 not joined or connected

inveterate
/ɪnˈvetərət/
中 *adj.* 根深蒂固的
英 firmly and long established; deep-rooted
中 *adj.* 习惯性的
英 persisting in an ingrained habit; habitual

backhanded
/ˌbækˈhændɪd/
中 *adj.* 不直接的
英 oblique or indirect
中 *adj.* 含沙射影的，讽刺挖苦的
英 having derogatory or insulting implications

affable
/ˈæfəbl/
中 *adj.* 和蔼可亲的
英 easy and pleasant to speak to

whimsy
/ˈwɪmzi/
中 *n.* 突发奇想
英 an unusual, unexpected or fanciful idea

tenacious
/təˈneɪʃəs/
中 *adj.* 坚定的
英 very determined to do something
中 *adj.* 持续的
英 continuing for a long time

sardonic
/saːrˈdaːnɪk/
中 *adj.* 嘲讽的，讥笑的
英 scornfully or cynically mocking

skullduggery
/skʌlˈdʌgəri/
中 *n.* 欺骗，作假
英 secret or dishonest behavior or activity

legitimate /lɪ'dʒɪtɪmət/	中 adj. 合法的
	英 being in compliance with the law
	中 adj. 合理的
	英 valid or justifiable
	中 v. 使…合理，合法
	英 to make (something) real, accepted or official; to show that (something) is fair or reasonable
plagiarize /'pleɪdʒəraɪz/	中 v. 抄袭
	英 to reproduce or otherwise use as one's own
disavow /ˌdɪsə'vaʊ/	中 v. 否认
	英 to say that you are not responsible for
deplete /dɪ'pliːt/	中 v. 耗尽
	英 to use most or all of
ridicule /'rɪdɪkjuːl/	中 v. 嘲笑，耻笑
	英 to laugh at and make jokes about
undermine /ˌʌndər'maɪn/	中 v. 削弱
	英 to make (someone or something) weaker or less effective
self-serving /self'sɜːrvɪŋ/	中 adj. 自私的
	英 having or showing concern only about your own needs and interests
perishable /'perɪʃəbl/	中 adj. 易消亡的，易腐烂的
	英 likely to spoil or decay quickly
capricious /kə'prɪʃəs/	中 adj. 变化多端的
	英 changing often and quickly
egotism /'iːgoʊɪzəm/	中 n. 自大
	英 an inflated sense of one's own importance

unqualified /ˌʌnˈkwɑːlɪfaɪd/	中 *adj.* 完全的
	英 complete or total
	中 *adj.* 不合格的
	英 not having the skills, knowledge or experience needed to do a particular job or activity

| **magisterial** /ˌmædʒɪˈstɪriəl/ | 中 *adj.* 权威的 |
| | 英 authoritative |

| **chauvinistic** /ˌʃoʊvɪˈnɪstɪk/ | 中 *adj.* 盲目爱国的 |
| | 英 believing that your country is better than any other |

sleek /sliːk/	中 *adj.* 光滑的
	英 straight and smooth in design or shape
	中 *adj.* 时髦的，吸引人的
	英 stylish and attractive

| **astringent** /əˈstrɪndʒənt/ | 中 *adj.* 严厉的，尖刻的 |
| | 英 very critical in a sharp and often clever way |

| **ambivalent** /æmˈbɪvələnt/ | 中 *adj.* （情感、态度）矛盾的 |
| | 英 simultaneous and contradictory attitudes or feelings toward an object, person or action |

| **ameliorate** /əˈmiːliəreɪt/ | 中 *v.* 改善，提升 |
| | 英 to make better or more tolerable |

| **exemplar** /ɪgˈzemplɑːr/ | 中 *n.* 典型 |
| | 英 a typical example |

grudge /grʌdʒ/	中 *v.* 不愿给予或承认
	英 to be unwilling to give or admit
	中 *n.* 怨恨
	英 a deep-seated feeling of resentment or rancor

sweeping /'swiːpɪŋ/	中 *adj.* 广泛的 英 extensive 中 *adj.* 全面的 英 marked by wholesale and indiscriminate inclusion
extirpate /'ekstərpeɪt/	中 *v.* 根除 英 to destroy or remove completely
~~**parity**~~ /'pærəti/	中 *n.* 平等 英 equality
~~**utilitarian**~~ /juːtɪlɪ'teriən/	中 *adj.* 实用的 英 made to be useful rather than to be decorative or comfortable 中 *adj.* 功利的，实用主义的 英 of or relating to utilitarianism
~~**elicit**~~ /i'lɪsɪt/	中 *v.* 引起 英 to call forth or draw out
~~**intoxicate**~~ /ɪn'tɑːksɪkeɪt/	中 *v.* 使…陶醉，沉醉 英 to excite or elate to the point of enthusiasm or frenzy
~~**inchoate**~~ /ɪn'kouət/	中 *adj.* 早期的 英 being in a beginning or early stage 中 *adj.* 不成熟的，仅初具规模的 英 imperfectly informed or developed
~~**rebuff**~~ /rɪ'bʌf/	中 *n.* （粗鲁的）回复 英 a blunt or abrupt repulse or refusal 中 *v.* （粗鲁地）拒绝 英 to reject bluntly, often disdainfully
~~**construe**~~ /kən'struː/	中 *v.* 理解 英 to understand the meaning of

fallacy
/'fæləsi/
中 *n.* 错误，谬论
英 a false or mistaken idea

increment
/'ɪŋkrəmənt/
中 *n.* 增长，递增
英 the action or process of increasing especially in quantity or value

deteriorate
/dɪ'tɪriəreɪt/
中 *v.* 恶化
英 to make (something) worse

grandiose
/'grændioʊs/
中 *adj.* 宏伟壮观的
英 impressive because of uncommon largeness, scope, effect or grandeur
中 *adj.* 妄自尊大的
英 excessive self-importance or affected grandeur

truncate
/'trʌŋkeɪt/
中 *v.* 缩短
英 to make shorter

haphazard
/hæp'hæzərd/
中 *adj.* 无序的，凌乱的
英 having no plan, order or direction

quizzical
/'kwɪzɪkl/
中 *adj.* 诧异的；感到好奇的
英 expressive of puzzlement, curiosity or disbelief

provincial
/prə'vɪnʃl/
中 *adj.* 眼光狭隘的
英 limited in outlook
中 *adj.* 乡下的
英 lacking the polish of urban society

insensitive
/ɪn'sensətɪv/
中 *adj.* 漠视的，不在乎的
英 not responsive or susceptible

shackle
/'ʃækl/
中 *v. / n.* 阻碍
英 *v.* to deprive of freedom especially of action by means of restrictions or handicaps

cumbersome
/ˈkʌmbərsəm/
中 adj. 笨拙的
英 unwieldy because of heaviness and bulk

encomium
/enˈkoʊmiəm/
中 n. 赞美
英 glowing and warm enthusiastic praise

decelerate
/ˌdiːˈseləreɪt/
中 v. 减缓
英 to decrease the rate of or the progress of

revitalize
/ˌriːˈvaɪtəlaɪz/
中 v. 使…复活
英 to make active, healthy or energetic again

indisputable
/ˌɪndɪˈspjuːtəbl/
中 adj. 不容置疑的
英 impossible to question or doubt

roost
/ruːst/
中 v. 栖息
英 to settle down for rest or sleep

corroborate
/kəˈrɑːbəreɪt/
中 v. 佐证，提供证据证明
英 to support with evidence or authority

proclivity
/prəˈklɪvəti/
中 n. 倾向，偏好
英 a strong natural liking for something

hysteria
/hɪˈstɪriə/
中 n. 歇斯底里，情绪失控
英 excessive or uncontrollable emotion, such as fear or panic

speculate
/ˈspekjuleɪt/
中 v. 推测，猜测
英 to think about something and make guesses about it

conducive
/kənˈduːsɪv/
中 adj. 有益的，有帮助的
英 tending to promote or assist

vexation
/vekˈseɪʃn/
中 n. 烦恼
英 something that worries or annoys you

disdain /dɪsˈdeɪn/	中 v. 蔑视，鄙视
	英 to strongly dislike or disapprove of (someone or something)
caterwaul /ˈkætərwɔːl/	中 v. 发出难听的声音
	英 to make a very loud and unpleasant sound
	中 v. 强烈抗议
	英 to protest or complain noisily
efficacious /ˌefɪˈkeɪʃəs/	中 adj. 有效果的
	英 having the power to produce a desired result or effect
alienate /ˈeɪliəneɪt/	中 v. 疏远
	英 to cause (someone) to feel that she or he no longer belongs in a particular group, society, etc.
	中 v. 使…变得不友好
	英 to cause (someone) to stop being friendly, helpful, etc., towards you
analgesic /ˌænəlˈdʒiːzɪk/	中 n. 止痛药
	英 a drug that relieves pain
	中 adj. 止痛的
	英 capable of relieving pain
anatomize /əˈnætəˌmaɪz/	中 v. 解剖
	英 to cut in pieces in order to display or examine the structure and use of the parts
	中 v. 分析
	英 to analyze
embargo /ɪmˈbɑːrgoʊ/	中 n. 贸易禁令
	英 a government order that limits trade in some way

contemplate
/ˈkɑːntəmpleɪt/
中 v. 深入思考
英 to think deeply or carefully about

dogmatic
/dɔːgˈmætɪk/
中 adj. 教条的
英 expressing personal opinions or beliefs as if they are certainly correct and cannot be doubted

concrete
/ˈkɑːŋkriːt/
中 adj. 真实的
英 naming a real thing or class of things
中 adj. 详细的
英 specific or particular

equitable
/ˈekwɪtəbl/
中 adj. 平等的，公平的
英 just or fair

fervent
/ˈfɜːrvənt/
中 adj. 情感强烈的，热烈的
英 exhibiting or marked by great intensity of feeling

alleviate
/əˈliːvieɪt/
中 v. 减轻
英 to reduce the pain or trouble of

contagious
/kənˈteɪdʒəs/
中 adj. 传染性的，有感染力的
英 communicable by contact

pedantic
/pɪˈdæntɪk/
中 adj. 卖弄知识的
英 narrowly, stodgily and often ostentatiously learned

unwieldy
/ʌnˈwiːldi/
中 adj. 体积庞大而笨重的
英 difficult to handle, control or deal with because of being large, heavy or complex

vociferous
/voʊˈsɪfərəs/
中 adj. 吵吵嚷嚷的
英 expressing feelings or opinions in a very loud or forceful way

~~profess~~ /prə'fes/	中 *v.* 宣称 英 to say or declare (something) openly
~~obeisance~~ /oʊ'biːsns/	中 *n.* 尊敬，敬意 英 respect for someone or something
~~diffuse~~ /dɪ'fjuːs/	中 *v.* 扩散 英 to spread about or scatter; disseminate 中 *adj.* 啰唆的 英 characterized by verbosity; wordy
✓ fulminate /'fʌlmɪneɪt/	中 *v.* 抨击，辱骂 英 to utter or send out with denunciation
~~voluble~~ /'vɑːljəbl/	中 *adj.* 健谈的，话多的 英 talking a lot in an energetic and rapid way
✓ sterling /'stɜːrlɪŋ/	中 *adj.* 优秀的，一流的 英 conforming to the highest standard
~~surmount~~ /sər'maʊnt/	中 *v.* 克服，战胜 英 to prevail over 中 *v.* 站在…的顶峰 英 to stand or lie at the top of

Word List 2

音频

prying /'praɪɪŋ/	中 *adj.* 窥视的 英 trying to find out about other people's private lives
inhibit /ɪn'hɪbɪt/	中 *v.* 抑制，限制 英 to hold in check
censure /'senʃər/	中 *v.* 指责 英 to criticize severely; blame
peripatetic /ˌperɪpə'tetɪk/	中 *adj.* 巡游的 英 itinerant
stringent /'strɪndʒənt/	中 *adj.* 非常严格的 英 very strict or severe
dwindle /'dwɪndl/	中 *v.* 减少，下降 英 to gradually become smaller
underrate /ˌʌndə'reɪt/	中 *v.* 低估 英 to rate or value (someone or something) too low
incursion /ɪn'kɜːrʒn/	中 *n.* 侵入，侵犯 英 a hostile entrance into a territory 中 *n.* 进入 英 an entering in or into
pastiche /pæ'stiːʃ/	中 *n.* 【贬】模仿作品 英 a work that imitates the style of previous works 中 *n.* 混合物 英 a mixture of different things
dishearten /dɪs'hɑːrtn/	中 *v.* 使…士气低落 英 to cause (a person or group of people) to lose hope, enthusiasm or courage

emulate /ˈemjuleɪt/	中 *v.* 通过模仿而超越，模仿 英 to strive to equal or excel
adduce /əˈduːs/	中 *v.* 引用…证明 英 to mention or provide (something such as a fact or example) as evidence or proof to support an argument
emblematic /ˌembləˈmætɪk/	中 *adj.* 象征的，代表的 英 representing something (such as an idea, state or emotion) that cannot be seen by itself
indict /ɪnˈdaɪt/	中 *v.* 指控 英 to charge with a fault or offense
discontinue /ˌdɪskənˈtɪnjuː/	中 *v.* 终止 英 to end (something)
wary /ˈweri/	中 *adj.* 谨慎小心的 英 marked by keen caution, cunning and watchfulness especially in detecting and escaping danger
opprobrium /əˈproʊbriəm/	中 *n.* 辱骂 英 very strong disapproval or criticism of a person or thing especially by a large number of people
aesthetic /esˈθetɪk/	中 *adj.* 美学的 英 of or relating to art or beauty
expedite /ˈekspədaɪt/	中 *v.* 加速，加快 英 to cause (something) to happen faster

captivate /ˈkæptɪveɪt/	中 v. 吸引
	英 to attract and hold the attention of (someone) by being interesting, pretty, etc.

irreversible /ˌɪrɪˈvɜːrsəbl/	中 adj. 不可逆的
	英 impossible to change back to a previous condition or state

emotive /iˈmoʊtɪv/	中 adj. 引起情绪的
	英 causing strong emotions for or against something

refine /rɪˈfaɪn/	中 v. 提纯
	英 to remove the unwanted substances in (something)
	中 v. 改进，改善
	英 to improve (something) by making small changes

exhilarate /ɪgˈzɪləreɪt/	中 v. 使…喜悦或兴奋
	英 to cause (someone) to feel very happy and excited

solitary /ˈsɑːləteri/	中 adj. 单独的
	英 not involving or including anyone or anything else

jar /dʒɑːr/	中 v. 使…不安
	英 to make (someone) feel uneasy
	中 v. 抵触，冲突
	英 to clash or conflict

unfettered /ʌnˈfetərd/	中 adj. 不受限制的，自由的
	英 not controlled or restricted

flummery /ˈflʌməri/	中 n. 假恭维
	英 meaningless or deceptive language

implacable /ɪmˈplækəbl/	中 *adj.* 不能安抚的，毫不妥协的 英 opposed to someone or something in a very angry or determined way that cannot be changed
~~arduous~~ /ˈɑːrdʒuəs/	中 *adj.* 困难的 英 demanding great effort or labor; difficult 中 *adj.* 艰难的 英 testing severely the powers of endurance; strenuous
~~conciliatory~~ /kənˈsɪliətɔːri/	中 *adj.* 安抚的，调和的 英 having the intention or effect of making angry people calm
~~optimism~~ /ˈɑːptɪmɪzəm/	中 *n.* 乐观 英 a feeling or belief that good things will happen in the future
~~vindicate~~ /ˈvɪndɪkeɪt/	中 *v.* 证明…的清白 英 to show that (someone) should not be blamed for a crime, mistake, etc.
~~malady~~ /ˈmælədi/	中 *n.* 疾病 英 a disease or illness
~~warrant~~ /ˈwɔːrənt/	中 *v.* 保证 英 to give assurance 中 *v.* 为…提供依据 英 to serve as or give adequate ground or reason for
~~puncture~~ /ˈpʌŋktʃər/	中 *v.* 刺穿 英 to make a hole in (something) with a sharp point 中 *v.* 削弱，使…无效 英 to make useless or ineffective as if by a puncture

ascribe /ə'skraɪb/	中 *v.* 归因于 英 to think of as coming from a specified cause, source or author
clandestine /klæn'destɪn/	中 *adj.* 秘密的，隐蔽的 英 done secretly
equivocal /ɪ'kwɪvəkl/	中 *adj.* 模棱两可的，有歧义的 英 having two or more possible meanings
elucidate /i'luːsɪdeɪt/	中 *v.* 阐释，阐明 英 to make (something that is hard to understand) clear or easy to understand
propaganda /ˌprɑːpə'gændə/	中 *n.* 政治宣传 英 ideas or statements that are often false or exaggerated and that are spread in order to help a cause, a political leader, a government, etc.
putative /'pjuːtətɪv/	中 *adj.* 公认的，假定的 英 generally believed or assumed to be something
conjecture /kən'dʒektʃər/	中 *v. / n.* 猜测 英 *v.* to form an opinion or idea without proof or sufficient evidence
coalesce /ˌkoʊə'les/	中 *v.* 聚合，团结 英 to come together to form one group or mass
tractable /'træktəbl/	中 *adj.* 易管理的，易控制的 英 easily managed or controlled
warble /'wɔːrbl/	中 *v.* 低吟浅唱 英 to sing a melody of low pleasing sounds

~~knotty~~ /ˈnɑːti/	中 *adj.* 复杂的 英 difficult or complicated
~~dichotomy~~ /daɪˈkɑːtəmi/	中 *n.* 矛盾的事物 英 something with seemingly contradictory qualities 中 *n.* 一分为二 英 bifurcation
restive /ˈrestɪv/	中 *adj.* 不服管理的 英 stubbornly resisting control 中 *adj.* 不安的，没有耐心的 英 marked by impatience or uneasiness
~~courteous~~ /ˈkɜːrtiəs/	中 *adj.* 有礼貌的 英 very polite in a way that shows respect
~~invigorate~~ /ɪnˈvɪɡəreɪt/	中 *v.* 使…有活力 英 to give life and energy to
truculent /ˈtrʌkjələnt/	中 *adj.* 好争斗的 英 easily annoyed or angered and likely to argue 中 *adj.* 言语刻薄的 英 scathingly harsh
~~congenial~~ /kənˈdʒiːniəl/	中 *adj.* 友善的 英 very friendly 中 *adj.* 和气的，令人愉悦的 英 pleasant and harmonious 中 *adj.* 性格相似的 英 having the same nature, disposition or tastes
~~insouciance~~ /ɪnˈsuːsiəns/	中 *n.* 无忧无虑，不操心 英 a feeling of not worrying about anything

~~devastate~~ /'devəsteɪt/	中 *v.* 严重破坏 英 to destroy much or most of (something) 中 *v.* 使…痛苦 英 to cause (someone) to feel extreme emotional pain
keen /kiːn/	中 *adj.* 对…感兴趣 英 very excited about and interested in something 中 *adj.* 犀利的，尖刻的 英 pungent; acrid 中 *adj.* 聪明的，敏锐的 英 having or marked by intellectual quickness and acuity
ethos /'iːθɑːs/	中 *n.* （团体的）气质，氛围，信仰等 英 the distinguishing character, sentiment, moral nature or guiding beliefs of a person, group or organization
flagrant /'fleɪɡrənt/	中 *adj.* 臭名昭著的 英 so bad as to be impossible to overlook
solitude /'sɑːlətuːd/	中 *n.* 孤独 英 a state or situation in which you are alone usually because you want to be
anachronism /ə'nækrənɪzəm/	中 *n.* 时代错乱 英 something (such as a word, an object or an event) that is mistakenly placed in a time where It does not belong in a story, movie, etc. 中 *n.* 不合时宜，过时 英 one that is out of its proper or chronological order, especially a person or practice that belongs to an earlier time

turbid
/'tɜːrbɪd/

中 *adj.* 浑浊的
英 having sediment or foreign particles stirred up or suspended
中 *adj.* 混乱的
英 in a state of turmoil

confine
/kən'faɪn/

中 *v.* 限制
英 to keep within limits

venerate
/'venəreɪt/

中 *v.* 尊敬
英 to feel or show deep respect for

premeditate
/ˌpriː'medɪteɪt/

中 *v.* 预谋，提前谋划
英 to think, consider or deliberate beforehand

insular
/'ɪnsələr/

中 *adj.* 孤立的
英 separated from other people or cultures
中 *adj.* 思想狭隘、守旧的
英 not knowing or interested in new or different ideas

consolidate
/kən'sɑːlɪdeɪt/

中 *v.* 巩固
英 to make (something, such as a position of power or control) stronger or more secure

upheaval
/ʌp'hiːvl/

中 *n.* （引起混乱的）剧变
英 a major change or period of change that causes a lot of conflict, confusion, anger, etc.

unyielding
/ʌn'jiːldɪŋ/

中 *adj.* 不妥协的，固执的
英 not changing or stopping

mendacious
/men'deɪʃəs/

中 *adj.* 欺骗的，不诚实的
英 not honest

sonorous
/'sɑːnərəs/

中 *adj.* 声音洪亮的
英 having a sound that is deep, loud, and pleasant

fertile
/ˈfɜːrtl/
中 *adj.* 多产的（即可指农作物，也可以指思想、想法）
英 producing a large amount of something

decadent
/ˈdekədənt/
中 *adj.* （思想）堕落的，颓废的
英 having low morals and a great love of pleasure, money, fame, etc.
中 *adj.* 三俗的 (庸俗、低俗、媚俗的)
英 attractive to people of low morals who are only interested in pleasure

indispensable
/ˌɪndɪˈspensəbl/
中 *adj.* 不可缺少的
英 extremely important and necessary

covert
/ˈkoʊvɜːrt/
中 *adj.* 秘密的，隐蔽的
英 secret or hidden

instinct
/ˈɪnstɪŋkt/
中 *n.* 本能
英 a natural or inherent aptitude, impulse or capacity

discern
/dɪˈsɜːrn/
中 *v.* 识别，察觉
英 to detect or recognize

orientation
/ˌɔːriənˈteɪʃn/
中 *n.* 取向，态度
英 a usually general or lasting direction of thought, inclination or interest
中 *n.* 方向
英 the relative position or direction of something

riddle
/ˈrɪdl/
中 *n.* 难题，谜题
英 a mystifying, misleading or puzzling question posed as a problem to be solved or guessed

jejune
/dʒɪˈdʒuːn/
中 *adj.* 无聊的
英 not interesting

clownish
/'klaʊnɪʃ/
中 adj. 小丑般的，滑稽的
英 acting in a silly or funny way

indifferent
/ɪn'dɪfrənt/
中 adj. 冷漠的
英 not interested in or concerned about something
中 adj. 客观公正的
英 characterized by a lack of partiality; unbiased

lethargic
/lə'θɑːrdʒɪk/
中 adj. 无生气的，缺乏热情的
英 feeling a lack of energy or a lack of interest in doing things

clique
/kliːk/
中 n. 小团体
英 a small exclusive group of friends or associates

fungible
/'fʌndʒəbl/
中 adj. 可替代的
英 interchangeable or replaceable

complimentary
/ˌkɑːmplɪ'mentri/
中 adj. 赞美的
英 expressing praise or admiration for someone or something

empirical
/ɪm'pɪrɪkl/
中 adj. 根据观察或经验的
英 originating in or based on observation or experience

conform
/kən'fɔːrm/
中 v. 符合，遵守
英 to obey or agree with something
中 v. 随大流，从众
英 to do what other people do

solicitous
/sə'lɪsɪtəs/
中 adj. 关心的，殷切的
英 showing great attention or concern to another

Word List 3

音频

~~insult~~ /ɪn'sʌlt/	中 v. 侮辱，辱骂 英 to do or say something that is offensive to (someone)
~~acrimony~~ /'ækrɪmoʊni/	中 n. 尖刻，犀利 英 harsh or biting sharpness especially of words, manner or disposition
~~misconception~~ /ˌmɪskən'sepʃn/	中 n. 误解，错觉 英 a false idea or belief
~~mundane~~ /mʌn'deɪn/	中 adj. 平凡的，无聊的 英 dull and ordinary
~~ambiguous~~ /æm'bɪgjuəs/	中 adj. 有歧义的，模糊不清的 英 able to be understood in more than one way
~~allure~~ /ə'lʊr/	中 v. 引诱 英 to entice by charm or attraction
cagey /'keɪdʒi/	中 adj. 小心的；谨慎的 英 wary; careful 中 adj. 狡猾的；机敏的 英 crafty; shrewd
~~heresy~~ /'herəsi/	中 n. 与主流观点相悖的观点 英 a belief or opinion that does not agree with the official belief or opinion of a particular religion

~~parsimony~~ /'pɑːrsəmouni/	中 n. 吝啬 英 the quality of being very unwilling to spend money
~~cunning~~ /'kʌnɪŋ/	中 adj. 狡猾机智的 英 getting what is wanted in a clever and often deceptive way 中 adj. 技艺高超的 英 dexterous or crafty in the use of special resources
~~highlight~~ /'haɪlaɪt/	中 v. 使⋯突出 英 to make or try to make people notice or be aware of
~~judicious~~ /dʒuˈdɪʃəs/	中 adj. 有正确判断力的 英 having or showing good judgment
~~disguise~~ /dɪsˈgaɪz/	中 v. 隐藏，伪装 英 to obscure the existence, true state or character of
~~far-fetched~~ /fɑːrˈfetʃt/	中 adj. 不切实际的 英 not likely to happen or be true
~~eclipse~~ /ɪˈklɪps/	中 v. 使⋯不重要 英 to make (something) less important or popular 中 v. 超出 英 to surpass 中 n. 日食，月食
~~impulsive~~ /ɪmˈpʌlsɪv/	中 adj. 冲动的，不加思索的 英 doing things or tending to do things suddenly and without careful thought
~~exculpate~~ /'ekskʌlpeɪt/	中 v. 开脱罪责 英 to prove that someone is not guilty of doing something wrong

overblow /ˌoʊvərˈbloʊ/	中 v. 夸大 英 to exaggerate
obfuscate /ˈɑːbfʌskeɪt/	中 v. 使…困惑 英 to make (something) more difficult to understand 中 v. 使…昏暗 英 to darken
droll /droʊl/	中 adj. 古怪的，搞笑的 英 having an odd and amusing quality
inconclusive /ˌɪnkənˈkluːsɪv/	中 adj. 无结果的，不确定的 英 leading to no conclusion or definite result
disperse /dɪˈspɜːrs/	中 v. 使…分散 英 to go or move in different directions
amplify /ˈæmplɪfaɪ/	中 v. 详细阐述 英 to speak or write about (something) in a more complete way 中 v. 夸大 英 to make larger or greater
exaggerate /ɛɡˈzædʒərˌeɪt/	中 v. 夸大 英 to make (something) larger or greater than normal
unwitting /ʌnˈwɪtɪŋ/	中 adj. 不知情的 英 not aware of what is really happening 中 adj. 不是故意的 英 not intended or planned; unintentional
inclusive /ɪnˈkluːsɪv/	中 adj. 包罗万象的，全面的 英 taking a great deal or everything within its scope; comprehensive

diatribe /'daɪətraɪb/	中 *n.* 谩骂 英 a bitter, abusive denunciation
promulgate /'prɑːmlgeɪt/	中 *v.* 传播 英 to make (an idea, belief, etc.) known to many people 中 *v.* 颁布（法律） 英 to make (a new law) known officially and publicly
consilience /kən'sɪlɪəns/	中 *n.* 一致，符合 英 the linking together of principles from different disciplines especially when forming a comprehensive theory
ebullient /ɪ'bʌliənt/	中 *adj.* 热情洋溢的 英 lively and enthusiastic
bolster /'boʊlstər/	中 *v.* 支持 英 to give support to
dispute /dɪ'spjuːt/	中 *n. / v.* 争辩，反对 英 *v.* to engage in argument or oppose
exposition /ˌekspə'zɪʃn/	中 *n.* 阐释，解释 英 clear explanation 中 *n.* 展览会 英 a public show or exhibition
coddle /'kɑːdl/	中 *v.* 溺爱 英 to treat (someone) with too much care or kindness
nuance /'nuːɑːns/	中 *n.* 细微差异 英 a very small difference in color, tone, meaning, etc.

peculiar /pɪˈkjuːliər/	中 *adj.* 不寻常的 英 not usual or normal
egalitarian /iˌɡælɪˈteriən/	中 *adj.* 主张人人平等的 英 aiming for equal wealth, status, etc., for all people
propitiate /prəˈpɪʃieɪt/	中 *v.* 安抚 英 to make (someone) pleased or less angry by giving or saying something desired
futile /ˈfjuːtl/	中 *adj.* 无用的 英 pointless or useless
unassuming /ˌʌnəˈsuːmɪŋ/	中 *adj.* 谦虚的，低调的 英 not having or showing a desire to be noticed, praised
amicable /ˈæmɪkəbl/	中 *adj.* 和善的 英 showing a polite and friendly desire to avoid disagreement and argument
unfounded /ʌnˈfaʊndɪd/	中 *adj.* 毫无根据的 英 lacking a sound basis
plastic /ˈplæstɪk/	中 *adj.* 虚假的，不真诚的 英 not real or sincere 中 *adj.* 可塑的 英 capable of being made into different shapes
apocalypse /əˈpɑːkəlɪps/	中 *n.* 大灾难 英 a great disaster
authoritative /əˈθɔːrəteɪtɪv/	中 *adj.* 权威的，可信的 英 clearly accurate or knowledgeable
clamorous /ˈklæmərəs/	中 *adj.* 吵吵闹闹的 英 noisily insistent

placate /ˈpleɪkeɪt/	中 v. 安抚
	英 to cause (someone) to feel less angry about something

far-reaching /ˈfɑːˈriːtʃɪŋ/	中 adj. 影响广泛的
	英 having a wide range or effect

disinterested /dɪsˈɪntrɛstəd/	中 adj. 客观公正的
	英 not influenced by personal feelings, opinions or concerns

embolden /ɪmˈbouldən/	中 v. 鼓舞，鼓励
	英 to make (someone) more confident

incompatible /ˌɪnkəmˈpætəbl/	中 adj. 无法共存的，不可兼容的
	英 not able to exist together without trouble or conflict; not able to be used together

stale /steɪl/	中 adj. 不新鲜的
	英 having an unpleasant taste or smell
	中 adj. 缺乏新鲜感的
	英 boring or unoriginal

lionize /ˈlaɪənaɪz/	中 v. 重视，尊敬
	英 to treat (someone) as a very important and famous person

preachy /ˈpriːtʃi/	中 adj. 说教的，好为人师的
	英 trying to teach something (such as proper or moral behavior) in a way that is annoying or unwanted

illusory /ɪˈluːsəri/	中 adj. 虚假的
	英 based on something that is not true or real

profit-monger /ˈprɑːfɪtˌmʌŋgər/	中 n. 贪婪的人
	英 a person, business or profession marked by avarice and greed

felicitous /fəˈlɪsɪtəs/	中 *adj.* 合适的 英 very well suited for some purpose or situation 中 *adj.* 喜悦的，令人愉悦的 英 pleasant or delightful
averse /əˈvɜːrs/	中 *adj.* 反感的 英 having an active feeling of repugnance or distaste
trigger /ˈtrɪɡər/	中 *v. / n.* 触发 英 *v.* to cause (something) to start or happen
integrity /ɪnˈteɡrəti/	中 *n.* 正直 英 the quality of being honest and fair
conservation /ˌkɑːnsərˈveɪʃn/	中 *n.* 保护 英 a careful preservation and protection of something 中 *n.* 环保 英 The controlled use and systematic protection of natural resources, such as forests, soil, and water systems.
spontaneous /spɑːnˈteɪniəs/	中 *adj.* 自主的，自发的 英 controlled and directed internally 中 *adj.* 自然的，不刻意的 英 not apparently contrived or manipulated
pushover /ˈpʊʃoʊvər/	中 *n.* 易被打败的人 英 an opponent that is easy to defeat 中 *n.* 容易做到的事 英 something that is easy to do

comprehensive
/ˌkɑːmprɪˈhensɪv/
中 adj. 全面的
英 covering completely or broadly

insufferable
/ɪnˈsʌfrəbl/
中 adj. 无法忍受的
英 too unpleasant to deal with or accept

sequential
/sɪˈkwenʃl/
中 adj. 有序的
英 happening in a series or sequence

surreptitious
/ˌsɜːrəpˈtɪʃəs/
中 adj. 秘密的，鬼鬼祟祟的
英 done in a secret way

dispassionate
/dɪsˈpæʃənət/
中 adj. 客观的
英 not influenced or affected by emotions

transient
/ˈtrænʃnt/
中 adj. 短暂的
英 not lasting long

vacant
/ˈveɪkənt/
中 adj. 空的
英 not filled, used or lived in
中 adj. 面无表情的，茫然的
英 devoid of thought, reflection or expression

canned
/kænd/
中 adj. 千篇一律的
英 lacking originality or individuality as if mass-produced
中 adj. 预先录制的
英 prepared or recorded in advance

soft-pedal
/ˈsɔːftˈpedl/
中 v. 弱化，减缓…的影响
英 to treat or describe (something) as less important than it really is

feign
/feɪn/
中 v. 假装
英 to give a false appearance of

daunting
/ˈdɔːntɪŋ/
中 adj. 令人畏惧的，望而生怯的
英 very difficult to do or deal with

downright /'daʊnraɪt/	中 adv. 完全地 英 completely
autonomous /ɔː'tɑːnəməs/	中 adj. 自治的 英 having the power or right to govern itself 中 adj. 独立自主的 英 responding, reacting, or developing independently of the whole
~~indeterminate~~ /ˌɪndɪ'tɜːrmɪnət/	中 adj. 不确定的 英 not able to be stated or described in an exact way
~~opulent~~ /'ɑːpjələnt/	中 adj. 昂贵的 英 very comfortable and expensive 中 adj. 富裕的 英 very wealthy
~~pervasive~~ /pər'veɪsɪv/	中 adj. 普遍的 英 existing in or spreading through every part of something
~~offset~~ /'ɔːfset/	中 v. 抵消 英 to cancel or reduce the effect of (something)
~~omnipresent~~ /ˌɑːmnɪ'preznt/	中 adj. 处处都有的 英 present everywhere simultaneously
~~entangle~~ /ɪn'tæŋgl/	中 v. 纠缠 英 to cause (something) to get caught in or twisted with something else 中 v. 使…卷入困境 英 to get (someone) involved in a confusing or difficult situation
~~dilatory~~ /'dɪlətɔːri/	中 adj. 拖延的 英 tending or intended to cause delay

generic /dʒəˈnerɪk/	中 *adj.* 一般的，通有的，通用的
	英 relating to or descriptive of an entire group or class; general
sensational /senˈseɪʃənl/	中 *adj.* 极好的
	英 exceedingly or unexpectedly excellent or great
	中 *adj.*（通过可怕的细节）令人兴奋的，骇人听闻的
	英 causing very great excitement or interest with shocking details
explicable /ˈeksplɪkəbl/	中 *adj.* 可以解释的
	英 possible to explain
pernicious /pərˈnɪʃəs/	中 *adj.* 有害的，致命的
	英 causing great harm or damage often in a way that is not easily seen or noticed
convoluted /ˈkɑːnvəluːtɪd/	中 *adj.* 难懂的，复杂的
	英 very complicated and difficult to understand
bureaucracy /bjʊˈrɑːkrəsi/	中 *n.* 官僚机构
	英 a system of government or business that has many complicated rules and ways of doing things
widespread /ˈwaɪdspred/	中 *adj.* 广泛的
	英 common over a wide area or among many people
compliant /kəmˈplaɪənt/	中 *adj.* 顺从的，迎合的
	英 ready and willing to comply
trifling /ˈtraɪflɪŋ/	中 *adj.* 不重要的
	英 having little value or importance

compunction
/kəm'pʌŋkʃn/
中 n. 犯罪感，后悔感
英 a feeling of guilt or regret

cynical
/'sɪnɪkl/
中 adj. 认为人性自私的，愤世嫉俗的
英 believing or showing the belief that people are motivated chiefly by base or selfish concerns

pretentious
/prɪ'tenʃəs/
中 adj. 炫耀的
英 having or showing the unpleasant quality of people who want to be regarded as more impressive, successful or important than they really are

customary
/'kʌstəmeri/
中 adj. 惯常的
英 usual or typical of a particular person

vilify
/'vɪlɪfaɪ/
中 v. 诽谤，辱骂
英 to utter slanderous and abusive statements against

tantamount
/'tæntəmaʊnt/
中 adj. （数量，效果）相同的
英 equal to something in value, meaning or effect

unflinching
/ʌn'flɪntʃɪŋ/
中 adj. 坚定的，不退缩的
英 staying strong and determined even when things are difficult
中 adj. （表达）直白的
英 looking at or describing something or someone in a very direct way

prototype
/'proʊtətaɪp/
中 n. 典型
英 a standard or typical example
中 n. 原型
英 an original model on which something is patterned

Word List 4

音频

equanimity /ˌekwəˈnɪməti/	中 n. 平静，镇定 英 calm emotions when dealing with problems or pressure
~~espouse~~ /ɪˈspaʊz/	中 v. 支持 英 to express support for (a cause, belief, etc.)
~~inattention~~ /ˌɪnəˈtenʃn/	中 n. 不留心，不注意 英 failure to carefully think about, listen to or watch someone or something
fractious /ˈfrækʃəs/	中 adj. 愤怒的 英 full of anger and disagreement 中 adj. 爱惹事的，不服管的 英 inclined to make trouble
~~disorganize~~ /dɪsˈɔːrgənaɪz/	中 v. 打乱，破坏 英 to destroy or interrupt the orderly structure or function of
~~figurative~~ /ˈfɪgjərətɪv/	中 adj.（形象化）比喻的 英 based on or making use of figures of speech; metaphorical
~~entail~~ /ɪnˈteɪl/	中 v. 包括，包含，使…必然，牵涉 英 to have (something) as a part, step or result
impeccable /ɪmˈpekəbl/	中 adj. 完美无瑕的 英 having no flaws
stifle /ˈstaɪfl/	中 v. 抑制 英 to not allow yourself to do or express (something) 中 v. 使…窒息 英 to kill by depriving of oxygen

pragmatic /præɡ'mætɪk/	中 *adj.* 实际的 英 practical
didactic /daɪ'dæktɪk/	中 *adj.* (过分的道德层面的)说教 英 excessively moralizing
dazzle /'dæzl/	中 *v.* 使…目眩，使…惊叹 英 to greatly impress or surprise (someone) by being very attractive or exciting
stalwart /'stɔːlwərt/	中 *adj.* 坚定的，忠诚的 英 loyal and resolute 中 *adj.* 结实的，强壮的 英 strong and imposing
archaic /ɑːr'keɪɪk/	中 *adj.* 过时的 英 old and no longer used
palliate /'pælieɪt/	中 *v.* 减缓 英 to make the effects of (something, such as an illness) less painful, harmful or harsh
accede /ək'siːd/	中 *v.* 同意 英 to agree to a request or a demand 中 *v.* 加入 英 to become a party (as to an agreement)
consort /'kɑːnsɔːrt/	中 *v.* 陪伴 英 to keep company
hostile /'hɑːstl/	中 *adj.* 不友好的，敌对的 英 not friendly
ubiquitous /juː'bɪkwɪtəs/	中 *adj.* 到处存在的，广泛的 英 seeming to be seen everywhere
authenticate /ɔː'θentɪkeɪt/	中 *v.* 验证，证明…是真实的 英 to prove that something is real, true or genuine

~~condescend~~ /ˌkɑːndɪ'send/	中 v. 带着优越感的态度对待人 英 to deal with people in a patronizingly superior manner 中 v. 屈尊 英 to descend to the level of one considered inferior; lower oneself
~~predilection~~ /ˌpredl'ekʃn/	中 n. 倾向，偏好 英 a natural liking for something
~~diminutive~~ /dɪ'mɪnjətɪv/	中 adj. 极小的 英 extremely or extraordinarily small
illustrious /ɪ'lʌstriəs/	中 adj. 杰出的 英 admired and respected very much because a lot was achieved
unconscionable /ʌn'kɑːnʃənəbl/	中 adj. 违背良心的，丧心病狂的 英 not guided or controlled by conscience 中 adj. 过分的，不合理的 英 beyond prudence or reason; excessive
~~trivial~~ /'trɪviəl/	中 adj. 不重要的 英 not important
~~callow~~ /'kæloʊ/	中 adj. 幼稚的，稚嫩的 英 lacking adult sophistication
~~sketchy~~ /'sketʃi/	中 adj. 粗略的 英 done quickly without many details
bemuse /bɪ'mjuːz/	中 v. 使…困惑 英 to cause (someone) to be confused and often also somewhat amused 中 v. 吸引 英 to occupy the attention of

exotic
/ɪgˈzɑːtɪk/

中 adj. 外来的
英 introduced from another country
中 adj. 奇异的，异域风情的
英 strikingly, excitingly or mysteriously different or unusual

intuition
/ˌɪntuˈɪʃn/

中 n. 直觉
英 a feeling that guides a person to act a certain way without fully understanding why

episodic
/ˌepɪˈsɑːdɪk/

中 adj. 暂时的
英 limited to the duration of an episode
中 adj. 不连续的，（时间上）分散的
英 happening or appearing at different times

dovish
/ˈdʌvɪʃ/

中 adj. 爱好和平的
英 advocating peace, conciliation or negotiation in preference to confrontation or armed conflict

realm
/relm/

中 n. 领域
英 an area of activity, interest or knowledge
中 n. 王国
英 a country that is ruled by a king or queen

presage
/ˈpresɪdʒ/

中 v. 预测，预言
英 to give or be a sign of (something that will happen or develop in the future)

distinctive
/dɪˈstɪŋktɪv/

中 adj. 独特的，显著区别的
英 different in a way that is easy to notice

concomitant
/kənˈkɑːmɪtənt/

中 adj. 伴随的，与…同时发生的
英 accompanying especially in a subordinate or incidental way

abstemious
/əbˈstiːmiəs/

中 adj. 生活有节制的
英 not eating and drinking too much

versatile
/'vɜːrsətl/

中 adj. 易变的
英 changing or fluctuating readily
中 adj. 多功能的
英 having many uses or applications

vacillate
/'væsəleɪt/

中 v. 犹豫不决
英 to swing indecisively from one course of action or opinion to another
中 v. 摇摆
英 to fluctuate or oscillate

devious
/'diːviəs/

中 adj. 欺骗的
英 willing to lie and trick people in order to get what is wanted
中 adj. 弯曲的，蜿蜒的
英 not straight or direct

suffice
/sə'faɪs/

中 v. 足够
英 to be or provide as much as is needed

astute
/ə'stuːt/

中 adj. 敏锐的
英 having or showing an ability to notice and understand things clearly

outrage
/'aʊtreɪdʒ/

中 v. 使…生气
英 to make (someone) very angry

consensus
/kən'sensəs/

中 n. 意见一致
英 a general agreement about something

metaphor
/'metəfər/

中 n. 比喻
英 a word or phrase for one thing that is used to refer to another thing in order to show or suggest that they are similar
中 n. 象征
英 an object, activity or idea that is used as a symbol of something else

outstrip /ˌaʊt'strɪp/	中 v. 胜出，超出 英 to be or become better, greater or larger than (someone or something)
querulous /'kwerələs/	中 adj. 抱怨的 英 complaining in an annoyed way
salient /'seɪliənt/	中 adj. 明显的，显眼的 英 very important or noticeable
culmination /ˌkʌlmɪ'neɪʃn/	中 n. 最终，结果 英 the end or final result of something
camaraderie /ˌkɑːmə'rɑːdəri/	中 n. 志同道合之情谊 英 a feeling of good friendship among the people in a group
cordial /'kɔːrdʒəl/	中 adj. 热情友好的 英 politely pleasant and friendly
tribute /'trɪbjuːt/	中 n. 赞美，致敬 英 something done, said or given to show respect, gratitude or affection
observant /əb'zɜːrvənt/	中 adj. 观察仔细的，善于观察的 英 paying strict attention or good at noticing what is going on around you
collegiality /kəˌliːdʒi'æləti/	中 n. 共同掌权 英 the cooperative relationship of colleagues
pensive /'pensɪv/	中 adj. （悲伤的）思考的 英 lost in serious or sad thought
penance /'penəns/	中 n. 忏悔 英 something that you do or are given to do in order to show that you are sad or sorry about doing something wrong

| rile /raɪl/ | 中 v. 使…生气 |
| | 英 to make agitated and angry |

| ~~lambaste~~ /læm'beɪst/ | 中 v. 严厉批评 |
| | 英 to criticize (someone or something) very harshly |

| undercut /ˌʌndər'kʌt/ | 中 v. 削弱 |
| | 英 to make (something) weaker or less effective |

| ~~harrow~~ /'hærou/ | 中 v. 折磨，使…痛苦 |
| | 英 to torment or vex |

| ~~paradigm~~ /'pærədaɪm/ | 中 n. 典范 |
| | 英 a model or pattern for something that may be copied |

| ~~dissent~~ /dɪ'sent/ | 中 v. 持不同意见 |
| | 英 to publicly disagree with an official opinion, decision or set of beliefs |

~~initiate~~ /ɪ'nɪʃieɪt/	中 v. 开始，启动
	英 to begin
	中 v. 介绍入门知识
	英 to teach (someone) the basic facts or ideas about something

| ~~mutual~~ /'mju:tʃuəl/ | 中 adj. 相互的，共同的 |
| | 英 shared between two or more people or groups |

~~robust~~ /rou'bʌst/	中 adj. 强壮的
	英 strong and healthy
	中 adj. 稳定无误的
	英 capable of performing without failure under a wide range of conditions

betoken /bɪˈtoʊkən/	中 v. 预示 英 to be a sign of (something)
conceal /kənˈsiːl/	中 v. 隐藏 英 to hide (something or someone) from sight
~~outnumber~~ /ˌaʊtˈnʌmbər/	中 v.（数量上）超过 英 to be more than (someone or something) in number
~~itinerant~~ /aɪˈtɪnərənt/	中 adj. 巡游的 英 traveling from place to place especially covering a circuit
demonize /ˈdiːmənaɪz/	中 v. 妖魔化 英 to represent as diabolically evil
~~sober~~ /ˈsoʊbər/	中 adj. 严肃认真的 英 having or showing a very serious attitude or quality
~~incendiary~~ /ɪnˈsendieri/	中 adj. 纵火的 英 tending to inflame 中 adj. 引起愤怒的 英 causing anger 中 n. 煽动者 英 a person who excites factions, quarrels or sedition : agitator
~~salutary~~ /ˈsæljəteri/	中 adj. 有益的，有益健康的 英 producing a beneficial effect
~~replete~~ /rɪˈpliːt/	中 adj. 充满的 英 having much or plenty of something
~~snobbish~~ /ˈsnɑːbɪʃ/	中 adj. 自命不凡的 英 having or showing the attitude of people who think they are better than other people

seditious /sɪ'dɪʃəs/	中 *adj.* 煽动叛乱的
	英 disposed to arouse or take part in or guilty of sedition
expatriate /ˌeks'peɪtriət/	中 *v.* 驱逐
	英 to banish
synopsis /sɪ'nɑːpsɪs/	中 *n.* 概要
	英 a short description of the most important information about something
affirmative /ə'fɜːrmətɪv/	中 *adj.* 积极的
	英 positive
	中 *adj.* 肯定的
	英 asserting that something is true or correct
emendation /ˌiːmen'deɪʃn/	中 *n.* 校订
	英 the act or practice of emending
collective /kə'lektɪv/	中 *adj.* 集体的
	英 shared or done by a group of people
synonymous /sɪ'nɑːnɪməs/	中 *adj.* 意思相同的
	英 having the same meaning
	中 *adj.* 与…意义相当的
	英 having the same connotations, implications or reference
modicum /'mɑːdɪkəm/	中 *n.* 少量
	英 a small amount
retrenchment /rɪ'trentʃmənt/	中 *n.* 削减（尤指经费）
	英 reduction or curtailment
magnify /'mæɡnɪfaɪ/	中 *v.* 放大
	英 to make greater
	中 *v.* 夸大
	英 to exaggerate

obligatory /ə'blɪɡətɔːri/	中 *adj.* 强制的，必需的
	英 compulsory
commensurate /kə'menʃərət/	中 *adj.* 相等的，相似的
	英 equal or similar to something in size, amount or degree
long-winded /lɔːŋ'wɪndɪd/	中 *adj.* 冗长的，啰唆的
	英 tediously long in speaking or writing
slippery /'slɪpəri/	中 *adj.* 滑的
	英 difficult to stand on because of being smooth, wet, icy. etc.
	中 *adj.* 难懂的
	英 not easy to understand or identify in an exact way
	中 *adj.* 不可靠的
	英 not able to be trusted
hefty /'hefti/	中 *adj.* 又大又重的
	英 large and heavy
forbidding /fər'bɪdɪŋ/	中 *adj.* 令人畏惧的，可怕的
	英 not friendly or appealing
wide-ranging /waɪd'reɪndʒɪŋ/	中 *adj.* 广泛的
	英 extensive in scope
diligent /'dɪlɪdʒənt/	中 *adj.* 努力的，刻苦的
	英 characterized by steady, earnest and energetic effort
punctilious /pʌŋk'tɪliəs/	中 *adj.* （对行为）谨慎小心的
	英 very careful about behaving properly and doing things in a correct and accurate way
engaging /ɪn'ɡeɪdʒɪŋ/	中 *adj.* 吸引人的
	英 very attractive or pleasing in a way that holds your attention

evanescent /ˌevə'nesnt/	中 *adj.* 短暂的 英 lasting a very short time
free-for-all /friːfər,ɔːl/	中 *n.* 混战，多人为所欲为的失控场面 英 an uncontrolled fight or competition that involves many people
rudimentary /ˌruːdɪ'mentri/	中 *adj.* 基本的 英 basic or simple
bustling /'bʌslɪŋ/	中 *adj.* 忙乱的 英 full of energetic and noisy activity

Word List 5

音 频

prioritize /praɪˈɔːrətaɪz/	中 v. 使…优先 英 to organize (things) so that the most important thing is done or dealt with first
envision /ɪnˈvɪʒn/	中 v. 想象 英 to think of (something that you believe might exist or happen in the future)
circumscribe /ˈsɜːrkəmskraɪb/	中 v. 限制 英 to limit the size or amount of (something)
reminiscent /ˌremɪˈnɪsnt/	中 adj. 引起回忆的 英 reminding you of someone or something else 中 adj. 思念的 英 having many thoughts of the past
symmetrical /sɪˈmetrɪkl/	中 adj. 对称的 英 having sides or halves that are the same
overthrow /ˌoʊvərˈθroʊ/	中 v. 推翻 英 to remove (someone or something) from power especially by force
juvenile /ˈdʒuːvənl/	中 adj. 幼稚，不成熟的 英 reflecting psychological or intellectual immaturity
elude /iˈluːd/	中 v. 逃跑，逃避 英 to avoid or escape (someone or something) by being quick, skillful or clever 中 v. 使…无法理解 英 to fail to be understood or remembered by (someone) 中 v. 使…无法得到 英 to fail to be achieved by (someone)

| jettison /ˈdʒetɪsn/ | 中 v. 拒绝，放弃 |
| | 英 to reject (something, such as a plan or idea) |

| detriment /ˈdetrɪmənt/ | 中 n. 损坏，破坏 |
| | 英 something that will cause damage or injury to something or someone |

| baroque /bəˈrouk/ | 中 adj. 奢华的，复杂的 |
| | 英 characterized by grotesqueness, extravagance, complexity or flamboyance |

quixotic /kwɪkˈsɑːtɪk/	中 adj. 不切实际的
	英 foolishly impractical especially in the pursuit of ideals
	中 adj. 变化多端的，变幻莫测的
	英 capricious or unpredictable

| mockery /ˈmɑːkəri/ | 中 n. 嘲笑 |
| | 英 insulting or contemptuous action or speech |

| tactful /ˈtæktfl/ | 中 adj. 得体的，圆滑的 |
| | 英 careful not to offend or upset other people |

| trendy /ˈtrendi/ | 中 adj. 时髦的 |
| | 英 very fashionable |

| subsidize /ˈsʌbsɪdaɪz/ | 中 v. 资助，赞助 |
| | 英 to help someone or something pay for the costs of (something) |

| numinous /ˈnuːmɪnəs/ | 中 adj. 超自然的 |
| | 英 supernatural, mysterious |

| anomalous /əˈnɑːmələs/ | 中 adj. 不寻常的，异常的 |
| | 英 not expected or usual |

| mawkish /ˈmɔːkɪʃ/ | 中 adj. 恶心做作的 |
| | 英 sad or romantic in a foolish or exaggerated way |

invidious /ɪnˈvɪdiəs/	中 adj. 令人反感的
	英 unpleasant and likely to cause bad feelings in other people

austere /ɔːˈstɪr/	中 adj. 朴素的，没有装饰的
	英 simple or unadorned
	中 adj. 严肃的
	英 having a serious and unfriendly quality
	中 adj. 生活简朴的
	英 relating to or having a strict and simple way of living that avoids physical pleasure

impede /ɪmˈpiːd/	中 v. 阻碍
	英 to slow the movement, progress or action of (someone or something)

frank /fræŋk/	中 adj. 真诚的
	英 marked by free, forthright and sincere expression

disjunction /dɪsˈdʒʌŋkʃn/	中 n. 分离，分裂
	英 a lack of connection between things that are related or should be connected

finicky /ˈfɪnɪki/	中 adj. 挑剔的
	英 very hard to please

hazardous /ˈhæzərdəs/	中 adj. 危险的
	英 involving risk or danger

chicanery /ʃɪˈkeɪnəri/	中 n. 欺骗，诡计
	英 deception by artful subterfuge or sophistry

verifiable /ˈverɪfaɪəbl/	中 adj. 可验证的
	英 capable of being verified

demonstrable /ˈdemənstrəbl/	中 adj. 可证明的
	英 able to be proven or shown
	中 adj. 明显的
	英 apparent, evident
pertinacious /ˌpɜːrtnˈeɪʃəs/	中 adj. 坚持的，固执的
	英 holding tenaciously to a purpose, belief, opinion, or course of action
searce /skers/	中 adj. 缺乏的
	英 not plentiful or abundant
lavish /ˈlævɪʃ/	中 adj. 奢华的
	英 having a very rich and expensive quality
	中 adj. 大量使用的，浪费的
	英 giving or using a large amount of something
	中 v. 挥霍，浪费
	英 to expend or bestow with profusion
sanguine /ˈsæŋɡwɪn/	中 adj. 乐观的
	英 confident and hopeful
waver /ˈweɪvər/	中 v. 摇摆不定
	英 to become unsteady because of weakness, emotion, tiredness, etc.
engender /ɪnˈdʒendər/	中 v. 产生
	英 to cause to exist or to develop
elusive /iˈluːsɪv/	中 adj. 难懂的
	英 hard to understand, define or remember
	中 adj. 难以捕捉的
	英 hard to find or capture
ponder /ˈpɑːndər/	中 v. 沉思，仔细思考
	英 to think about or consider (something) carefully

| proliferate /prə'lɪfəreɪt/ | 中 v. 快速增长 |
| | 英 to increase in number or amount quickly |

| paucity /'pɔːsəti/ | 中 n. 少量 |
| | 英 a small amount of something |

univocal /juː'nɪvoʊkl/	中 adj.（意思）唯一的
	英 having one meaning only
	中 adj. 明确的，不模糊的
	英 unambiguous

| dejected /dɪ'dʒektɪd/ | 中 adj. 沮丧的 |
| | 英 sad because of failure, loss, etc. |

| surplus /'sɜːrpləs/ | 中 n. 多余，过量 |
| | 英 an amount (such as an amount of money) that is more than the amount that is needed |

impertinent /ɪm'pɜːrtnənt/	中 adj. 粗鲁的
	英 rude and showing a lack of respect
	中 adj. 不相关的
	英 not pertinent

| one-of-a-kind /wʌn'əvə'kaɪnd/ | 中 n. 独一无二 |
| | 英 a person or thing that is not like any other person or thing |

apropos /ˌæprə'poʊ/	中 adj. 合适的
	英 being both relevant and opportune
	中 prep. 关于…
	英 with regard to

| ingratiate /ɪn'greɪʃieɪt/ | 中 v. 讨好 |
| | 英 to gain favor or approval for (yourself) by doing or saying things that people like |

| concoct /kən'kɑːkt/ | 中 v. 编造，捏造 |
| | 英 to invent or develop (a plan, story, etc.) especially in order to trick or deceive someone |

disgorge /dɪsˈɡɔːrdʒ/	中 v. 吐
	英 to empty whatever is in the stomach through the mouth
	中 v. 涌出
	英 to discharge the contents of

| baseless /ˈbeɪsləs/ | 中 adj. 毫无根据的 |
| | 英 groundless or unwarranted |

| momentary /ˈmoʊmənteri/ | 中 adj. 短暂的 |
| | 英 lasting a very short time |

| debilitate /dɪˈbɪlɪteɪt/ | 中 v. 使…衰弱，使…虚弱 |
| | 英 to impair the strength of |

acute /əˈkjuːt/	中 adj. 重要的
	英 important or critical
	中 adj. 思维敏锐的
	英 marked by keen discernment or intellectual perception especially of subtle distinctions
	中 adj. 短暂的
	英 lasting a short time
	中 adj. 急性的
	英 having a rapid onset and following a short but severe course
	中 adj. 敏感的
	英 reacting readily to stimuli or impressions

| resent /rɪˈzent/ | 中 v. 憎恨，生气 |
| | 英 to be angry or upset about (someone or something that you think is unfair) |

| delightful /dɪˈlaɪtfl/ | 中 adj. （形容事物）令人愉悦的，令人高兴的 |
| | 英 highly pleasing |

~~decisive~~ /dɪˈsaɪsɪv/	中 *adj.* 果断的，坚定的
	英 resolute or determined
	中 *adj.* 决定性的
	英 determining what the result of something will be
	中 *adj.* 明显的
	英 very clear and obvious
~~testimony~~ /ˈtestɪmoʊni/	中 *n.* 证词，证据
	英 proof or evidence that something exists or is true
nominal /ˈnɑːmɪnl/	中 *adj.* 名义上的
	英 existing as something in name only
	中 *adj.* 微不足道的
	英 very small in amount
simultaneous /ˌsaɪmlˈteɪniəs/	中 *adj.* 同时的
	英 happening at the same time
~~monotonous~~ /məˈnɑːtənəs/	中 *adj.* 单调的
	英 tediously uniform or unvarying
divination /ˌdɪvɪˈneɪʃn/	中 *n.* 预言，占卜
	英 a prediction uttered under divine inspiration
~~virtuosity~~ /ˌvɜːrtʃuˈɑːsəti/	中 *n.* 精湛的技艺
	英 great ability or skill shown by a musician, performer, etc.
~~manifest~~ /ˈmænɪfest/	中 *adj.* 显然的，明显的
	英 easy to understand or recognize
	中 *v.* 清晰地展示，显露出
	英 to show (something) clearly
purview /ˈpɜːrvjuː/	中 *n.* 视野
	英 an area within which someone or something has authority, influence or knowledge

annex /əˈneks/	中 v. 附加
	英 to add to something earlier, larger or more important
	中 v. 吞并
	英 to incorporate (a country or other territory) within the domain of a state

| shriek /ʃriːk/ | 中 v. 叫喊，尖叫 |
| | 英 to make a loud, high-pitched cry |

| ephemeral /ɪˈfemərəl/ | 中 adj. 短暂的 |
| | 英 lasting for a markedly brief time |

| erudite /ˈerudaɪt/ | 中 adj. 博学的 |
| | 英 having or showing knowledge that is learned by studying |

plague /pleɪɡ/	中 v. 困扰
	英 to cause worry or distress to
	中 n. 瘟疫，灾害
	英 a disease that causes death and that spreads quickly to a large number of people

| counterintuitive /ˈkaʊntərɪnˈtuːɪtɪv/ | 中 adj. 违反常理的，与直觉相反的 |
| | 英 not agreeing with what seems right or natural |

| intriguing /ɪnˈtriːɡɪŋ/ | 中 adj. 非常有趣的 |
| | 英 extremely interesting |

| magnanimous /mæɡˈnænɪməs/ | 中 adj. 大度的，宽宏大量的 |
| | 英 having or showing a generous and kind nature |

| untether /ʌnˈteðər/ | 中 v. 释放，脱离 |
| | 英 to free from or as if from a tether |

formulaic
/ˌfɔːrmjuˈleɪɪk/
中 adj. 刻板的，俗套的
英 containing or made from ideas or expressions that have been used many times before and are therefore not very new or interesting

gambit
/ˈɡæmbɪt/
中 n. 计谋，策略
英 a calculated move

vivacious
/vɪˈveɪʃəs/
中 adj. 活力四射的
英 happy and lively in a way that is attractive

stratify
/ˈstrætɪfaɪ/
中 v. 分层级
英 to divide or arrange into classes, castes or social strata

exceptional
/ɪkˈsepʃənl/
中 adj. 不寻常的
英 not usual
中 adj. 杰出的，超常的
英 better than average

slump
/slʌmp/
中 v. 急速下跌
英 to decrease suddenly and by a large amount

pessimistic
/ˌpesɪˈmɪstɪk/
中 adj. 悲观的
英 having or showing a lack of hope for the future

dilute
/daɪˈluːt/
中 v. 削弱，减轻
英 to lessen the strength of (something)
中 v. 稀释
英 to make thinner or less strong by adding water or another liquid

palatable
/ˈpælətəbl/
中 adj. 美味的
英 having a pleasant or agreeable taste
中 adj. 称心如意的
英 pleasant or acceptable to someone

| stagnate /'stægneɪt/ | 中 v. 停滞 |
| | 英 to stop developing, progressing, moving, etc. |

| esoteric /ˌesəˈterɪk/ | 中 adj. 难懂的 |
| | 英 difficult to understand |

| befuddle /bɪˈfʌdl/ | 中 v. 使…困惑 |
| | 英 to confuse |

deliberate /dɪˈlɪbərət/	中 v. 深思熟虑
	英 to think about or discuss something very carefully in order to make a decision
	中 adj. 故意的
	英 done or said in a way that is planned or intended

| antithesis /ænˈtɪθəsɪs/ | 中 n. 相反，对立 |
| | 英 the exact opposite of something or someone |

| valediction /ˌvælɪˈdɪkʃn/ | 中 n. 告别 |
| | 英 an act of bidding farewell |

| hamstring /ˈhæmstrɪŋ/ | 中 v. 损坏 |
| | 英 to damage or ruin the force or effectiveness of (something or someone) |

| complacent /kəmˈpleɪsnt/ | 中 adj. 自我感觉良好的，自满的 |
| | 英 marked by self-satisfaction especially when accompanied by unawareness of actual dangers or deficiencies |

| hinder /ˈhɪndər/ | 中 v. 阻碍 |
| | 英 to make (something, such as a task or action) slow or difficult |

~~formidable~~ /'fɔːrmɪdəbl/	中 adj. 可怕的 英 causing fear, dread or apprehension 中 adj. 令人惊叹的，令人敬畏的 英 tending to inspire awe or wonder 中 adj. 艰巨的 英 very difficult to deal with
~~impenetrable~~ /ɪm'penɪtrəbl/	中 adj. 难懂的 英 impossible to understand 中 adj. 无法穿透的 英 incapable of being penetrated or pierced
obtrude /əb'truːd/	中 v. 强迫，强加于 英 to force or impose (as oneself or one's ideas) without warrant or request 中 v. 强行闯入 英 to become involved with something or to become noticeable in an unpleasant or annoying way
~~debunk~~ /ˌdiː'bʌŋk/	中 v. 拆穿，揭露…的错误 英 to show that something (such as a belief or theory) is not true
~~umbrage~~ /'ʌmbrɪdʒ/	中 n. 生气，不悦 英 a feeling of being offended by what someone has said or done
affinity /ə'fɪnəti/	中 n. 倾向，偏好 英 a liking for or an attraction to something 中 n. 密切联系 英 likeness based on relationship or causal connection
~~ramification~~ /ˌræmɪfɪ'keɪʃn/	中 n. 结果，后果 英 something that is the result of something else 中 n. 分支 英 branch

immerse /ɪ'mɜːrs/	中 *v.* 浸润，浸泡 英 to put (something) in a liquid so that all parts are completely covered 中 *v.* 全心沉浸在…中 英 to make (yourself) fully involved in some activity or interest
demise /dɪ'maɪz/	中 *n. / v.* 死亡，灭亡 英 *v.* to die 中 *v.* 让位 英 to transmit by succession or inheritance
compassionate /kəm'pæʃənət/	中 *adj.* 同情的 英 feeling or showing concern for someone who is sick, hurt, poor, etc.

Word List 6

音 频

ignorant /ˈɪgnərənt/	中 adj. 无知的 英 destitute of knowledge or education 中 adj. 不知情的，无意识的 英 unaware or uninformed
immortal /ɪˈmɔːrtl/	中 adj. 不朽的，永存的 英 marked by the quality or state of someone or something that will never die or be forgotten
assuage /əˈsweɪdʒ/	中 v. 安抚，缓和 英 to make (something, such as an unpleasant feeling) less painful, severe, etc.
expiation /ˌekspiˈeɪʃn/	中 n. 赎罪 英 the act of making atonement
loquacious /ləˈkweɪʃəs/	中 adj. 话多的 英 liking to talk and talking smoothly and easily
marginal /ˈmɑːrdʒɪnl/	中 adj. 边缘的，不重要的 英 not very important
adjuration /ˌædʒʊˈreɪʃən/	中 n. 恳求 英 an earnest, solemn appeal
dreary /ˈdrɪri/	中 adj. 令人悲伤的 英 causing unhappiness or sad feelings
callous /ˈkæləs/	中 adj. 冷漠的 英 not feeling or showing any concern about the problems or suffering of other people

| discount | 中 *v.* 低估，轻视 |
| /'dɪskaʊnt/ | 英 to minimize the importance of |

| ostentatious | 中 *adj.* 炫耀的 |
| /ˌɑːstenˈteɪʃəs/ | 英 marked by or fond of conspicuous or vainglorious and sometimes pretentious display |

| thwart | 中 *v.* 阻挠，阻止 |
| /θwɔːrt/ | 英 to prevent (someone) from doing something or to stop (something) from happening |

| distress | 中 *v. / n.* 使…紧张，忧虑，不适 |
| /dɪˈstres/ | 英 *v.* to worry or upset (someone) |

| raillery | 中 *n.* 打趣 |
| /ˈreɪləri/ | 英 friendly joking about or with somebody |

| exasperate | 中 *v.* 使…生气 |
| /ɪɡˈzæspəreɪt/ | 英 to make (someone) very angry or annoyed |

feckless	中 *adj.* 虚弱的，无能的
/ˈfekləs/	英 weak or ineffective
	中 *adj.* 粗心的，不负责任的
	英 careless and irresponsible

| stigma | 中 *n.* 污点 |
| /ˈstɪɡmə/ | 英 a set of negative and often unfair beliefs that a society or group of people have about something |

attenuate	中 *v.* 使减弱
/əˈtenjueɪt/	英 to make (something) weaker or less in amount, effect or force
	中 *adj.* 变弱的
	英 reduced especially in thickness, density or force

enigmatic /ˌenɪɡˈmætɪk/	中 adj. 难懂的 英 full of mystery and difficult to understand
condemn /kənˈdem/	中 v. 谴责 英 to say in a strong and definite way that someone or something is bad or wrong
impugn /ɪmˈpjuːn/	中 v.（因人不诚实而）批评抨击 英 to criticize (a person's character, intentions, etc.) by suggesting that someone is not honest and should not to be trusted
elaborate /ɪˈlæbərət/	中 adj. 精心的，精细的 英 planned or carried out with great care 中 v. 详细阐述 英 to expand something in detail
pejorative /pɪˈdʒɔːrətɪv/	中 adj. 轻蔑的（话语） 英 having negative connotations, tending to disparage or belittle
blithe /blaɪð/	中 adj. 无忧无虑的，轻松的 英 of a happy lighthearted character or disposition 中 adj. 轻率的 英 lacking due thought or consideration
refute /rɪˈfjuːt/	中 v. 驳倒，否认 英 to prove that (something) is not true
vacuous /ˈvækjuəs/	中 adj. 空的，空洞的 英 emptied of or lacking content 中 adj. 愚蠢的 英 marked by lack of ideas or intelligence
enervate /ˈenərveɪt/	中 v. 使…衰弱 英 to make (someone or something) very weak or tired 中 adj. 虚弱的 英 lacking physical, mental or moral vigor

| honorific /ˌɑːnəˈrɪfɪk/ | 中 adj. 尊敬的 |
| | 英 giving or expressing honor or respect |

| disprove /ˌdɪsˈpruːv/ | 中 v. 驳斥 |
| | 英 to show that (something) is false or wrong |

extinguish /ɪkˈstɪŋgwɪʃ/	中 v. 熄灭
	英 to cause (something) to stop burning
	中 v. 使…灭绝
	英 to cause the end or death of (something)

| excoriate /ˌeksˈkɔːrieɪt/ | 中 v. 强烈斥责 |
| | 英 to censure scathingly |

| immutable /ɪˈmjuːtəbl/ | 中 adj. 不变的 |
| | 英 not subject or susceptible to change |

| hypercritical /ˌhaɪpərˈkrɪtɪkl/ | 中 adj. 吹毛求疵的 |
| | 英 criticizing other people or things too strongly or too often |

| momentous /moʊˈmentəs/ | 中 adj. 重要的 |
| | 英 very important |

| esteem /ɪˈstiːm/ | 中 n. 尊敬 |
| | 英 respect and affection |

| traumatic /traʊˈmætɪk/ | 中 adj. 心灵受创伤的 |
| | 英 emotionally upset |

| secretive /ˈsiːkrətɪv/ | 中 adj. 鬼鬼祟祟的，秘密的 |
| | 英 not letting people see or know what you are doing or thinking |

delegate /ˈdelɪgət/	中 n. 代表
	英 a person who is chosen or elected to vote or act for others
	中 v. 委托
	英 to give (control, responsibility, authority, etc.) to someone

abeyance /əˈbeɪəns/	中 *n.* 中止，暂停 英 temporary inactivity
blatant /ˈbleɪtnt/	中 *adj.* 吵吵闹闹的 英 noisy especially in a vulgar or offensive manner 中 *adj.* 明目张胆的 英 completely obvious, conspicuous or obtrusive especially in a crass or offensive manner
flamboyant /flæmˈbɔɪənt/	中 *adj.* 引人注意的，酷炫的 英 having a very noticeable quality that attracts a lot of attention
lucid /ˈluːsɪd/	中 *adj.* 清晰的 英 very clear and easy to understand
opaque /oʊˈpeɪk/	中 *adj.* 难懂的 英 difficult to understand or explain 中 *adj.* 不透明的 英 not letting light through
alarmism /əˈlɑːrmɪzəm/	中 *n.* （毫无根据的）担忧，危言耸听 英 the often unwarranted exciting of fears or warning of danger
divisive /dɪˈvaɪsɪv/	中 *adj.* 引起争议的，引起分裂的 英 causing a lot of disagreement between people and causing them to separate into different groups
torpor /ˈtɔːrpər/	中 *n.* 麻木，迟钝，懒散 英 a state of not being active and having very little energy
indolent /ˈɪndələnt/	中 *adj.* 懒惰的 英 not liking to work or be active

| compulsory /kəm'pʌlsəri/ | 中 *adj.* 强制的 |
| | 英 having the power of forcing someone to do something |

| revelation /ˌrevə'leɪʃn/ | 中 *n.* 揭露 |
| | 英 an act of revealing to view or making known |

| contingency /kən'tɪndʒənsi/ | 中 *n.* 可能事件 |
| | 英 something (such as an emergency) that might happen |

| prolific /prə'lɪfɪk/ | 中 *adj.* 多产的 |
| | 英 producing a large amount of something |

| alacrity /ə'lækrəti/ | 中 *n.* 欣然同意 |
| | 英 a quick and cheerful readiness to do something |

transcend /træn'send/	中 *v.* 超越
	英 to rise above or go beyond the limits of
	中 *v.* 胜出，超出
	英 to outstrip or outdo in some attribute, quality, or power
	中 *v.* 克服，战胜
	英 to triumph over the negative or restrictive aspects of

resonate /'rezəneɪt/	中 *v.* 回响
	英 to produce or exhibit resonance
	中 *v.* 引起共鸣
	英 to evoke a feeling of shared emotion or belief

| uncharacteristic /ˌʌnˌkærəktə'rɪstɪk/ | 中 *adj.* 不典型的，不寻常的 |
| | 英 not typical or distinctive |

| impetuous /ɪm'petʃuəs/ | 中 *adj.* 鲁莽的，仓促的 |
| | 英 acting or done quickly and without thought |

| disparate /ˈdɪspərət/ | 中 adj. 不同的 |
| | 英 different from each other |

| respite /ˈrespɪt/ | 中 n. 暂歇，休息 |
| | 英 an interval of rest or relief |

| rankle /ˈræŋkl/ | 中 v. 使…生气，愤怒 |
| | 英 to cause (someone) to feel angry or irritated especially for a long time |

| acquiesce /ˌækwiˈes/ | 中 v. 默许，默认 |
| | 英 to accept, agree or allow something to happen by staying silent or by not arguing |

remedy /ˈremədi/	中 v. 补救，完善
	英 to solve, correct or improve (something)
	中 n. 治疗的方法，治疗的药物
	英 a medicine or treatment that relieves pain or cures a usually minor illness

| congruous /ˈkɒŋgruəs/ | 中 adj. 一致的，适合的 |
| | 英 being in agreement, harmony or correspondence |

| gadfly /ˈgædflaɪ/ | 中 n. 讨厌的人 |
| | 英 someone who annoys people by being very critical |

shrink /ʃrɪŋk/	中 v. 缩小
	英 to become smaller in amount, size or value
	中 v. 畏缩
	英 to quickly move away from something shocking, frightening or disgusting

| overwrought /ˌoʊvərˈrɔːt/ | 中 adj. 情绪激动或不高兴的 |
| | 英 very excited or upset |

| purposeful
/'pɜːrpəsfl/ | 中 *adj.* 有目的的，有意图的 |
| | 英 having a clear aim or purpose |

prognosis /praɪɡ'noʊsɪs/	中 *n.* 诊断
	英 a doctor's opinion about how someone will recover from an illness or injury
	中 *n.* 预言
	英 a judgment about what is going to happen in the future

| malleable
/'mæliəbl/ | 中 *adj.* 易适应的，能适应的 |
| | 英 able to adjust to changing circumstances; adaptable |

| forgo
/fɔːr'ɡoʊ/ | 中 *v.* 放弃（优势） |
| | 英 to give up the enjoyment or advantage of:do without |

| encumber
/ɪn'kʌmbər/ | 中 *v.* 阻碍 |
| | 英 to cause problems or difficulties for |

| barbarity
/bɑːr'bærəti/ | 中 *n.* 野蛮，残忍 |
| | 英 extreme cruelty |

| sanctimonious
/ˌsæŋktɪ'moʊniəs/ | 中 *adj.* 假装道德高尚的，假正经的 |
| | 英 pretending to be morally better than other people |

| repugnant
/rɪ'pʌɡnənt/ | 中 *adj.* 令人厌恶的 |
| | 英 causing a strong feeling of dislike or disgust |

| pseudonym
/'suːdənɪm/ | 中 *n.* 假名 |
| | 英 a name that someone (such as a writer) uses instead of his or her real name |

| explicit /ɪkˈsplɪsɪt/ | 中 *adj.* 明白的，清楚的 |
| | 英 very clear and complete and leaving no doubt about the meaning |

| inexorable /ɪnˈeksərəbl/ | 中 *adj.* 无动于衷的，无情的 |
| | 英 not capable of being persuaded by entreaty; relentless |

| dissemble /dɪˈsembl/ | 中 *v.* 隐藏，掩饰（感情、意见） |
| | 英 to hide your true feelings, opinions, etc. |

| scintillating /ˈsɪntɪleɪtɪŋ/ | 中 *adj.* 生动有趣的，机智幽默的 |
| | 英 very clever, amusing and interesting |

| luminary /ˈluːmɪneri/ | 中 *n.* 杰出人物 |
| | 英 a very famous or successful person |

empower /ɪmˈpaʊər/	中 *v.* 授权
	英 to give power to (someone)
	中 *v.* 提升…的影响力
	英 to promote the self-actualization or influence of

| deference /ˈdefərəns/ | 中 *n.* （因地位高或年长而）尊敬 |
| | 英 respect and esteem due a superior or an elder |

| lugubrious /ləˈɡuːbriəs/ | 中 *adj.* 悲伤的 |
| | 英 full of sadness or sorrow |

| denounce /dɪˈnaʊns/ | 中 *v.* 批评 |
| | 英 to criticize (someone or something) harshly and publicly |

parochial /pəˈroʊkiəl/	中 *adj.* 地方的
	英 limited to only the things that affect your local area
	中 *adj.* 狭隘的，范围有限的
	英 limited in range or scope

| **lament** /lə'ment/ | 中 v. 哀叹，哀悼 |
| | 英 to express sorrow, regret or unhappiness about something |

primitive /'prɪmətɪv/	中 adj. 原始的
	英 of, belonging to or seeming to come from an early time in the very ancient past
	中 adj. 基本的
	英 very simple and basic

| **hamper** /'hæmpər/ | 中 adj. 阻碍 |
| | 英 to slow the movement, progress or action of (someone or something) |

distill /dɪ'stɪl/	中 v. 蒸馏
	英 to let fall, exude or precipitate in drops or in a wet mist
	中 v. 提炼
	英 to extract the essence of

| **imitate** /'ɪmɪteɪt/ | 中 v. 模仿 |
| | 英 to do the same thing as |

| **encyclopedic** /ɪnˌsaɪklə'piːdɪk/ | 中 adj.（如大百科全书般）全面的 |
| | 英 dealing with or knowing a subject thoroughly or completely |

| **euphemism** /'juːfəmɪzəm/ | 中 n. 委婉语 |
| | 英 a mild or pleasant word or phrase that is used instead of one that is unpleasant or offensive |

| **nondescript** /'nɑːndɪskrɪpt/ | 中 adj. 平庸的 |
| | 英 lacking distinctive qualities; having no individual character or form |

| **adverse** /'ædvɜːrs/ | 中 adj. 不利的，有害的 |
| | 英 bad or unfavorable |

~~enduring~~ /ɪn'dʊrɪŋ/	中 *adj.* 长期的 英 lasting, continuing
~~enliven~~ /ɪn'laɪvn/	中 *v.* 使活跃 英 to give life, action or spirit to
half-formulated /hæf'fɔːrmjuleɪtɪd/	中 *adj.* 新出现的 英 coming into view, existence or notice
~~dubious~~ /'duːbiəs/	中 *adj.* 可疑的，不确定的 英 causing doubt, uncertainty or suspicion
churlish /'tʃɜːrlɪʃ/	中 *adj.* 不礼貌的 英 not polite
~~outlandish~~ /aʊt'lændɪʃ/	中 *adj.* 奇异的 英 very strange or unusual 中 *adj.* 外来的，异国的 英 of or relating to another country
~~serendipitous~~ /ˌserən'dɪpətəs/	中 *adj.* 偶然发现的 英 happening by luck

Word List 7

音 频

mercurial /mɜːrˈkjʊriəl/	中 *adj.* 性格多变的 英 changing moods quickly and often
deceive /dɪˈsiːv/	中 *v.* 欺骗 英 to make (someone) believe something that is not true
fortuitous /fɔːrˈtuːɪtəs/	中 *adj.* 偶然的 英 happening by chance 中 *adj.* 幸运的 英 having or showing good luck
fathom /ˈfæðəm/	中 *v.* 理解 英 to understand the reason for (something)
remuneration /rɪˌmjuːnəˈreɪʃn/	中 *n.* 酬金 英 an amount of money paid to someone for the work that person has done
sparkling /ˈspɑːrklɪŋ/	中 *adj.* 闪闪发光的 英 shining with brilliant points of light like stars
luxuriant /lʌgˈʒʊriənt/	中 *adj.* 繁茂的 英 having heavy and thick growth 中 *adj.* 奢华的 英 having an appealingly rich quality
credential /krəˈdenʃl/	中 *n.* 证明 英 something that gives a title to credit or confidence
recoil /rɪˈkɔɪl/	中 *v.* 畏缩 英 to quickly move away from something that is shocking, frightening or disgusting; to react to something with shock or fear

~~scandalous~~ /'skændələs/	中 *adj.* 令人震惊的，反感的 英 shocking or offensive
~~erode~~ /ɪ'roʊd/	中 *v.* 腐蚀 英 to diminish or destroy by degrees
tenuous /'tenjuəs/	中 *adj.* 站不住脚的 英 not certain, definite or strong; flimsy, weak or uncertain 中 *adj.* 稀薄的 英 very thin
~~fluctuate~~ /'flʌktʃueɪt/	中 *v.* 波动，起伏，上上下下 英 to change level, strength or value frequently
~~contentious~~ /kən'tenʃəs/	中 *adj.* 引起争议的 英 likely to cause people to argue or disagree 中 *adj.* 爱争吵的 英 likely or willing to argue
patchwork /'pætʃwɜːrk/	中 *n.* 混合物 英 something made of miscellaneous or incongruous parts or elements
~~flabbergast~~ /'flæbər,gæst/	中 *v.* 使…惊讶 英 to shock or surprise (someone) very much
~~temperate~~ /'tempərət/	中 *adj.* （气温）温和的 英 having temperatures that are not too hot or too cold 中 *adj.* 自我克制的，脾气温和的 英 emotionally calm and controlled 中 *adj.* 适度的 英 keeping or held within limits

benighted /bɪˈnaɪtɪd/	中 *adj.* 无知的，愚昧的 英 having no knowledge or education
undiscriminating /ˌʌndɪˈskrɪmɪneɪtɪŋ/	中 *adj.* 不加区分的 英 indiscriminate 中 *adj.* 没有鉴别力的 英 lacking sensitivity, taste or judgment
palpable /ˈpælpəbl/	中 *adj.* 可感知的 英 capable of being touched or felt 中 *adj.* 明显的 英 easily perceptible
effusive /ɪˈfjuːsɪv/	中 *adj.* 表达过多感情的 英 expressing a lot of emotion
habitable /ˈhæbɪtəbl/	中 *adj.* 宜居的 英 suitable or fit to live in
codify /ˈkɑːdɪfaɪ/	中 *v.* 整理 英 to put (things) in an orderly form
duplicate /ˈduːplɪkeɪt/	中 *v.* 复制 英 to make an exact copy of (something)
sluggish /ˈslʌgɪʃ/	中 *adj.* 迟钝的 英 moving slowly or lazily
sway /sweɪ/	中 *v.* 影响，控制 英 to exert a guiding or controlling influence on 中 *v.* 摇摆 英 to cause to sway; set to swinging, rocking or oscillating
ornamental /ˌɔːrnəˈmentl/	中 *adj.* 装饰性的，美观的 英 used to make something more attractive

| convivial /kən'vɪvɪəl/ | 中 adj. 好交际的，欢聚的 |
| | 英 of or relating to social events where people can eat, drink and talk in a friendly way with others |

| multifarious /ˌmʌltɪ'feriəs/ | 中 adj. 各种各样的 |
| | 英 of many and various kinds |

| panacea /ˌpænə'siːə/ | 中 n. 万能灵药 |
| | 英 a remedy for all ills or difficulties |

| countenance /'kaʊntənəns/ | 中 v. / n. 赞同 |
| | 英 v. to accept, support or approve of (something) |

| inflammatory /ɪn'flæmətɔːri/ | 中 adj. 煽动性的 |
| | 英 tending to excite anger, disorder or tumult; seditious |

| taint /teɪnt/ | 中 v. 玷污，破坏 |
| | 英 to hurt or damage the good condition of (something) |

rigorous /'rɪɡərəs/	中 adj. 严格的
	英 very strict and demanding
	中 adj. 细致的，准确的
	英 done carefully and with a lot of attention to detail

| delude /dɪ'luːd/ | 中 v. 迷惑，欺骗 |
| | 英 to cause (someone) to believe something that is not true |

| ill-advised /ˌɪləd'vaɪzd/ | 中 adj. 不明智的，不合理的 |
| | 英 not wise or sensible |

prosaic
/prə'zeɪɪk/
- 中 *adj.* 普通寻常的
- 英 everyday or ordinary
- 中 *adj.* 散文的
- 英 characteristic of prose as distinguished from poetry
- 中 *adj.* 缺乏创意的
- 英 dull or unimaginative

malfeasance
/mæl'fizns/
- 中 *n.* 违法行为
- 英 wrongdoing or misconduct especially by a public official

egregious
/ɪ'gri:dʒiəs/
- 中 *adj.* 极坏的
- 英 conspicuously bad or offensive

counterfeit
/'kaʊntərfɪt/
- 中 *adj.* 伪造的
- 英 made in imitation of what is genuine with the intent to defraud

volatile
/'vɑːlətl/
- 中 *adj.* 性格多变的
- 英 having or showing extreme or sudden changes of emotion

conundrum
/kə'nʌndrəm/
- 中 *n.* 难题
- 英 a confusing or difficult problem

contrive
/kən'traɪv/
- 中 *v.* 设计
- 英 to plan with cleverness or ingenuity; devise

gratify
/'grætɪfaɪ/
- 中 *v.* 使…满意
- 英 to make (someone) happy or satisfied

deflate
/dɪ'fleɪt/
- 中 *v.* 使…泄气，使…挫败
- 英 to make (someone) lose confidence or pride
- 中 *v.* 使…漏气
- 英 to lose air or gas from inside
- 中 *v.* 缩小，减轻
- 英 to reduce in size, importance or effectiveness

anthropogenic /ˌænθrəpə'dʒənɪk/	中 adj. 人为的 英 caused by human
conflate /kən'fleɪt/	中 v. 合并 英 to combine (as two readings of a text) into a composite whole
animate /'ænɪmeɪt/	中 adj. 活着的，有生命的 英 having life 中 v. 鼓励，使…有活力 英 to give spirit and support to
contemporary /kən'tempəreri/	中 adj. 当代的，现代的 英 happening or beginning now or in recent times 中 adj. 同时代的 英 from the same time period
underlie /ˌʌndər'laɪ/	中 v. 成为…的根据，基础 英 to form the basis or foundation of (an idea, a process, etc.) 中 v. 位于…最下面 英 to lie or be located under (something)
anecdote /'ænɪkdoʊt/	中 n. 趣闻，轶事 英 a short account of an interesting or humorous incident
ministration /ˌmɪnɪ'streɪʃən/	中 n. 帮助 英 the act or process of ministering
banal /bə'nɑːl/	中 adj. 无聊的，平庸的 英 boring or ordinary
flippant /'flɪpənt/	中 adj. 轻率无礼的，不严肃的 英 lacking proper respect or seriousness
invective /ɪn'vektɪv/	中 n. 辱骂，侮辱 英 harsh or insulting words

anemia
缺乏活力

paltry
/'pɔːltri/

中 n. 少量
英 very small or too small in amount

miserly
/'maɪzərli/

中 adj. 吝啬的
英 hating to spend money

renowned
/rɪ'naʊnd/

中 adj. 出名的
英 known and admired by many people for some special quality or achievement

exhaustive
/ɪg'zɔːstɪv/

中 adj. 全面的
英 including all possibilities

polemical
/pə'lemɪkl/

中 adj. （好）争辩的
英 of or involving strongly critical or disputatious writing or speech

facile
/'fæsl/

中 adj. 轻率的，肤浅的
英 too simple and not showing enough thought or effort
中 adj. 【贬】轻而易举的
英 done or achieved in a way that is too easy

transparent
/træns'pærənt/

中 adj. 透明的
英 able to be seen through
中 adj. 易懂的
英 easy to notice or understand
中 adj. 坦诚的
英 honest and open

unimpeachable
/ˌʌnɪm'piːtʃəbl/

中 adj. 毋庸置疑的
英 not able to be doubted or questioned

tortuous
/'tɔːrtʃuəs/

中 adj. 复杂难懂的
英 complicated, long and confusing

perturb
/pər'tɜːrb/

中 v. 使…不安
英 to cause (someone) to be worried or upset

flighty /ˈflaɪti/	中 *adj.* 多变的
	英 given to capricious or unstable behavior
	中 *adj.* 易激动的
	英 easily excited

| infectious /ɪnˈfekʃəs/ | 中 *adj.* 传染的 |
| | 英 spreading or capable of spreading rapidly to others |

gall /ɡɔːl/	中 *v.* 使…生气
	英 to make (someone) feel annoyed or angry
	中 *n.* 愤怒
	英 a state of exasperation

compelling /kəmˈpelɪŋ/	中 *adj.* 有趣的
	英 very interesting
	中 *adj.* 有说服力的
	英 capable of causing someone to believe or agree

| overt /oʊˈvɜːrt/ | 中 *adj.* 明显的 |
| | 英 open to view |

| fraudulent /ˈfrɔːdʒələnt/ | 中 *adj.* 欺诈的 |
| | 英 done to trick someone for the purpose of getting something valuable |

| perilous /ˈperələs/ | 中 *adj.* 危险的 |
| | 英 full of danger |

| cataclysm /ˈkætəklɪzəm/ | 中 *n.* 灾难 |
| | 英 something that causes great destruction, violence, etc. |

| concede /kənˈsiːd/ | 中 *v.* 承认 |
| | 英 to admit (something) usually in an unwilling way |

~~horrific~~ /hə'rɪfɪk/	中 *adj.* 可怕的 英 causing horror or shock
~~multitudinous~~ /ˌmʌltɪ'tuːdɪnəs/	中 *adj.* 很多的 英 very many
~~downplay~~ /ˌdaʊn'pleɪ/	中 *v.* 轻描淡写 英 to make (something) seem smaller or less important
purport /pər'pɔːrt/	中 *n.* 中心思想 英 meaning conveyed, professed or implied 中 *v.* （虚假地）声称 英 to claim to be or do a particular thing when this claim may not be true
~~mediocre~~ /ˌmiːdi'oʊkər/	中 *adj.* 平庸的，平凡的 英 of moderate or low quality, value, ability or performance
~~irritate~~ /'ɪrɪteɪt/	中 *v.* 使…不高兴 英 to provoke impatience, anger or displeasure in
~~stilted~~ /'stɪltɪd/	中 *adj.* 不自然的，僵硬的 英 awkward especially because of being too formal
~~placid~~ /'plæsɪd/	中 *adj.* 平静的 英 not easily upset or excited
~~erratic~~ /ɪ'rætɪk/	中 *adj.* 飘忽不定的，没规律的 英 acting, moving or changing in ways that are not expected or usual 中 *adj.* 古怪的 英 deviating from what is ordinary or standard
~~ingenious~~ /ɪn'dʒiːniəs/	中 *adj.* 机敏的，聪明的 英 very smart or clever

renaissance
/'renəsɑːns/
- 中 *n.* 复苏
- 英 revival
- 中 *n.* 文艺复兴时期（首字母大写）

endorse
/ɪn'dɔːrs/
- 中 *v.* 公开支持
- 英 to publicly or officially say that you support or approve of (someone or something)
- 中 *v.* 代言…产品
- 英 to publicly say that you like or use (a product or service) in exchange for money

harbinger
/'hɑːrbɪndʒər/
- 中 *n.* 前兆
- 英 something that shows what is coming
- 中 *v.* 预兆
- 英 to be a harbinger of

malign
/mə'laɪn/
- 中 *adj.* 邪恶的，恶毒的
- 英 having or showing intense often vicious ill will
- 中 *v.* 贬损，诋毁
- 英 to say bad things about (someone or something) publicly

imperative
/ɪm'perətɪv/
- 中 *adj.* 重要的
- 英 very important
- 中 *n.* 命令，要求
- 英 a command, rule, duty, etc. that is very important or necessary

ethical
/'eθɪkl/
- 中 *adj.* 道德的
- 英 morally right and good

consequential
/ˌkɑːnsə'kwenʃl/
- 中 *adj.* 重要的
- 英 having significant consequences
- 中 *adj.* 自以为是的
- 英 self-important
- 中 *adj.* 结果的
- 英 happening as a result

(77)

~~perpetuate~~ /pər'petʃueɪt/	中 *v.* 持续，使…继续 英 to cause (something that should be stopped, such as a mistaken idea or a bad situation) to continue
~~anathema~~ /ə'næθəmə/	中 *n.* 诅咒，强烈的谴责 英 a vehement denunciation; a curse
illuminate /ɪ'luːmɪneɪt/	中 *v.* 阐述清楚 英 to make (something) clear and easier to understand
~~enchanting~~ /ɪn'tʃæntɪŋ/	中 *adj.* 迷人的 英 charming
~~mishandle~~ /ˌmɪs'hændl/	中 *v.* 虐待 英 to treat roughly 中 *v.* 错误地处理，处理不当 英 to deal with or manage wrongly or ignorantly
fickle /'fɪkl/	中 *adj.* 多变的 英 changing opinions often
~~countermand~~ /'kaʊntərmænd/	中 *v.* 撤销（命令） 英 to cancel (an order) especially by giving a new order
~~mollify~~ /'maːlɪfaɪ/	中 *v.* 安抚 英 to make (someone) less angry; to calm (someone) down
~~gloomy~~ /'gluːmi/	中 *adj.* 悲伤的 英 causing feelings of sadness

Word List 8

音 频

~~methodical~~ /məˈθɑːdɪkl/	中 *adj.* 有条理的 英 arranged, characterized by or performed with method or order
✓ **hortatory** /ˈhɔrtəˌtɔri/	中 *adj.* 劝告的，激励的 英 marked by exhortation or strong urging
innate /ɪˈneɪt/	中 *adj.* 天生的 英 existing from the time a person or animal is born
~~displace~~ /dɪsˈpleɪs/	中 *v.* 驱逐 英 to force (people or animals) to leave the area where they live 中 *v.* 取代，代替 英 to take the job or position of (someone or something)
~~apprehend~~ /ˌæprɪˈhend/	中 *v.* 逮捕 英 to arrest or seize 中 *v.* 理解 英 to notice and understand (something) 中 *v.* 害怕，恐惧 英 to anticipate especially with anxiety, dread or fear
~~disarray~~ /ˌdɪsəˈreɪ/	中 *n.* 杂乱，混乱 英 a lack of order 中 *v.* 使混乱 英 to throw into disorder
~~tedious~~ /ˈtiːdiəs/	中 *adj.* 冗长无聊的 英 boring and too slow or long

~~irascible~~ /ɪˈræsəbl/	中 *adj.* 易怒的，坏脾气的 英 becoming angry very easily
~~fastidious~~ /fæˈstɪdiəs/	中 *adj.* 小心谨慎的，挑剔的 英 very careful about how you do something
occlude /əˈkluːd/	中 *v.* 阻塞 英 to close up or block off
~~impair~~ /ɪmˈper/	中 *v.* 损害 英 to make (something) weaker or worse
~~laudatory~~ /ˈlɔːdətɔːri/	中 *adj.* 赞美的 英 expressing or containing praise
~~prevalent~~ /ˈprevələnt/	中 *adj.* 流行的，普遍的 英 common or widespread
~~deprecate~~ /ˈdeprəkeɪt/	中 *v.* 贬损，诋毁 英 to criticize or express disapproval of (someone or something)
portend /pɔːrˈtend/	中 *v.* 预示，预兆 英 to be a sign or warning that something usually bad or unpleasant is going to happen
~~self-defeating~~ /ˈselfdɪˈfiːtɪŋ/	中 *adj.* 违背自己利益的，弄巧成拙的 英 injurious to one's or its own purposes or welfare
~~proclaim~~ /prəˈkleɪm/	中 *v.* 宣布 英 to say or state (something) in a public, official or definite way
~~meddle~~ /ˈmedl/	中 *v.* 干涉 英 to interest oneself in what is not one's concern

~~overshadow~~ /ˌoʊvərˈʃædoʊ/	中 *v.* 使黯然失色 英 to exceed in importance 中 *v.* 遮盖 英 to cast a shadow over
~~somnolent~~ /ˈsɑːmnələnt/	中 *adj.* 无聊的，令人昏昏欲睡的 英 very boring or causing a person to fall asleep
~~precipitate~~ /prɪˈsɪpɪteɪt/	中 *v.* 加速 英 to cause (something) to happen quickly or suddenly 中 *adj.* 鲁莽的 英 happening very quickly or too quickly without enough thought or planning
~~onerous~~ /ˈɑːnərəs/	中 *adj.* 繁重的，费力的 英 difficult and unpleasant to do or deal with
~~comity~~ /ˈkɑːməti/	中 *n.* 友好，和谐 英 friendly social atmosphere
~~douse~~ /daʊs/	中 *v.* 熄灭 英 to extinguish
asseverate /əˈsevəˌreɪt/	中 *v.* 郑重声明 *assevert* ? 英 to affirm or declare positively or earnestly
~~arbitrary~~ /ˈɑːrbətreri/	中 *adj.* 武断的，任性的 英 not planned or chosen for a particular reason 中 *adj.* 随意的 英 existing or coming about seemingly at random or by chance or as a capricious and unreasonable act of will

81

discretion /dɪ'skreʃn/	中 n. 自由决定
	英 power of free decision or latitude of choice within certain legal bounds
	中 n. 谨慎
	英 the quality of having or showing discernment or good judgment; the quality of being discreet : circumspection
sacrosanct /'sækroʊsæŋkt/	中 adj. 神圣而不可侵犯的
	英 most sacred or holy
quiescent /kwi'esnt/	中 adj. 静止的，不活跃的
	英 not active
evasive /ɪ'veɪsɪv/	中 adj. 回避的，闪烁其词的
	英 not honest or direct
defer /dɪ'fɜːr/	中 v. 推迟
	英 put off, delay
	中 v. 顺从
	英 to submit to another's wishes, opinion or governance usually through deference or respect
innocuous /ɪ'nɑːkjuəs/	中 adj. 无害的
	英 having no adverse effect; harmless
	中 adj. 平淡乏味的
	英 not likely to offend or provoke to strong emotion; insipid
arcane /ɑːr'keɪn/	中 adj. 难懂的
	英 known or understood by only a few people
permanent /'pɜːrmənənt/	中 adj. 长期稳定的
	英 continuing or enduring without fundamental or marked change; stable

entice /ɪnˈtaɪs/	中 v. 诱惑 英 to attract artfully or adroitly or by arousing hope or desire
unmistakable /ˌʌnmɪˈsteɪkəbl/	中 adj. 清晰的，一目了然的 英 not capable of being mistaken or misunderstood
antecedent /ˌæntɪˈsiːdnt/	中 n. 先前的 英 something that came before something else and may have influenced or caused it
overstate /ˌoʊvərˈsteɪt/	中 v. 夸大 英 to say that (something) is larger or greater than it really is
relish /ˈrelɪʃ/	中 v. 喜爱 英 to enjoy or take pleasure in (something)
trepidation /ˌtrepɪˈdeɪʃn/	中 n. 恐惧，害怕 英 a nervous or fearful feeling of uncertain agitation
synergy /ˈsɪnərdʒi/	中 n. 协同作用 英 the increased effectiveness that results when two or more people or businesses work together
universal /ˌjuːnɪˈvɜːrsl/	中 adj. 普世的 英 existing or true at all times or in all places 中 adj. 普遍的 英 present or occurring everywhere
dampen /ˈdæmpən/	中 v. 抑制，削弱 英 to check or diminish the activity or vigor of
predate /ˌpriːˈdeɪt/	中 v. 先于 英 to exist or happen at an earlier time than (something or someone)

| premise /ˈpremɪs/ | 中 n. 前提 |
| | 英 a proposition antecedently supposed or proved as a basis of argument or inference |

| motivate /ˈmoʊtɪveɪt/ | 中 v. 激励 |
| | 英 to provide with a motive |

| linkage /ˈlɪŋkɪdʒ/ | 中 n. 连接，联结 |
| | 英 a connection or relationship between two or more things |

| hypocrisy /hɪˈpɑːkrəsi/ | 中 n. 虚伪，伪善 |
| | 英 one feigning to be what one is not or to believe what one does not, especially the false assumption of an appearance of virtue or religion |

| redundant /rɪˈdʌndənt/ | 中 adj. 重复的，冗余的，赘述的 |
| | 英 needlessly wordy or repetitive in expression |

| mitigate /ˈmɪtɪɡeɪt/ | 中 v. 减缓 |
| | 英 to make less severe or intense |

wane /weɪn/	中 v. 减少，衰退
	英 to decrease gradually in size, amount, intensity, or degree; decline
	中 v. 结束
	英 to approach an end
	中 v.（月亮的）亏
	英 to show a progressively smaller illuminated area, as the moon does in passing from full to new

accountable /əˈkaʊntəbl/	中 adj.（对某事）负责任的
	英 required to be responsible for something
	中 adj. 可以解释的
	英 capable of being explained

~~fecund~~ /ˈfiːkənd/	中 *adj.* 多产的 英 fruitful in offspring or vegetation 中 *adj.* 有创造力的，硕果颇丰的 英 intellectually productive or inventive
~~reflective~~ /rɪˈflektɪv/	中 *adj.* 反思的，沉思的 英 characterized by or given to serious thinking or contemplation
~~precedent~~ /ˈpresɪdənt/	中 *n.* 先例 英 an easier occurrence of something similar
✓ recant /rɪˈkænt/	中 *v.* （公开正式的）否认 英 to withdraw or repudiate (a statement or belief) formally and publicly
~~rambling~~ /ˈræmblɪŋ/	中 *adj.* 跑题的，冗长的 英 lengthy and digressive 中 *adj.* 闲逛的 英 habitually roaming
inure /ɪˈnjʊr/	中 *v.* 习惯于（不好的事物） 英 to habituate to something undesirable
~~eccentric~~ /ɪkˈsentrɪk/	中 *adj.* 古怪的 英 strange or unusual
~~mercenary~~ /ˈmɜːrsəneri/	中 *adj.* 唯利是图的 英 serving merely for pay or sordid advantage
~~negligible~~ /ˈneglɪdʒəbl/	中 *adj.* 可忽略的，不重要的 英 not significant or important enough to be worth considering; trifling

puerile
/'pjʊrəl/

中 *adj.* 稚嫩的，幼稚的
英 silly or childish especially in a way that shows a lack of seriousness or good judgment

plausible
/'plɔːzəbl/

中 *adj.* 看起来合理的
英 superficially fair, reasonable or valuable but often specious
中 *adj.* 表面上可行的
英 appearing worthy of belief

baffle
/'bæfl/

中 *v.* 使…困惑
英 to confuse (someone) completely

simplistic
/sɪm'plɪstɪk/

中 *adj.* 过于简化的
英 too simple

chivalrous
/'ʃɪvəlrəs/

中 *adj.* 勇敢的
英 valiant
中 *adj.* 绅士风度的，礼貌的
英 showing respect and politeness especially toward women

apathetic
/ˌæpə'θetɪk/

中 *adj.* 漠不关心的
英 not having or showing much emotion or interest

dedicate
/'dedɪkeɪt/

中 *v.* 致力于，奉献于
英 to commit to a goal or way of life

blemish
/'blemɪʃ/

中 *v.* 玷污，破坏
英 to hurt or damage the good condition of (something)
中 *n.* 污点
英 a mark that makes something imperfect or less beautiful

~~inertia~~ /ɪˈnɜːrʃə/	中 n. 不动，不活跃 英 lack of movement or activity especially when movement or activity is wanted or needed 中 n.（思想上的）惰性 英 a feeling of not having the energy or desire that is needed to move, change, etc.
~~intelligible~~ /ɪnˈtelɪdʒəbl/	中 adj. 可以理解的 英 able to be understood
~~primacy~~ /ˈpraɪməsi/	中 n. 首要，首位 英 the state of being most important or strongest
~~untenable~~ /ʌnˈtenəbl/	中 adj.（论点）经不起反驳的，站不住脚的 英 not capable of being defended against attack or criticism
~~incivility~~ /ˌɪnsəˈvɪləti/	中 n. 不礼貌 英 a rude or impolite attitude or behavior
~~laconic~~ /ləˈkɑːnɪk/	中 adj. 简洁的，用词少的 英 using few words in speech or writing
~~confess~~ /kənˈfes/	中 v. 坦白，承认 英 to admit that you did something wrong or illegal
~~demoralize~~ /dɪˈmɔːrəlaɪz/	中 v. 使…泄气 英 to weaken the morale of (a person or group)
paragon /ˈpærəgɑːn/	中 n. 典范，模范 英 a model of excellence or perfection
~~outmoded~~ /ˌaʊtˈmoʊdɪd/	中 adj. 过时的 英 no longer useful or acceptable

~~fleeting~~ /ˈfliːtɪŋ/	中 adj. 短暂的 英 passing swiftly
~~scrutinize~~ /ˈskruːtənaɪz/	中 v. 仔细检查 英 to examine something carefully especially in a critical way
~~incentive~~ /ɪnˈsentɪv/	中 n. 激励 英 something that encourages a person to do something or to work harder
~~contradictory~~ /ˌkɑːntrəˈdɪktəri/	中 adj. 对立的 英 involving, causing or constituting a contradiction
~~sectarian~~ /sekˈteriən/	中 adj. 狭隘的 英 limited in character or scope 中 adj. 派系的 英 relating to religious or political sects and the differences between them
moribund /ˈmɔːrɪbʌnd/	中 adj. 濒临死亡的 英 approaching death
~~galvanize~~ /ˈgælvənaɪz/	中 v. 刺激 英 to stimulate or shock with an electric current 中 v. 激起…意识，激发…行动 英 to arouse to awareness or action
~~interchangeable~~ /ˌɪntərˈtʃeɪndʒəbl/	中 adj. 可交换的，相似的 英 capable of being used in place of each other
exiguous /egˈzɪgjuəs/	中 adj. 极其缺乏的 英 excessively scanty
truism /ˈtruːɪzəm/	中 n. 真理 英 an undoubted or self-evident truth

利他主义 → altruism

valorize
/'væləraɪz/
中 v. 规定价格（引申为赞美）
英 to give or assign a value to, especially a higher value

meticulous
/mə'tɪkjələs/
中 adj. 谨慎的
英 very careful about doing something in an extremely accurate and exact way

satire
/'sætaɪər/
中 n. 讽刺，嘲讽
英 humor that shows the weaknesses or bad qualities of a person, government, society, etc.

proprietary
/prə'praɪəteri/
中 adj. 私有的
英 kept private by an owner

evenhanded
/'iːvn,hændɪd/
中 adj. 公平的
英 not favoring one side or group over another

amorphous
/ə'mɔːrfəs/
中 adj. 无固定形状的
英 having no definite or clear shape or form
中 adj. 难以归类的
英 of no particular type; anomalous

apolitical
/,eɪpə'lɪtɪkl/
中 adj. 对政治不感兴趣的
英 not interested or involved in politics

obviate
/'ɑːbvieɪt/
中 v. 免除
英 to make (something) no longer necessary
中 v. 避免
英 to prevent or avoid

prescience
/'presiəns/
中 n. 先知
英 the ability to know what will or might happen in the future

audacious	中 *adj.* 大胆的，无畏的
/ɔːˈdeɪʃəs/	英 intrepidly daring
	中 *adj.* 无礼的
	英 contemptuous of law, religion or decorum
	中 *adj.* 大胆创新的
	英 marked by originality and verve

| animadversion | 中 *n.* 批判，责骂 |
| /ˌænɪmədˈvɜrʒən/ | 英 a critical and usually censorious remark |

Word List 9

音 频

adorn /ə'dɔːrn/	中 v. 装饰 英 to make (someone or something) more attractive by adding something beautiful
duplicitous /duː'plɪsɪtəs/	中 adj. 欺骗的 英 deceptive in words or action
~~**vehement**~~ /'viːəmənt/	中 adj. 情绪激动的 英 showing strong and often angry feelings
~~**revive**~~ /rɪ'vaɪv/	中 v. 使…复苏 英 to make (someone or something) strong, healthy or active again
antediluvian /ˌæntidɪ'luːviən/	中 adj. 极为过时的 英 very old or old-fashioned
~~**facet**~~ /'fæsɪt/	中 n. 某一方面 英 a part or element of something
~~**ponderous**~~ /'pɑːndərəs/	中 adj. 笨重的 英 slow or awkward because of weight and size 中 adj. 无聊的 英 very boring or dull
~~**detract**~~ /dɪ'trækt/	中 v. 贬低 英 to diminish the importance, value or effectiveness of something
~~**specific**~~ /spə'sɪfɪk/	中 adj. 独特的 英 relating to a particular person, situation, etc. 中 adj. 清晰的，明确的 英 clearly and exactly presented or stated

aggrandize /ə'græn,daɪz/	中 *v.* 夸大，吹捧
	英 to make appear great or greater
	中 *v.* 抬高身价，提高地位
	英 to enhance the power, wealth, position or reputation of

| prospect /'prɑːspekt/ | 中 *n.* 前景 |
| | 英 someone or something that is likely to succeed or to be chosen |

chagrin /ʃə'grɪn/	中 *n.* 苦恼，烦恼
	英 a feeling of being frustrated or annoyed because of failure or disappointment
	中 *v.* 使烦恼
	英 to vex or unsettle by disappointing or humiliating

seclusion /sɪ'kluːʒn/	中 *n.* 隔离，隐居
	英 the act of placing or keeping someone away from other people; the act of secluding someone
	中 *n.* 偏僻
	英 a secluded or isolated place

| commence /kə'mens/ | 中 *v.* 开始 |
| | 英 to begin |

| mordant /'mɔːrdnt/ | 中 *adj.* 尖酸刻薄的 |
| | 英 expressing harsh criticism especially in a way that is funny |

| disconcerting /,dɪskən'sɜːrtɪŋ/ | 中 *adj.* 令人不安的 |
| | 英 causing an emotional disturbance |

| embellish /ɪm'belɪʃ/ | 中 *v.* 装饰 |
| | 英 to make beautiful with ornamentation |

| pugnacious /pʌg'neɪʃəs/ | 中 *adj.* 好争斗的 |
| | 英 showing a readiness or desire to fight or argue |

exacerbate /ɪɡ'zæsərbeɪt/	中 v. 使…恶化 英 to make (a bad situation, a problem, etc.) worse
furtive /'fɜːrtɪv/	中 adj. 鬼鬼祟祟的 英 done in a quiet and secret way to avoid being noticed
bewilder /bɪ'wɪldər/	中 v. 使…困惑 英 to confuse (someone) very much
unidimensional /ˌjuːnɪdɪ'menʃənl/	中 adj. 肤浅的 英 lacking depth
jaded /'dʒeɪdɪd/	中 adj. 厌倦的，无聊的 英 feeling or showing a lack of interest and excitement caused by having done or experienced too much of something
visionary /'vɪʒəneri/	中 adj. 有远见的 英 having or showing clear ideas about what should happen or be done in the future
archetypal /ˌɑːrki'taɪpl/	中 n. 典型 英 a perfect example of something
humility /hjuː'mɪləti/	中 n. 谦虚 英 the quality or state of being humble
disclose /dɪs'kloʊz/	中 v. 揭发，揭露 英 to make (something) known to the public
adversarial /ˌædvər'seriəl/	中 adj. 敌对的 英 involving two people or two sides who oppose each other
beneficiary /ˌbenɪ'fɪʃieri/	中 n. 受帮助的人 _beneficial_ 英 a person, organization, etc., that is helped by something

premature /ˌpriːməˈtʃʊr/	中 adj. 过早的 英 happening too soon or earlier than usual
jeopardize /ˈdʒepərdaɪz/	中 v. 使…危险 英 to put (something or someone) in danger
conjure /ˈkʌndʒər/	中 v. 想象出 英 to create or imagine (something)
persevere /ˌpɜːrsəˈvɪr/	中 v. 坚持 英 to continue doing something or trying to do something even though it is difficult
enormous /ɪˈnɔːrməs/	中 adj. 大量的 英 very great in size or amount 中 adj. 穷凶极恶的 英 exceedingly wicked
inverse /ˌɪnˈvɜːrs/	中 adj. 相反的 英 opposite in order, nature or effect
indiscriminate /ˌɪndɪˈskrɪmɪnət/	中 adj. 不加区分的，不加选择的 英 not marked by careful distinction 中 adj. （因为不加区别而）多样的 英 heterogeneous or motley
defy /dɪˈfaɪ/	中 v. 不遵守，不服从，抵抗 英 to refuse to obey
admonish /ədˈmɑːnɪʃ/	中 v. 警告，批评 英 to criticize or warn gently but seriously 中 v. 劝告 英 to give friendly advice or encouragement
preclude /prɪˈkluːd/	中 v. 阻止 英 to prevent (someone) from doing something

forswear /fɔːr'swer/	中 v. 放弃 英 to promise to give up (something) or to stop doing (something)
solidarity /ˌsɑːlɪ'dærəti/	中 n. 团结 英 unity (as of a group or class) that produces or is based on community of interests, objectives and standards
conspicuous /kən'spɪkjuəs/	中 adj. 显眼的，明显的 英 very easy to see or notice 中 adj. 吸引人的 英 attracting attention
disinformation /ˌdɪsˌɪnfər'meɪʃn/	中 n. 假情报，假消息 英 false information deliberately and often covertly spread
preempt /pri'empt/	中 v. 阻止，先发制人 英 to prevent (something) from happening 中 v. 取代 英 to take the place of 中 v. 抢占 英 to acquire by preemption
recapitulate /ˌriːkə'pɪtʃuleɪt/	中 v. 总结 英 to give a brief summary of something
paralyze /'pærəlaɪz/	中 v. 使…瘫痪 英 to make (a person or animal) unable to move or feel all or part of the body 中 v. 使…无效或无力 英 to make powerless or ineffective
inexpressible /ˌɪnɪk'spresəbl/	中 adj. 无以言表的 英 too strong or great to be expressed or described

absorbing /əb'zɔːrbɪŋ/	中 *adj.* 吸引人的 英 fully taking one's attention
plethora /'pleθərə/	中 *n.* 大量 英 a very large amount or number
disregard /ˌdɪsrɪ'gɑːrd/	中 *v.* 无视，忽视 英 to ignore (something) or treat (something) as unimportant
turbulent /'tɜːrbjələnt/	中 *adj.* 混乱的 英 causing unrest, violence or disturbance
antagonistic /ænˌtægə'nɪstɪk/	中 *adj.* 敌对的 英 showing dislike or opposition
commonplace /'kɑːmənpleɪs/	中 *n.* 常见的事，平常的事 英 something that happens or appears in many places and is not unusual
meager /'miːgər/	中 *adj.* 不足的，少的 英 deficient in quality or quantity
tendentious /ten'denʃəs/	中 *adj.* 偏袒的，偏向的 英 strongly favoring a particular point of view in a way that may cause argument
prestige /pre'stiːʒ/	中 *n.* 声望，声誉 英 the respect and admiration that someone or something gets for being successful or important
burlesque /bɜːr'lesk/	中 *v.* 通过滑稽的模仿而讽刺 英 to imitate in a humorous or derisive manner
attain /ə'teɪn/	中 *v.* 达到，获得 英 to accomplish or achieve (something); to succeed in getting or doing (something)

upsurge /ˈʌpsɜːrdʒ/	中 n. 猛增 英 a rapid or sudden increase or rise
grouchy /ˈgraʊtʃi/	中 adj. 易怒的，脾气不好的 英 having a bad temper
pliable /ˈplaɪəbl/	中 adj. 易受影响的 英 too easily influenced or controlled by other people 中 adj. 能适应的 英 adjustable to varying conditions
reproach /rɪˈproʊtʃ/	中 v. 斥责，批评 英 to express disapproval or disappointment to (someone)
histrionic /ˌhɪstriˈɑːnɪk/	中 adj. 戏剧性的，做作的 英 deliberately affected
abnegate /ˈæbnəˌgeɪt/	中 v. 否认 英 to deny or renounce 中 v. 放弃，屈服 英 to relinquish or surrender
provoke /prəˈvoʊk/	中 v. 激起 英 to cause the occurrence of (a feeling or action) 中 v. 激怒 英 to incite to anger
avaricious /ˌævəˈrɪʃəs/	中 adj. 贪婪的 英 excessively acquisitive especially in seeking to hoard riches
brag /bræg/	中 v. 吹嘘，炫耀 英 to talk about yourself, your achievements, your family, etc., in a way that shows too much pride

heed /hiːd/	中 *v.* 留心，注意
	英 to pay attention to (advice, a warning, etc.)
sagacious /səˈgeɪʃəs/	中 *adj.* 聪明的，睿智的
	英 having or showing an ability to understand difficult ideas and situations and to make good decisions
penalty /ˈpenəlti/	中 *n.* 惩罚
	英 punishment for breaking a rule or law
prefigure /ˌpriːˈfɪgjər/	中 *v.* 预示
	英 to show or suggest (something that will happen or exist at a future time)
glorify /ˈglɔːrɪfaɪ/	中 *v.* 赞美
	英 to represent as glorious
animus /ˈænɪməs/	中 *n.* 敌意
	英 a strong feeling of dislike or hatred
justification /ˌdʒʌstɪfɪˈkeɪʃn/	中 *n.* 理由
	英 an acceptable reason for doing something
pertain /pərˈteɪn/	中 *v.* 与…相关
	英 to relate to
	中 *v.* 适用，适合
	英 to be appropriate to something
aggrieve /əˈgriv/	中 *v.* 使痛苦
	英 to give pain or trouble to; distress
	中 *v.* 侵害
	英 to inflict injury on
dearth /dɜːrθ/	中 *n.* 缺乏
	英 the state or condition of not having enough of something

enemy

~~calumny~~ /'kæləmni/	中 n. 诽谤 英 an untrue statement that is made to damage someone's reputation
~~rampant~~ /'ræmpənt/	中 adj. 广泛的 英 profusely widespread 中 adj. 猖獗的 英 growing quickly and in a way that is difficult to control
~~vulnerable~~ /'vʌlnərəbl/	中 adj. 易受伤害的 英 easily hurt or harmed physically, mentally or emotionally
~~pertinent~~ /'pɜːrtnənt/	中 adj. 相关的 英 having a clear decisive relevance to the matter in hand
~~distort~~ /dɪ'stɔːrt/	中 v. 曲解 英 to twist out of the true meaning or proportion 中 v. 扭曲 英 to twist out of a natural, normal or original shape or condition
~~overextend~~ /ˌoʊvərɪk'stend/	中 v. 过分扩展，承担过多义务 英 to extend or expand beyond a safe or reasonable point, especially to commit (oneself) financially beyond what can be paid
~~precocious~~ /prɪ'koʊʃəs/	中 adj. 早熟的 英 exhibiting mature qualities at an unusually early age
repudiate /rɪ'pjuːdieɪt/	中 v. 否认，拒绝 英 to refuse to accept or support

quirky /ˈkwɜːrki/	中 *adj.* 奇怪的，古怪的
	英 unusual especially in an interesting way
proponent /prəˈpoʊnənt/	中 *n.* 支持者
	英 a person who argues for or supports something
reiterate /riˈɪtəreɪt/	中 *v.* 重复强调
	英 to repeat something you have already said in order to emphasize
conscientious /ˌkɑːnʃiˈenʃəs/	中 *adj.* 本着良心的
	英 very careful about doing what you are supposed to do; concerned with doing something correctly
	中 *adj.* 勤奋的
	英 thorough and assiduous
rapacious /rəˈpeɪʃəs/	中 *adj.* 贪婪的
	英 having or showing a strong or excessive desire to acquire money or possess things
disquisition /ˌdɪskwɪˈzɪʃn/	中 *n.* 演讲，报告
	英 a long speech or written report on a subject
foretell /fɔːrˈtel/	中 *v.* 预言，预测
	英 to tell of or indicate beforehand
understate /ˌʌndərˈsteɪt/	中 *v.* 少说，少报
	英 to represent less than the case
	中 *v.* 带有限制地表达
	英 to state or present with restraint especially for effect

discredit /dɪsˈkredɪt/	中 *v.* 拒绝承认 英 to refuse to accept as true or accurate 中 *v.* 使被怀疑 英 to cause disbelief in the accuracy or authority of 中 *v.* 破坏名声 英 to deprive of good repute
underscore /ˌʌndərˈskɔːr/	中 *v.* 强调 英 to emphasize (something) or show the importance of (something)
predetermine /ˌpriːdɪˈtɜːrmɪn/	中 *v.* 预先决定 英 to decide (something) before it happens or in advance
provisional /prəˈvɪʒənl/	中 *adj.* 临时的 英 serving for the time being
circumspect /ˈsɜːrkəmspekt/	中 *adj.* 谨慎的 英 thinking carefully about possible risks before doing or saying something
majestic /məˈdʒestɪk/	中 *adj.* 庄严威武的 英 large and impressively beautiful
estrange /ɛˈstreɪndʒ/	中 *v.* 使疏远 英 to cause someone to be no longer friendly or close to another person or group

Word List 10

音频

~~falsehood~~ /ˈfɔːlshʊd/	中 *n.* 谎言，谬论 英 an untrue statement
~~manipulate~~ /məˈnɪpjuleɪt/	中 *v.* 操控 英 to move or control (something) with your hands or by using a machine
~~pathological~~ /ˌpæθəˈlɑːdʒɪkl/	中 *adj.* 极端的 英 being such to a degree that is extreme, excessive or markedly abnormal 中 *adj.* 病态的 英 indicative of disease
circuitous /sərˈkjuːɪtəs/	中 *adj.* 兜圈子的，不直接的 英 not being forthright or direct in language or action
propitious /prəˈpɪʃəs/	中 *adj.* 吉祥的，吉利的 英 likely to have or produce good results
~~insightful~~ /ˈɪnsaɪtfʊl/	中 *adj.* 有洞察力的 英 having or showing a very clear understanding of something; having or showing insight
~~nullify~~ /ˈnʌlɪfaɪ/	中 *v.* 使…无效 英 to cause (something) to lose its value or to have no effect
facilitate /fəˈsɪlɪteɪt/	中 *v.* 辅助，帮助 英 to make easier

appeal /ə'piːl/	中 *v.* 呼吁，恳求 英 to ask for something (such as help or support) in a serious way 中 *v.* 吸引 英 to be pleasing or attractive to someone
appease /ə'piːz/	中 *v.* 安抚，缓和 英 to make (someone) pleased or less angry by giving or saying something desired
deleterious /ˌdelə'tɪriəs/	中 *adj.* 有害的 英 damaging or harmful
ethereal /i'θɪriəl/	中 *adj.* 虚无的 英 lacking material substance; immaterial, intangible 中 *adj.* 天上的 英 of or relating to the regions beyond the earth
rehabilitate /ˌriːə'bɪlɪteɪt/	中 *v.* 恢复 英 to restore to a former capacity
cluster /'klʌstər/	中 *v.* 聚集 英 to come together to form a group
partisan /'pɑːrtəzn/	中 *n.* 坚定的支持者（盲目的，偏护的，不理性的支持） 英 a firm adherent to a party, faction, cause or person, especially one exhibiting blind, prejudiced and unreasoning allegiance
bypass /'baɪpæs/	中 *v.* 绕过 英 to go around or avoid (a place or area)
scrupulous /'skruːpjələs/	中 *adj.* 小心谨慎的 英 very careful about doing something correctly 中 *adj.* 有道德的，有良心的 英 acting in strict regard for what is considered right or proper

monolithic
/ˌmɑːnəˈlɪθɪk/
中 adj. 庞大而僵硬的
英 constituting a massive undifferentiated and often rigid whole

scathing
/ˈskeɪðɪŋ/
中 adj. 尖酸刻薄的
英 very harsh or severe

block
/blɑːk/
中 v. 阻碍，妨碍
英 to make unsuitable for passage or progress by obstruction

off-putting
/ˈɔːf pʊtɪŋ/
中 adj. 令人反感的
英 causing you to feel dislike of someone or something

profligate
/ˈprɑːflɪɡət/
中 adj. 奢侈的，花钱大手大脚的
英 carelessly and foolishly wasting money, materials

unctuous
/ˈʌŋktʃuəs/
中 adj. 虚情假意的
英 revealing or marked by a smug, ingratiating and false earnestness or spirituality
中 adj. 油腻的
英 rich in oil or fat

nimble
/ˈnɪmbl/
中 adj. 灵敏的，轻快的
英 able to move quickly, easily and lightly
中 adj. 机敏的
英 able to learn and understand things quickly and easily

shoddy
/ˈʃɑːdi/
中 adj. 劣质的
英 poorly done or made

heterogeneous
/ˌhetərəˈdʒiːniəs/
中 adj. 组成多样的，混合的
英 made up of parts that are different

verisimilitude
/ˌverɪsɪˈmɪlɪtuːd/

中 *n.* 逼真
英 the quality of seeming real

derivative
/dɪˈrɪvətɪv/

中 *adj.* 非原创的
英 unoriginal

sycophantic
/ˌsɪkəˈfæntɪk/

中 *adj.* 奉承的
英 fawning, obsequious

circumvent
/ˌsɜːrkəmˈvent/

中 *v.* 绕过，回避
英 to avoid being stopped by (something, such as a law or rule)

rigid
/ˈrɪdʒɪd/

中 *adj.* 僵硬的
英 not flexible
中 *adj.* 严格精确的
英 precise and accurate in procedure
中 *adj.* 思想僵化的
英 not willing to change opinions or behavior

plaintive
/ˈpleɪntɪv/

中 *adj.* 痛苦的
英 expressing suffering or sadness

detestation
/ˌdiːteˈsteɪʃn/

中 *n.* 厌恶，反感
英 extreme hatred or dislike

susceptible
/səˈseptəbl/

中 *adj.* 易受影响的
英 easily affected, influenced or harmed by something

tautology
/tɔːˈtɑːlədʒi/

中 *n.* 赘述
英 a statement in which you repeat a word, idea, etc. in a way that is not necessary

leaven
/ˈlevn/

中 *v.* 使…生动，使…更有趣
英 to make (something) less serious and often more exciting

| convulsion /kən'vʌlʃn/ | 中 *n.* 骚乱，动乱 |
| | 英 a sudden change or disturbance that affects a country, organization, etc. |

| exorbitant /ɪg'zɔːrbɪtənt/ | 中 *adj.* 过度的，超出合理范围的 |
| | 英 going far beyond what is fair, reasonable or expected |

| corollary /'kɔːrəleri/ | 中 *n.* 推论，结果 |
| | 英 something that naturally follows or results from another thing |

| perforce /pər'fɔːrs/ | 中 *adv.* 必然地 |
| | 英 used to say that something is necessary or must be done |

| proselytize /'prɑːsələtaɪz/ | 中 *v.* 劝诱，使变节 |
| | 英 to try to persuade people to join a religion, cause or group |

| fetishize /'fetɪʃaɪz/ | 中 *v.* 把…当成神物而崇拜 |
| | 英 to make a fetish of; treat or regard with fetishism |

omnivorous /ɑːm'nɪvərəs/	中 *adj.* 杂食的
	英 eating both plants and animals
	中 *adj.* 兴趣广泛的
	英 eager to learn about many different things

| urbane /ɜːr'beɪn/ | 中 *adj.* 礼貌的 |
| | 英 polite and confident |

| idiosyncrasy /ˌɪdiə'sɪŋkrəsi/ | 中 *n.* 独特的气质 |
| | 英 an unusual way in which a particular person behaves or thinks |

forthcoming /ˌfɔːrθ'kʌmɪŋ/	中 *adj.* 直白的
	英 honest and open
	中 *adj.* 即将到来的
	英 appearing, happening or arriving soon

pecuniary
/pɪˈkjuːnieri/
中 *adj.* 金钱的
英 relating to or in the form of money

pathos
/ˈpeɪθɑːs/
中 *n.* 怜悯，同情
英 an emotion of sympathetic pity

cosmopolitan
/ˌkɑːzməˈpɑːlɪtən/
中 *adj.* 见多识广的
英 having worldwide rather than limited or provincial scope or bearing
中 *adj.* 来自四面八方的
英 composed of persons, constituents or elements from all or many parts of the world
中 *adj.* 世界各地都有的
英 found in most parts of the world and under varied ecological conditions

panoply
/ˈpænəpli/
中 *n.* 大批，全副（装备）
英 a group or collection that is impressive because it is so big or because it includes so many different kinds of people or things

arboreal
/ɑːrˈbɔːriəl/
中 *adj.* 树的
英 of or relating to trees
中 *adj.* 树栖的
英 living in or often found in trees

nostalgia
/nəˈstældʒə/
中 *n.* 思乡
英 the state of being homesick
中 *n.* 思念过去
英 a wistful or excessively sentimental yearning for return to or of some past period or irrecoverable condition

peremptory
/pəˈremptəri/
中 *adj.* 不容反抗的，断然的
英 admitting of no contradiction
中 *adj.* 狂妄自大的
英 characterized by often imperious or arrogant self-assurance

avian
/ˈeɪviən/
中 *adj.* 与鸟有关的
英 of or relating to birds

ramshackle
/ˈræmʃækl/
中 *adj.* 摇摇欲坠的
英 appearing ready to collapse
中 *adj.* 组织松散的
英 not carefully made or put together

quiver
/ˈkwɪvər/
中 *v.* 战栗
英 to shake because of fear, cold, nervousness, etc.

rancor
/ˈræŋkər/
中 *n.* 憎恨
英 an angry feeling of hatred or dislike for someone who has treated you unfairly

dewy-eyed
/ˈduːiˌaɪd/
中 *adj.* 天真的，朴素的
英 innocent

epitome
/ɪˈpɪtəmi/
中 *n.* 典型
英 a perfect example

fissure
/ˈfɪʃər/
中 *n.* 裂缝
英 a narrow opening or crack
中 *n.* 分歧
英 a separation or disagreement in thought or viewpoint

parley
/ˈpɑːrli/
中 *v.* 谈判
英 to discuss terms with an enemy

immolate
/ˈɪməleɪt/
中 *v.* 用火摧毁
英 to kill or destroy (someone or something) by fire

lassitude
/ˈlæsɪtuːd/
中 *n.* 无精打采
英 lack of physical or mental energy

pompous /ˈpɑːmpəs/	中 adj. 过于华丽的
	英 excessively elevated or ornate
	中 adj. 傲慢的，自以为是的
	英 having or exhibiting self-importance
overreach /ˌoʊvərˈriːtʃ/	中 v. 野心勃勃而失败
	英 to defeat (oneself) by seeking to do or gain too much
	中 v. 不自量力做…
	英 to try to do something that is beyond your ability to do
demarcate /ˈdiːmɑːrkeɪt/	中 v. 划分边界
	英 to set the boundaries of; delimit
evince /ɪˈvɪns/	中 v. 显示
	英 to display clearly
veer /vɪr/	中 v. 改变方向
	英 to change direction or course
resilient /rɪˈzɪliənt/	中 adj. 能（从困境中）恢复的
	英 able to become strong, healthy or successful again after something bad happens
	中 adj. 有弹性的
	英 able to return to an original shape after being pulled, stretched, pressed, bent, etc.
revolt /rɪˈvoʊlt/	中 v. 反叛，反抗
	英 to fight in a violent way against the rule of a leader or government
	中 v. 反感
	英 to cause (someone) to feel disgust or shock

devolve /dɪˈvaːlv/	中 v. 衰落
	英 to gradually go from an advanced state to a less advanced state
	中 v. （权力、责任）移交
	英 to pass on from one person or entity to another

| adulation /ˌædʒəˈleɪʃn/ | 中 n. 恭维，吹捧 |
| | 英 excessive or slavish admiration or flattery |

demolish /dɪˈmaːlɪʃ/	中 v. 拆毁
	英 to forcefully tear down or take apart (a structure)
	中 v. 破坏
	英 to damage (something) so that it cannot be repaired

| timely /ˈtaɪmli/ | 中 adv. 合时宜地 |
| | 英 in time |

snapshot /ˈsnæpʃaːt/	中 n. 大致情况，简介
	英 a quick view of a small amount of information that tells you a little about what someone or something is like
	中 n. 快照
	英 an informal photograph that is taken quickly

| obsequious /əbˈsiːkwiəs/ | 中 adj. 谄媚的 |
| | 英 too eager to help or obey someone important |

gut /gʌt/	中 n. 内心深处
	英 innermost emotional or visceral response
	中 v. 摘取要点
	英 to extract essential or major parts of

guts ?

hierarchy
/'haɪərɑːrki/

中 *n.* 等级制度，有等级划分的组织
英 the classification of a group of people according to ability or to economic, social or professional standing or the group so classified
中 *n.* 权力机构
英 a body of persons in authority

terse
/tɜːrs/

中 *adj.* 简洁的
英 brief and direct in a way that may seem rude or unfriendly

abate
/ə'beɪt/

中 *v.* 减弱
英 to become weaker

fluster
/'flʌstər/

中 *v.* 使…不安
英 to make (someone) nervous and confused

flatter
/'flætər/

中 *v.* 谄媚，拍马屁
英 to praise (someone) in a way that is not sincere

accentuate
/ək'sentʃueɪt/

中 *v.* 强调
英 to make (something) more noticeable

augment
/ɔːg'ment/

中 *v.* 放大
英 to increase the size or amount of (something)
中 *v.* 补充
英 to supplement

certitude
/'sɜːrtɪtuːd/

中 *n.* 确信无疑
英 freedom from doubt

cachet
/kæ'ʃeɪ/

中 *n.* 声望，威望
英 an indication of approval carrying great prestige

| contrite /kən'traɪt/ | 中 adj. 后悔的 |
| | 英 feeling or showing regret for bad behavior |

| ✓ unanimous /ju'nænɪməs/ | 中 adj. 意见一致的 |
| | 英 having the same opinion |

| neologism /ni'ɑːlədʒɪzəm/ | 中 n. 新词，新义 |
| | 英 a new word or expression or a new meaning of a word |

| aristocracy /ˌærɪ'stɑːkrəsi/ | 中 n. 贵族统治，精英统治 |
| | 英 government by the best individuals or by a small privileged class |

| inimical /ɪ'nɪmɪkl/ | 中 adj. 有害的，不友好的 |
| | 英 likely to cause damage or have a bad effect |

| hallow /'hæloʊ/ | 中 v. 尊敬，崇敬 |
| | 英 to respect greatly; venerate |

| annals /'ænlz/ | 中 n. 历史记载 |
| | 英 historical records |

| execrate /'eksɪˌkreɪt/ | 中 v. 痛斥 |
| | 英 to dislike and criticize (someone or something) very strongly |

| unexampled /ˌʌnɪg'zæmpld/ | 中 adj. 史无前例的 |
| | 英 without precedent |

tug /tʌg/	中 v. 用力拉
	英 to pull something with a quick, forceful movement
	中 n. 竞争
	英 a struggle between two people or opposite forces

| claustrophobic /ˌklɔːstrəˈfoʊbɪk/ | 中 *adj.* 狭小而引起不适的 |
| | 英 uncomfortably closed or hemmed in |

atavism /ˈætəˌvɪzəm/	中 *n.* 重现
	英 the return of a trait or recurrence of previous behavior after a period of absence
	中 *n.* 返祖现象
	英 The reappearance of a characteristic in an organism after several generations of absence, usually caused by the chance recombination of genes.

| prepossessing /ˌpriːpəˈzesɪŋ/ | 中 *adj.* 有吸引力的 |
| | 英 appealing or attractive |

| perfidious /pərˈfɪdiəs/ | 中 *adj.* 不可信赖的 |
| | 英 not able to be trusted |

Word List 11

音 频

jubilation /ˌdʒuːbɪˈleɪʃn/	中 *n.* 高兴，喜悦 英 great happiness or joy
peregrination /ˌperəɡrɪˈneɪʃn/	中 *n.* 长途旅行，游历 英 a voyage, especially an extensive one
retribution /ˌretrɪˈbjuːʃn/	中 *n.* 惩罚 英 punishment for doing something wrong
charlatan /ˈʃɑːrlətən/	中 *n.* 骗子 英 a person who falsely pretends to know or be something in order to deceive people
malinger /məˈlɪŋɡər/	中 *v.* 装病以逃避工作 英 to feign illness or other incapacity in order to avoid duty or work
halcyon /ˈhælsiən/	中 *adj.* 岁月静好的，安宁的 英 very happy and successful
predominant /prɪˈdɑːmɪnənt/	中 *adj.* 最显著的，主导的 英 more important, powerful, successful or noticeable than other people or things
evocative /ɪˈvɑːkətɪv/	中 *adj.* 唤起的 英 bringing thoughts, memories or feelings into the mind
nonchalant /ˌnɑːnʃəˈlɑːnt/	中 *adj.* 漠不关心的 英 relaxed and calm in a way that shows that you do not care or are not worried about anything
ennoble /ɪˈnoʊbl/	中 *v.* 使…崇高 英 to make (someone or something) better or more worthy of admiration

eradicate
/ɪ'rædɪkeɪt/
中 v. 根除
英 to remove (something) completely

prodigal
/'prɑ:dɪgl/
中 adj. 奢侈浪费的
英 characterized by profuse or wasteful expenditure
中 adj. 多产的，大量的
英 yielding abundantly

disengage
/ˌdɪsɪn'geɪdʒ/
中 v. 使解脱
英 to release from something that engages or involves

rebound
/rɪ'baʊnd/
中 v. 从挫败中恢复
英 to recover from setback or frustration
中 v. 弹回
英 to bounce back off something after hitting it

adhere
/əd'hɪr/
中 v. 依附于，坚持
英 to stick to something

unilateral
/ˌjuːnɪ'lætrəl/
中 adj. 单方面的
英 involving only one group or country

equable
/'ekwəbl/
中 adj. 平静的
英 tending to remain calm
中 adj. 稳定不变的
英 free from sudden or harsh changes

instantiate
/ɪn'stænʃiˌeɪt/
中 v. 举例，例证
英 to represent (an abstraction) by a concrete instance

diverse
/daɪ'vɜːrs/
中 adj. 多样的，不同的
英 different from each other

protean
/'proʊtiən/
中 adj. 多样的
英 displaying great diversity or variety

pillory /ˈpɪləri/	中 v. 公开批评 英 to publicly criticize (someone) in a very harsh way
exuberant /ɪgˈzuːbərənt/	中 adj. 过量的 英 extreme or excessive in degree, size or extent 中 adj. 热情洋溢的 英 filled with energy and enthusiasm
plunder /ˈplʌndər/	中 v. 掠夺 英 to steal things from (a place, such as a city or town) especially by force
ennui /ɑːnˈwiː/	中 n. 无趣，无聊 英 a lack of spirit, enthusiasm or interest
conceive /kənˈsiːv/	中 v. 构想，创造 英 to think of or create (something) in the mind
devoid /dɪˈvɔɪd/	中 adj. 缺乏的 英 being without
sophisticated /səˈfɪstɪkeɪtɪd/	中 adj. 精于世故的，老练的 英 having or showing a lot of experience and knowledge about the world and about culture, art, literature, etc. 中 adj. 高度复杂的 英 highly developed and complex
conclusive /kənˈkluːsɪv/	中 adj. 终结的，最终的 英 putting an end to debate or question especially by reason of irrefutability
enlighten /ɪnˈlaɪtn/	中 v. 启迪，开导 英 to give knowledge or understanding to (someone)

| methodology /ˌmeθə'dɑːlədʒi/ | 中 n. 方法论 |
| | 英 a set of methods, rules or ideas that are important in a science or art; a particular procedure or set of procedures |

tectonic /tek'tɑːnɪk/	中 adj. 建筑的
	英 relating to construction or building
	中 adj. 地壳构造的
	英 of or relating to changes in the structure of the Earth's surface
	中 adj. 影响广泛的
	英 having a strong and widespread impact

| monogamy /mə'nɑːɡəmi/ | 中 n. 一夫一妻制 |
| | 英 the state or practice of being married to only one person at a time |

| pathogen /'pæθədʒən/ | 中 n. 病原体 |
| | 英 a specific causative agent (as a bacterium or virus) of disease |

| depict /dɪ'pɪkt/ | 中 v. 描述 |
| | 英 to describe (someone or something) using words |

dismissive /dɪs'mɪsɪv/	中 adj. 轻视的，无视的
	英 serving to dismiss
	中 adj. 轻蔑的
	英 showing indifference or disregard

invertebrate /ɪn'vɜːrtɪbrət/	中 adj. 软弱无力的
	英 lacking in strength or vitality
	中 n. 无脊椎动物

| discrepancy /dɪs'krepənsi/ | 中 n. 差异 |
| | 英 a difference especially between things that should be the same |

demographic /ˌdeməˈɡræfɪk/	中 *adj.* 与人口统计有关的 英 of or relating to the study of changes that occur in large groups of people over a period of time, of or relating to demography
forage /ˈfɔːrɪdʒ/	中 *v.* 寻找（食物） 英 to search for something (such as food or supplies)
~~**synchronous**~~ /ˈsɪŋkrənəs/	中 *adj.* 同时的 英 happening, moving or existing at the same time
hagiography /ˌhæɡiˈɑːɡrəfi/	中 *n.*（夸大的）传记 英 a book about someone's life that makes it seem better than it really is or was
~~**monochromatic**~~ /ˌmɑːnəkroʊˈmætɪk/	中 *adj.* 单调的 英 lacking variety, creativity or excitement
~~**employ**~~ /ɪmˈplɔɪ/	中 *v.* 使用 英 to make use of 中 *v.* 雇用 英 to give a job to
~~**indigenous**~~ /ɪnˈdɪdʒənəs/	中 *adj.* 当地的 英 originating and growing or living in an area or environment; native 中 *adj.* 与生俱来的 英 innate or inborn
insurrection /ˌɪnsəˈrekʃn/	中 *n.* 造反 英 a usually violent attempt to take control of a government
~~**ideology**~~ /ˌaɪdiˈɑːlədʒi/	中 *n.* 思想体系，意识形态 英 the set of ideas and beliefs of a group or political party

~~segregate~~ /'segrɪgeɪt/	中 v. 分离，隔离 英 to separate groups of people because of their particular race, religion 中 v. 强制隔离 英 to not allow people of different races to be together in (a place, such as a school)
propound /prə'paʊnd/	中 v. 提出…供考虑 英 to offer for discussion or consideration
~~adulterate~~ /ə'dʌltəreɪt/	中 v. 掺假 英 to make (something, such as a food or drink) impure or weaker by adding something of poor quality
~~expository~~ /ɪk'spɑːzətɔːri/	中 adj. 解释的，阐释的 英 used to describe writing that is done to explain something
anemia /ə'niːmiə/	中 n. 缺乏活力 英 lack of vitality
~~excavate~~ /'ekskəveɪt/	中 v. 开凿，挖出 英 to uncover (something) by digging away and removing the earth that covers it
~~acerbic~~ /ə'sɜːrbɪk/	中 adj.（语言）辛辣尖刻的 英 expressing harsh or sharp criticism in a clever way
~~resurgence~~ /rɪ'sɜːrdʒəns/	中 n. 复苏 英 a growth or increase that occurs after a period without growth or increase
~~colloquial~~ /kə'loʊkwiəl/	中 adj. 口头的，非正式的 英 using conversational style
~~interjection~~ /ˌɪntər'dʒekʃn/	中 n. 插话 英 the act of uttering exclamations

hoodwink /'hʊdwɪŋk/	中 v. 欺骗 英 to deceive or trick (someone)
analogous /ə'næləgəs/	中 adj. 相似的 英 similar in some way
latent /'leɪtnt/	中 adj. 潜藏的，潜在的 英 present but not visible or active
boycott /'bɔɪkaːt/	中 v. 抵制 英 to refuse to buy, use or participate in (something) as a way of protesting
sentimental /ˌsentɪ'mentl/	中 adj. 感情用事的 英 resulting from feeling rather than reason or thought 中 adj. 多愁善感的 英 marked or governed by feeling, sensibility or emotional idealism
castigate /'kæstɪgeɪt/	中 v. 严厉批评 英 to criticize (someone) harshly
preeminent /ˌpriː'emɪnənt/	中 adj. 杰出的，独一无二的 英 better than others
terminology /ˌtɜːrmə'naːlədʒi/	中 n. 术语 英 the special words or phrases that are used in a particular field
domesticate /də'mestɪkeɪt/	中 v. 驯服 英 to breed or train (an animal) to need and accept the care of human beings; to tame (an animal)
pedagogical /ˌpedə'gaːdʒɪk/	中 adj. 教育学的 英 of or relating to teachers or education

~~skew~~ /skjuː/	中 *v.* 歪曲，曲解 英 to change (something) so that it is not true or accurate
~~static~~ /ˈstætɪk/	中 *adj.* 静态的 英 showing little or no change, action or progress
~~discrete~~ /dɪˈskriːt/	中 *adj.* 分开的，分离的 英 separate and different from each other
~~corrode~~ /kəˈroʊd/	中 *v.* 削弱，破坏 英 to weaken or destroy gradually 中 *v.* 腐蚀 英 to slowly break apart and destroy (metal, an object, etc.) through a chemical process
protagonist /prəˈtægənɪst/	中 *n.* 重要人物 英 an important person who is involved in a competition, conflict or cause 中 *n.* 支持者 英 a supporter or champion
~~forerunner~~ /ˈfɔːrʌnər/	中 *n.* 先驱 英 someone or something that comes before another 中 *n.* 预兆 英 a sign of something that is going to happen
clutch /klʌtʃ/	中 *v.* 抓住 英 to hold onto (someone or something) tightly with your hand
straggle /ˈstrægl/	中 *v.* 迷路 英 to wander from the direct course or way 中 *v.* 散乱 英 to move away or spread out from others in a disorganized way

rhetorical /rɪ'tɔːrɪkl/	中 adj. 带有修饰色彩的 英 of, relating to or concerned with the art of speaking or writing formally and effectively especially as a way to persuade or influence people
equilibrium /ˌiːkwɪ'lɪbriəm/	中 n. 平衡 英 a state in which opposing forces or actions are balanced so that one is not stronger or greater than the other
quintessential /ˌkwɪntɪ'senʃl/	中 adj. 精华的，典型的 英 of, relating to or having the nature of a quintessence; being the most typical
regimen /'redʒɪmən/	中 n. 统治，政府统治 英 governmental rule or control
objective /əb'dʒektɪv/	中 adj. 客观的 英 dealing with facts without allowing personal feelings to confuse them
postulate /'pɑːstʃəleɪt/	中 v. 假设，假定 英 to suggest (something, such as an idea or theory) especially in order to start a discussion
onset /'ɑːnset/	中 n. 开始 英 the beginning of something
impinge /ɪm'pɪndʒ/	中 v. 猛烈撞击 英 to strike or dash especially with a sharp collision 中 v. 影响 英 to have an effect or make an impression 中 v. 妨碍，侵犯 英 encroach or infringe

thrive /θraɪv/	中 v. 兴旺发达
	英 to grow or develop successful
milieu /miːˈljɜː/	中 n. 环境
	英 the physical or social setting in which something occurs or develops
paradoxical /ˌpærəˈdɑːksɪkl/	中 adj. 不寻常的
	英 not being the normal or usual kind
	中 adj. 悖论的，矛盾的
	英 of the nature of a paradox
iterate /ˈɪtəreɪt/	中 v. 重说一遍，重做一遍
	英 to say or state or run again
prophetic /prəˈfetɪk/	中 adj. 预言的
	英 correctly stating what will happen in the future
delineate /dɪˈlɪnieɪt/	中 v. 描绘轮廓
	英 to mark the outline of
	中 v. 详细描述
	英 to clearly describe
condone /kənˈdoʊn/	中 v. 原谅，认可
	英 to forgive or approve (something that is considered wrong)
acumen /əˈkjuːmən/	中 n. 机智，精明
	英 keenness and depth of perception, discernment or discrimination especially in practical matters
agonize /ˈægənaɪz/	中 v. 感到痛苦，挣扎
	英 to suffer agony, torture or anguish
revere /rɪˈvɪr/	中 v. 尊敬
	英 to have great respect for (someone or something)

reckless /ˈrekləs/	中 adj. 粗心的，鲁莽的 英 not showing proper concern about the possible bad results of your actions
unsparing /ʌnˈspeərɪŋ/	中 adj. 无情的，苛求的 英 not merciful or forbearing 中 adj. 不节俭的 英 not frugal
belligerent /bəˈlɪdʒərənt/	中 adj. 好斗的 英 angry and aggressive
taciturn /ˈtæsɪtɜːrn/	中 adj. 沉默寡言的 英 tending to be quiet
penitential /ˌpenɪˈtenʃl/	中 adj. 后悔的，忏悔的 英 relating to the feeling of being sorry for doing something wrong
frivolous /ˈfrɪvələs/	中 adj. 无关紧要的 英 of little weight or importance 中 adj. 不严肃的，轻率的 英 silly and not serious
plead /pliːd/	中 v. 辩护 英 to argue a case or cause in a court of law
orthodox /ˈɔːrθədɑːks/	中 adj. 主流的 英 accepted as true or correct by most people 中 adj. 符合传统的 英 accepting and closely following the traditional beliefs and customs of a religion

Word List 12

音频

allege /ə'ledʒ/	中 v. 断言，宣称 英 to assert without proof or before proving
reconcile /'rekənsaɪl/	中 v. 调和 英 to cause people or groups to become friendly again after an argument or disagreement
improvise /'ɪmprəvaɪz/	中 v. 即兴表演 英 to speak or perform without preparation
eliminate /ɪ'lɪmɪneɪt/	中 v. 移除，去掉 英 to get rid of
disquiet /dɪs'kwaɪət/	中 v. 使…不安 英 to take away the peace or tranquility of
predicament /prɪ'dɪkəmənt/	中 n. 困境 英 a difficult or unpleasant situation
fester /'festər/	中 v. 恶化 英 to become worse as time passes
accord /ə'kɔːrd/	中 n. 和谐，一致 英 agreement; harmony
ascertain /ˌæsər'teɪn/	中 v. 查明 英 to learn or find out (something, such as information or the truth)
counterproductive /ˌkaʊntərprə'dʌktɪv/	中 adj. 起反作用的，事与愿违的 英 tending to hinder the attainment of a desired goal

125

misnomer /ˌmɪsˈnoʊmər/	中 *n.* 误称
	英 a name that is wrong or not proper or appropriate
precarious /prɪˈkerəriəs/	中 *adj.* 处境危险的
	英 characterized by a lack of security or stability that threatens with danger
unrelenting /ˌʌnrɪˈlentɪŋ/	中 *adj.* 不屈的
	英 having or exhibiting uncompromising determination; unyielding
	中 *adj.* 持续的，不减退的
	英 not letting up or weakening in vigor or pace
soporific /ˌsɑːpəˈrɪfɪk/	中 *adj.* 令人昏昏欲睡的
	英 causing a person to become tired and ready to fall asleep
disseminate /dɪˈsemɪneɪt/	中 *v.* 传播，散布
	英 to cause (something, such as information) to go to many people
lure /lʊr/	中 *v.* 诱惑
	英 to cause or persuade (a person or an animal) to go somewhere or to do something by offering some pleasure or gain
banish /ˈbænɪʃ/	中 *v.* 驱逐
	英 to send away
degrade /dɪˈɡreɪd/	中 *v.* 贬低
	英 to treat (someone or something) poorly and without respect
	中 *v.* 退化
	英 to make the quality of (something) worse

skittish /ˈskɪtɪʃ/	中 adj. 多变的 英 tending to change often; not dependable or stable 中 adj. 易受惊吓的，易激动的 英 easily frightened or excited; restive
tranquil /ˈtræŋkwɪl/	中 adj. 安静的 英 free from commotion or disturbance 中 adj. 心神安宁的 英 free from anxiety, tension or restlessness
seemly /ˈsiːmli/	中 adj. 有魅力的，好看的 英 good-looking and handsome 中 adj. 得体的 英 conventionally proper
unkempt /ˌʌnˈkempt/	中 adj. 不整洁的，邋遢的 英 not neat or orderly
decorous /ˈdekərəs/	中 adj. 得体的 英 correct and polite in a particular situation
tawdry /ˈtɔːdri/	中 adj. 俗气的 英 cheap and gaudy in appearance or quality 中 adj. 卑鄙的 英 morally low or bad
décor /deɪˈkɔːr/	中 n.（装修的）格调，风格 英 the way that a room or the inside of a building is decorated
lush /lʌʃ/	中 adj. 茂盛的，郁郁葱葱的 英 lavishly productive 中 adj. 奢华的 英 opulent or sumptuous
acidic /əˈsɪdɪk/	中 adj. 酸的，尖酸刻薄的 英 having a very sour or sharp taste

~~coarse~~ /kɔːrs/	中 *adj.* 粗糙的 英 having a rough quality 中 *adj.* 粗鲁的 英 rude or offensive
impoverished /ɪmˈpɑːvərɪʃt/	中 *adj.* 贫瘠的，贫穷的 英 represented by few species or individuals
threshold /ˈθreʃhoʊld/	中 *n.* 阈值，临界点 英 the point or level at which something begins or changes
~~disparage~~ /dɪˈspærɪdʒ/	中 *v.* 鄙视 英 to describe (someone or something) as unimportant, weak, bad, etc.
~~invalidate~~ /ɪnˈvælɪdeɪt/	中 *v.* 削弱，使…无效 英 to weaken or destroy the effect of (something)
~~hackneyed~~ /ˈhæknid/	中 *adj.* 陈词滥调的 英 not interesting, funny, etc., because of being used too often
ruminate /ˈruːmɪneɪt/	中 *v.* 仔细思考 英 to think carefully and deeply about something
~~meander~~ /miˈændər/	中 *v.* 漫无目的地走动 英 to move or cause to move in a sinuous, spiral or circular course
bucolic /bjuːˈkɑːlɪk/	中 *adj.* 乡间生活的 英 of or relating to the country or country life
pastoral /ˈpæstərəl/	中 *adj.* 乡间生活的 英 of or relating to the countryside or to the lives of people who live in the country

hard-nosed
/'hɑːrd,noʊzd/

中 *adj.* 顽强的
英 being tough, stubborn or uncompromising
中 *adj.* 精明而讲究实际的
英 concerned with or involving practical considerations

petty
/'peti/

中 *adj.* 不重要的，次要的
英 not very important or serious
中 *adj.* 小气的
英 marked by or reflective of narrow interests and sympathies

opportunistic
/,ɑːpərtuːˈnɪstɪk/

中 *adj.* 机会主义的，投机的
英 taking advantage of opportunities as they arise

menace
/'menəs/

中 *v.* 威胁
英 to threaten harm to (someone or something)

painstaking
/'peɪnzteɪkɪŋ/

中 *adj.* 勤奋努力的
英 diligent care and effort

humanitarian
/hjuː,mænɪˈteriən/

中 *adj.* 人道的，博爱的
英 relating to or characteristic of people who work to improve the lives and living conditions of other people

predispose
/,priːdɪˈspoʊz/

中 *v.* 使…易受感染
英 to make susceptible or liable

eminent
/'emɪnənt/

中 *adj.* 杰出的
英 successful, well-known and respected

declamatory
/dɪˈklæmətɔːri/

中 *adj.* 演说般的，慷慨激昂的
英 expressing feelings or opinions in a way that is loud and forceful

ascetic /ə'setɪk/	中 *adj.* 过清苦生活的
	英 relating to or having a strict and simple way of living that avoids physical pleasure
safeguard /'seɪfɡɑːrd/	中 *v.* 保护
	英 to make (someone or something) safe or secure
sinister /'sɪnɪstər/	中 *adj.* 邪恶的
	英 having an evil appearance
	中 *adj.* 不吉利的
	英 presaging ill fortune or trouble
convincing /kən'vɪnsɪŋ/	中 *adj.* 有说服力的
	英 causing someone to believe that something is true or certain
peak /piːk/	中 *n.* 顶点，顶峰
	英 the highest level or greatest degree
unrivaled /ʌn'raɪvld/	中 *adj.* 无法匹敌的
	英 better than anyone or anything else
pivotal /'pɪvətl/	中 *adj.* 非常重要的
	英 very important
recondite /'rekəndaɪt/	中 *adj.* 难懂的
	英 difficult or impossible for one of ordinary understanding or knowledge to comprehend
morbid /'mɔːrbɪd/	中 *adj.* 不健康的
	英 not healthy or normal
	中 *adj.* （话题）不愉快的
	英 relating to unpleasant subjects
staple /'steɪpl/	中 *adj.* （食物，商品等）必要的
	英 used, needed or enjoyed constantly by many people
	中 *adj.* 重要的，主要的
	英 principal, chief

herald /'herəld/	中 *n.* 前兆 英 a sign that something will happen 中 *v.* 预示 英 to be a sign of
cure-all /kjʊr,ɔl/	中 *n.* 万能灵药 英 a cure or solution for any illness or problem
ruthless /'ruːθləs/	中 *adj.* 无情的，残忍的 英 having no pity
scorn /skɔːrn/	中 *v.* 鄙视，嘲笑 英 to show disdain or derision
acquisitive /ə'kwɪzətɪv/	中 *adj.* 贪婪的 英 having a strong desire to own or acquire more things
clangorous /'klæŋgərəs/	中 *adj.* 叮当响的，响亮的 英 having a loud resonant metallic sound
rejuvenate /rɪ'dʒuːvəneɪt/	中 *adj.* 使…重新有活力 英 to give new strength or energy to
obsess /əb'ses/	中 *v.* 沉迷于… 英 to think and talk about someone or something too much
canonical /kə'nɑːnɪkl/	中 *adj.*（书籍等在某个领域）经典之作的 英 of or relating to the group of books, plays, poems, etc., that are traditionally considered to be very important
undo /ʌn'duː/	中 *v.* 撤销 英 to stop the effect of
obsolete /ˌɑːbsə'liːt/	中 *adj.* 过时的 英 no longer used because something newer exists

quotidian /kwoʊˈtɪdiən/	中 *adj.* 普通的 英 everyday; commonplace
pathetic /pəˈθetɪk/	中 *adj.* 可怜的 英 causing feelings of sadness and sympathy 中 *adj.* 差劲的，不足的 英 pitifully inferior or inadequate
bathetic /bəˈθetɪk/	中 *adj.* 陈腐的 英 marked by exceptional commonplaceness
veracious /vəˈreɪʃəs/	中 *adj.* 真实的 英 marked by truth 中 *adj.* 精确的 英 accurate; precise
voracious /vəˈreɪʃəs/	中 *adj.* 贪婪的 英 excessively eager 中 *adj.* 贪吃的 英 having a huge appetite
exploit /ɪkˈsplɔɪt/	中 *v.* 充分利用 英 to make productive use of 中 *v.* 剥削 英 to make use of meanly or unfairly for one's own advantage 中 *n.* 成就，功绩 英 an act or deed, especially a brilliant or heroic one
retrofit /ˈretroʊfɪt/	中 *v.* 翻新 英 to provide (something) with new parts that were not available when it was originally built
witty /ˈwɪti/	中 *adj.* 机智幽默的 英 funny and clever

provocative /prə'vɑːkətɪv/	中 *adj.* 引起争论的，启发的
	英 causing discussion, thought, argument, etc.
	中 *adj.* 刺激的
	英 causing excitement
impecunious /ˌɪmpɪ'kjuːniəs/	中 *adj.* 贫穷的
	英 having little or no money
assiduous /ə'sɪdʒuəs/	中 *adj.* 努力的
	英 showing great care, attention and effort
tacit /'tæsɪt/	中 *adj.* 不言而喻的，心照不宣的
	英 expressed or understood without being directly stated *tact?*
transgress /trænz'gres/	中 *v.* 违反，违背
	英 to disobey a command or law
abstruse /əb'struːs/	中 *adj.* 难以理解的
	英 difficult to comprehend
embed /ɪm'bed/	中 *v.* 嵌入
	英 to place or set (something) firmly in something else; to make something an integral part of
render /'rendər/	中 *v.* 使成为…
	英 to cause to become; make
	中 *v.* 复制
	英 to produce a copy or version of; reproduce
alter /'ɔːltər/	中 *v.* 改变
	英 to change (something)
penchant /'pentʃənt/	中 *n.* 倾向
	英 a strong liking for something or a strong tendency to behave in a certain way

~~tailor~~ /ˈteɪlər/	中 v. 修改 英 to make or change (something) so that it meets a special need or purpose 中 n. 裁缝
~~homogeneous~~ /ˌhoʊməˈdʒiːniəs/	中 adj. 同种的，相似的 英 of the same or similar nature or kind
immense /ɪˈmens/	中 adj. 巨大的 英 very great in size or amount
~~kindred~~ /ˈkɪndrəd/	中 adj. 相关的，相似的 英 closely related or similar
affiliate /əˈfɪlieɪt/	中 v. 附属 英 to closely connect (something or yourself) with or to something (such as a program or organization) as a member or partner
run-of-the-mill /rʌnəvðəmɪl/	中 adj. 平凡的 英 average or ordinary
~~refuge~~ /ˈrefjuːdʒ/	中 n. 避难所 英 a place that provides shelter or protection
oratorical /ˌɔːrəˈtɔːrɪkl/	中 adj. 演说的 英 of or relating to the skill or activity of giving speeches
~~incense~~ /ˈɪnsens/	中 v. 激怒 英 to arouse the extreme anger or indignation of
mortify /ˈmɔːrtɪfaɪ/	中 v. 使…尴尬 英 to cause (someone) to feel very embarrassed and foolish
~~heterodox~~ /ˈhetərədɑːks/	中 adj. 异端邪说的，非主流观点的 英 not agreeing with established beliefs or standards

doctrinaire /ˌdɑːktrəˈner/	中 *adj.* 空谈理论的，教条的 英 of, relating to, or characteristic of a person inflexibly attached to a practice or theory; dictatorial 中 *n.* 教条主义者（不顾实际而一味坚持某一经验或理论的人） 英 a person inflexibly attached to a practice or theory without regard to its practicality
sporadic /spəˈrædɪk/	中 *adj.* 不规律的，偶发的，随机的 英 occurring occasionally, singly, or in irregular or random instances
dictate /ˈdɪkteɪt/	中 *v.* 掌控，支配 英 to control or command 命令，口述
buoyant /ˈbɔɪənt/	中 *adj.* 愉悦的 英 happy and confident 中 *adj.* 漂浮的，可浮起来的 英 able to float or able to cause things to float

Word List 13

音频

---

premonitory
/prɪ'mɑːnɪtɔːri/

中 *adj.* 警告的
英 giving warning

---

abreast
/ə'brest/

中 *adj.* 平行的
英 side by side
中 *v.* 及时了解
英 up to date with

---

obstinate
/'ɑːbstɪnət/

中 *adj.* 固执的
英 refusing to change your behavior or your ideas

---

redeem
/rɪ'diːm/

中 *v.* 赎罪
英 to atone for
中 *v.* 赎回
英 to buy back

---

debacle
/deɪ'bɑːkl/

中 *n.* 大灾难
英 a great disaster
中 *n.* 彻底失败
英 a complete failure

---

omit
/ə'mɪt/

中 *v.* 省略，忽略
英 to not include or to leave undone

---

boon
/buːn/

中 *n.* 好处，福利
英 a benefit or advantage

---

hidebound
/'haɪdbaʊnd/

中 *adj.* 守旧的
英 not willing to accept new or different ideas

---

sullen
/'sʌlən/

中 *adj.* 不高兴的，性格阴郁的
英 dismal and gloomy
中 *adj.* 阴沉灰暗的
英 gray and dark

---

prudent /'pru:dnt/	中 *adj.* 谨慎的
	英 marked by circumspection
	中 *adj.* 节省的
	英 provident or frugal
	中 *adj.* 睿智的，精明的
	英 marked by wisdom or judiciousness
juxtapose /ˌdʒʌkstə'poʊz/	中 *v.* 并排放置
	英 to place two or more things side by side
noxious /'naːkʃəs/	中 *adj.* 有害的
	英 harmful to living things
obnoxious /əb'naːkʃəs/	中 *adj.* 极其令人反感的
	英 odiously or disgustingly objectionable
laborious /lə'bɔːriəs/	中 *adj.* 费力的
	英 requiring a lot of time and effort
	中 *adj.* 勤奋的
	英 devoted to labor
rhapsody /'ræpsədi/	中 *n.* 慷慨激昂的说辞
	英 a written or spoken expression of great enthusiasm, praise, etc.
stanch /stæntʃ/	中 *v.* 阻止
	英 to stop or check in its course
	中 *v.* 止血
	英 to stop blood from flowing
divert /daɪ'vɜːrt/	中 *v.* 分散，转移（注意力，精神）
	英 to distract
	中 *v.* 通过转移注意力使人愉悦
	英 to give pleasure to especially by distracting the attention from what burdens or distresses
bungle /'bʌŋgl/	中 *v.* 搞砸
	英 to not do (something) well or successfully

pendulum /'pendʒələm/	中 n.（局势）摇摆不定 英 something (as a state of affairs) that alternates between opposites
~~**fixate**~~ /'fɪkˌseɪt/	中 v. 注视，全神贯注 英 to give all of your attention to something
~~**aghast**~~ /ə'gæst/	中 adj. 吃惊的 英 shocked and upset
~~**obdurate**~~ /'ɑːbdərət/	中 adj. 固执的 英 stubbornly persistent in wrongdoing
~~**foresight**~~ /'fɔːrsaɪt/	中 n. 远见 英 the ability to see what will or might happen in the future
glamorous /'glæmərəs/	中 adj. 有吸引力的 英 very exciting and attractive
relegate /'relɪgeɪt/	中 v. 降低 英 to assign to a place of insignificance or of oblivion
apostle /ə'pɑːsl/	中 n. 狂热的支持者 英 an ardent supporter
foreground /'fɔːrgraʊnd/	中 v. 强调 英 to make (something) more important
pious /'paɪəs/	中 adj. 信仰虔诚的 英 deeply religious 中 adj. 假虔诚的；伪善的 英 marked by false devoutness; solemnly hypocritical
self-righteous /self'raɪtʃəs/	中 adj. 自以为是的 英 convinced of one's own righteousness especially in contrast with the actions and beliefs of others

brandish /ˈbrændɪʃ/	中 v. 炫耀
	英 to display ostentatiously
	中 v. 挥舞
	英 to shake or wave (as a weapon) menacingly
erroneous /ɪˈrouniəs/	中 adj. 错误的
	英 not correct
feasible /ˈfiːzəbl/	中 adj. 可行的
	英 possible to do
schism /ˈsɪzəm/	中 n. 分裂
	英 division or separation
notorious /nouˈtɔːriəs/	中 adj. 臭名昭著的
	英 well-known or famous especially for something bad
providential /ˌprɑːvɪˈdenʃl/	中 adj. 幸运的，凑巧的
	英 happening at a good time because of luck
tumultuous /tuːˈmʌltʃuəs/	中 adj. 混乱的
	英 involving a lot of violence, confusion or disorder
panache /pəˈnæʃ/	中 n. 炫
	英 dash or flamboyance in style and action
gawky /ˈgɔːki/	中 adj. 笨拙的
	英 awkward and clumsy
virulent /ˈvɪrjələnt/	中 adj. 有害的，有毒的
	英 extremely dangerous and deadly and usually spreading very quickly
	中 adj. 恶毒的
	英 full of malice

malignant /məˈlɪgnənt/	中 *adj.* 有害的 英 tending to produce death or deterioration 中 *adj.* 恶毒的 英 passionately and relentlessly malevolent
~~benign~~ /bɪˈnaɪn/	中 *adj.* 无害的 英 not causing harm or damage 中 *adj.* 温和的，善良的 英 showing kindness and gentleness
~~abridge~~ /əˈbrɪdʒ/	中 *v.* 缩短 英 to shorten by leaving out some parts
lurid /ˈlʊrɪd/	中 *adj.* 令人震惊的，骇人听闻的 英 causing shock or disgust
~~copious~~ /ˈkoʊpiəs/	中 *adj.* 大量的 英 very large in amount or number
~~negligent~~ /ˈneglɪdʒənt/	中 *adj.* 疏忽大意的 英 failing to take proper or normal care of something or someone
sartorial /sɑːrˈtɔːriəl/	中 *adj.* 与衣服相关的 英 of or relating to a tailor or tailored clothes
~~supersede~~ /ˌsuːpərˈsiːd/	中 *v.* 淘汰，取代 英 to take the place of (someone or something that is old, no longer useful, etc.)
~~thrill~~ /θrɪl/	中 *v.* 使…兴奋 英 to cause (someone) to feel very excited or happy
approbate /ˈæprəˌbeɪt/	中 *v.* 支持，赞成 英 to approve or sanction
~~relinquish~~ /rɪˈlɪŋkwɪʃ/	中 *v.* 放弃 英 to give up (something)

~~replenish~~ /rɪ'plenɪʃ/	中 v. 补充，修复 英 to fill or build up again
~~curtail~~ /kɜːr'teɪl/	中 v. 削减 英 to reduce or limit (something)
~~fabricate~~ /'fæbrɪkeɪt/	中 v. 编造，捏造 英 to make up for the purpose of deception 中 v. 生产，制造 英 to construct or manufacture
manacle /'mænəkl/	中 v. 限制 英 to restrain from movement, progress or action
~~rein~~ /reɪn/	中 v. 阻止，限制 英 to check or stop by or as if by a pull at the reins 中 n. （马的）缰绳
~~bridle~~ /'braɪdl/	中 v. 限制，管控 英 to restrain, check or control with or as if with a bridle 中 n. 马勒
grant /grænt/	中 v. 承认 英 to admit (something) although it does not agree with or support your opinion 中 v. 授予 英 to bestow or transfer formally 中 v. 允许 英 to agree to do, give or allow (something asked for or hoped for)
digress /daɪ'gres/	中 v. 偏题，跑题 英 to speak or write about something that is different from the main subject being discussed

entrench /ɪnˈtrentʃ/	中 v. 牢固地确立 英 to establish firmly or solidly
prowess /ˈprauəs/	中 n.（超凡的）技巧，能力 英 great ability or skill
secular /ˈsekjələr/	中 adj. 世俗的 英 of or relating to the physical world and not the spiritual world 中 adj. 非宗教的 英 not religious
ecstatic /ɪkˈstætɪk/	中 adj. 特别高兴的 英 very happy or excited
euphoria /juːˈfɔːriə/	中 n. 特别高兴 英 a feeling of great happiness and excitement
disgruntle /dɪsˈɡrʌntl/	中 v. 使…不高兴 英 to make ill-humored or discontented
gracious /ˈɡreɪʃəs/	中 adj. 有礼貌的 英 very polite in a way that shows respect 中 adj. 优雅的 英 graceful
humdrum /ˈhʌmdrʌm/	中 adj. 无聊的，千篇一律的 英 not interesting or dull
polarize /ˈpouləraɪz/	中 v. 使…两极化 英 to break up into opposing factions or groupings
hand-wringing /ˈhænd.rɪŋɪŋ/	中 n. 焦虑的、绝望的言谈举止 英 an overwrought expression of concern or guilt

prime /praɪm/	中 v. 使…准备好
	英 to make (someone) ready to do something
	中 adj. 最重要的
	英 most important

vanquish /'væŋkwɪʃ/	中 v. 打败，战胜
	英 to defeat (someone) completely in a war, battle, etc.

triumph /'traɪʌmf/	中 n. 胜利，成就
	英 a great or important victory

forge /fɔːrdʒ/	中 v. 伪造，造假
	英 to make or imitate falsely especially with intent to defraud
	中 v. 努力形成
	英 to form or bring into being especially by an expenditure of effort

garrulous /'gærələs/	中 adj. 话多的
	英 very talkative

prevaricate /prɪ'værɪˌkeɪt/	中 v. 搪塞，闪烁其词
	英 to avoid telling the truth by not directly answering a question

eclectic /ɪ'klektɪk/	中 adj. 多元的
	英 including things taken from many different sources

haughty /'hɔːti/	中 adj. 高傲的，傲慢的
	英 blatantly and disdainfully proud

dismantle /dɪs'mæntl/	中 v. 拆开
	英 to take to pieces
	中 v. 破坏
	英 to destroy (something) in an orderly way

propagate /ˈprɑːpəgeɪt/	中 v. 宣扬，宣传 英 to foster growing knowledge of, familiarity with or acceptance of (as an idea or belief)
caricature /ˈkærɪkətʃər/	中 n. 讽刺画 英 a drawing that makes someone look funny or foolish because some part of the person's appearance is exaggerated
~~**abrade**~~ /əˈbreɪd/	中 v. 磨损 英 to damage (something) by rubbing, grinding or scraping 中 v.（在精神上）折磨 英 to wear down in spirit
~~**blight**~~ /blaɪt/	中 v. 破坏 英 to impair the quality or effect of
pristine /ˈprɪsˌtin/	中 adj. 原始的 英 belonging to the earliest period or state 中 adj. 未被破坏的 英 not spoiled, corrupted or polluted and left in its natural state
~~**apposite**~~ /ˈæpəzɪt/	中 adj. 合适的，恰当的 英 highly pertinent or appropriate
~~**germane**~~ /dʒɜːrˈmeɪn/	中 adj. 相关的 英 relating to a subject in an appropriate way
fitful /ˈfɪtfl/	中 adj. 不规律的，一阵阵的 英 not regular or steady
~~**imperturbable**~~ /ˌɪmpərˈtɜːrbəbl/	中 adj. 镇定的，冷静的 英 very calm

exigent /'ɛksɪdʒənt/	中 *adj.* 紧急的 英 requiring immediate attention
surrogate /'sɜːrəgət/	中 *v.* 代理 英 to appoint as successor, deputy or substitute for oneself
erstwhile /'ɜːrstwaɪl/	中 *adv.* 过去地 英 in the past
onetime /'wʌn,taɪm/	中 *adj.* 过去的，之前的 英 having been someone or something specified in the past
florid /'flɔːrɪd/	中 *adj.* 过分修饰的，花哨的 英 elaborately decorated 中 *adj.* 红润的 英 having a red or reddish color
defame /dɪ'feɪm/	中 *n.* 贬损，玷污 英 to hurt the reputation of (someone or something) especially by saying things that are false or unfair
inveigle /ɪn'veɪgl/	中 *v.* 诱骗 英 to persuade (someone) to do something in a clever or deceptive way
timorous /'tɪmərəs/	中 *adj.* 胆小的 英 easily frightened
omniscient /ɑːm'nɪsiənt/	中 *adj.* 无所不知的 英 knowing everything
interminable /ɪn'tɜːrmɪnəbl/	中 *adj.* 持续的，没完没了的 英 continuing for a very long time

posture /ˈpɑːstʃər/	中 *n.* 态度，立场
	英 state or condition at a given time especially with respect to capability in particular circumstances
	中 *v.* 装腔作势
	英 to assume an artificial or pretended attitude
narcissism /ˈnɑːrsɪsɪzəm/	中 *n.* 自恋
	英 often excessive interest, in one's own appearance, comfort, importance, abilities, etc.
substantiate /səbˈstænʃieɪt/	中 *v.* 证明
	英 to prove the truth of (something)

Substant-
真的吗？

Word List 14

音 频

snare /sner/	中 n. 陷阱
	英 a position or situation from which it is difficult to escape
	中 v. 捕捉
	英 to cause (something) to become caught in something

| forestall /fɔːrˈstɔːl/ | 中 v. 阻止 |
| | 英 to stop (something) from happening |

| beholden /bɪˈhoʊldən/ | 中 adj. 亏欠的 |
| | 英 being under obligation for a favor or gift |

| indebted /ɪnˈdetɪd/ | 中 adj. 感激的 |
| | 英 owing gratitude or recognition to another |

| impute /ɪmˈpjuːt/ | 中 v. 归罪于，归咎于 |
| | 英 to say or suggest that someone or something has or is guilty of (something) |

| brazen /ˈbreɪzn/ | 中 adj. 厚颜无耻的 |
| | 英 acting or done in a very open and shocking way without shame or embarrassment |

| nettle /ˈnetl/ | 中 v. 使…生气 |
| | 英 to make (someone) angry |

| contemptuous /kənˈtemptʃuəs/ | 中 adj. 鄙视的 |
| | 英 feeling or showing deep hatred or disapproval |

| objurgation /ˈɑbdʒərˌgeɪt/ | 中 n. 斥责，非难 |
| | 英 a harsh rebuke |

nascent /'næsnt/	中 *adj.* 初始的 英 beginning to exist
token /'toʊkən/	中 *n.* 象征 英 something that signifies or evidences authority, validity, or identity 中 *adj.* 象征性的 英 done as an indication or a pledge
residual /rɪ'zɪdʒuəl/	中 *adj.* 剩余的，残留的 英 leaving a residue that remains effective for some time 中 *n.* 剩余，残渣 英 the part that is left when the other people or things are gone, used
deft /deft/	中 *adj.* 灵巧的 英 able to do something quickly and accurately
eloquent /'eləkwənt/	中 *adj.* 能说会道的，能言善辩的 英 having or showing the ability to use language clearly and effectively
adroit /ə'drɔɪt/	中 *adj.* 灵巧的 英 very clever or skillful
plentiful /'plentɪfl/	中 *adj.* 慷慨的 英 giving or providing many desired things
bountiful /'baʊntɪfl/	中 *adj.* 丰富的 英 given or provided abundantly 中 *adj.* 慷慨的 英 liberal in bestowing gifts or favors
clearheaded /'klɪr'hedɪd/	中 *adj.* 思路清晰的 英 having or showing an ability to think clearly

interweave /ˌɪntər'wiːv/	中 *v.* 混合 英 to mix or blend together
~~**impolitic**~~ /ɪm'pɑːlətɪk/	中 *adj.* 不明智的 英 unwise
~~**feeble**~~ /'fiːbl/	中 *adj.* 衰弱的，虚弱的 英 very weak
prerogative /prɪ'rɑːgətɪv/	中 *n.* 特权 英 a right or privilege
~~**vigilant**~~ /'vɪdʒɪlənt/	中 *adj.* 警惕的 英 carefully noticing problems or signs of danger
~~**clumsy**~~ /'klʌmzi/	中 *adj.* 笨拙的 英 lacking dexterity, nimbleness or grace
~~**fringe**~~ /frɪndʒ/	中 *adj.* 次要的，边缘的，不重要的 英 something that is marginal, additional or secondary to some activity, process or subject
~~**denigrate**~~ /'denɪgreɪt/	中 *v.* 攻击，贬损 英 to attack the reputation of
implore /ɪm'plɔːr/	中 *v.* 恳求，哀求 英 to ask or beg for (something) in a very serious or emotional way
supplicate /'sʌplɪˌkeɪt/	中 *v.* 恳求 英 to make a humble entreaty
willful /'wɪlfl/	中 *adj.* 固执任性的 英 refusing to change your ideas or opinions or to stop doing something 中 *adj.* 故意的 英 done deliberately

entreaty /ɪnˈtriːti/	中 *n.* 恳求 英 a serious request for something
notwithstanding /ˌnɑːtwɪθˈstændɪŋ/	中 *prep.* 尽管 英 despite
insipid /ɪnˈsɪpɪd/	中 *adj.* 无聊的 英 not interesting or exciting
modish /ˈmoʊdɪʃ/	中 *adj.* 时髦的 英 fashionable or stylish
salubrious /səˈluːbriəs/	中 *adj.* 有益健康的 英 making good health possible or likely
treacherous /ˈtretʃərəs/	中 *adj.* 不可靠的，背叛的 英 not able to be trusted 中 *adj.* 危险的 英 marked by hidden dangers, hazards or perils
objectionable /əbˈdʒekʃənəbl/	中 *adj.* 令人反感的 英 causing people to be offended
recrudesce /ˌriːkruːˈdes/	中 *v.* 复发 英 to break out or become active again
tangible /ˈtændʒəbl/	中 *adj.* 可感知的，实实在在的 英 able to be touched or felt
nebulous /ˈnebjələs/	中 *adj.* 模糊的，不清楚的 英 not clear
utter /ˈʌtər/	中 *adj.* 完全的 英 complete, absolute or entire 中 *v.* 发出声音 英 to send forth as a sound
aberrant /æˈberənt/	中 *adj.* 不正常的 英 deviating from the usual or natural type

doom /duːm/	中 v. 注定（失败） 英 to make certain the failure or destruction of
slender /'slendər/	中 adj. 缺少的，不足的 英 limited or inadequate in amount or scope 中 adj. 窄的，瘦的 英 thin, very narrow or not wide
garner /'gɑːrnər/	中 v. 收集 英 to collect or gather (something) 中 v. 通过努力获得… 英 to acquire by effort
recruit /rɪ'kruːt/	中 v. 招募 英 to find suitable people and get them to join a company, an organization, the armed forces, etc.
provision /prə'vɪʒn/	中 n. 预备，预先采取的措施 英 something that is done in advance to prepare for something else 中 n. 提供，供应 英 the act or process of supplying or providing something
prompt /prɑːmpt/	中 v. 促进，激起 英 to serve as the inciting cause of 中 adj. 敏捷的，迅速的 英 of or relating to prompting actors
assail /ə'seɪl/	中 v. 批评，攻击 英 to attack or criticize (someone or something) in a violent or angry way

~~endow~~ /ɪnˈdaʊ/	中 *v.* 赋予 英 to freely or naturally provide (someone or something) with something 中 *v.* 捐赠 英 to give a large amount of money to a school, hospital, etc., in order to pay for the creation or continuing support of (something)
intrude /ɪnˈtruːd/	中 *v.* 闯入 英 to come or go into a place where you are not wanted or welcome
~~designate~~ /ˈdezɪɡneɪt/	中 *adj.* 指定的，选定的 英 chosen for a particular job but not officially doing that job yet 中 *v.* 指定，指派 英 to officially choose (someone or something) to do or be something
~~tackle~~ /ˈtækl/	中 *v.* 着手处理 英 to begin working on 中 *v.* 抓住并摔倒 英 to seize and throw (a person) to the ground
prosecute /ˈprɑːsɪkjuːt/	中 *v.* 从事 英 to engage in 中 *v.* 起诉，检举 英 to bring legal action against for redress or punishment of a crime or violation of law
abolish /əˈbɑːlɪʃ/	中 *v.* 废除，废止 英 to officially end or stop (something, such as a law)

endow

confer

| bestow /bɪˈstoʊ/ | 中 v. 授予，给予 |
| | 英 to give (something) as a gift or honor |

| compile /kəmˈpaɪl/ | 中 v. 编辑 |
| | 英 to collect and edit into a volume |

| requisite /ˈrekwɪzɪt/ | 中 adj. 必要的 |
| | 英 needed for a particular purpose 先决条件？ |

| splendor /ˈsplendər/ | 中 n. 光辉，壮丽 |
| | 英 great and impressive beauty |

exempt /ɪɡˈzempt/	中 adj. 被免除的
	英 not required to do something that others are required to do
	中 v. 免除
	英 to say that (someone or something) does not have to do something that others are required to do

invoke /ɪnˈvoʊk/	中 v. 引述
	英 to appeal to or cite in support or justification
	中 v. 恳求，祈求
	英 to call for earnestly; solicit

| entrust /ɪnˈtrʌst/ | 中 v. 委托，托付 =cosign |
| | 英 to give someone the responsibility of doing something or of caring for someone or something |

| alliance /əˈlaɪəns/ | 中 n. 联盟，联合 |
| | 英 the state of being joined in some activity or effort |

| periodical /ˌpɪriˈɑːdɪkl/ | 中 adj. 周期的 |
| | 英 happening regularly over a period of time |

spacious /ˈspeɪʃəs/	中 *adj.* 宽敞的 英 having a large amount of space
eligible /ˈelɪdʒəbl/	中 *adj.* 合格的 英 able to be chosen for something
strenuous /ˈstrenjuəs/	中 *adj.* 费力的 英 requiring or showing great energy and effort 中 *adj.* 活跃的 英 vigorously active
adjacent /əˈdʒeɪsnt/	中 *adj.* 相邻的 英 close or near
wrench /rentʃ/	中 *v.* 猛扭 英 to move with a violent twist 中 *v.* 歪曲，曲解 英 to distort
confiscate /ˈkɑːnfɪskeɪt/	中 *v.* 没收 英 appropriated by the government
ferocious /fəˈroʊʃəs/	中 *adj.* 凶猛的，残忍的 英 very fierce or violent 中 *adj.* 十分强烈的 英 very great or extreme
velocity /vəˈlɑːsəti/	中 *n.* 速度，迅速 英 quickness of motion
consign /kənˈsaɪn/	中 *v.* 委托，转交 英 to give, transfer or deliver into the hands or control of another
grapple /ˈɡræpl/	中 *v.* 抓住 英 to seize with or as if with a grapple 中 *v.* 握紧 英 to bind closely

| **deviate** /ˈdiːvieɪt/ | 中 *v.* 脱离，偏离 |
| | 英 to do something that is different or to be different from what is usual or expected |

prodigious /prəˈdɪdʒəs/	中 *adj.* 惊人的
	英 amazing or wonderful, very impressive
	中 *adj.* 巨大的
	英 very big

| **induce** /ɪnˈduːs/ | 中 *v.* 诱导 |
| | 英 to lead or move, as to a course of action, by influence or persuasion |

assimilate /əˈsɪməleɪt/	中 *v.* 吸收
	英 to learn (something) so that it is fully understood and can be used
	中 *v.* 使同化
	英 to make similar

| **encroach** /ɪnˈkroʊtʃ/ | 中 *v.* 侵占 |
| | 英 to gradually move or go into an area that is beyond the usual or desired limits |

| **embody** /ɪmˈbɑːdi/ | 中 *v.* 体现 |
| | 英 to represent (something) in a clear and obvious way |

coincide /ˌkoʊɪnˈsaɪd/	中 *v.* 碰巧
	英 to happen at the same time as something else
	中 *v.* 与…相一致
	英 to agree with something exactly

confer /kənˈfɜːr/	中 *v.* 授予，给予
	英 to give (as a property or characteristic) to someone or something
	中 *v.* 协商
	英 to discuss something important in order to make a decision

subdue /səb'duː/	中 v. 征服，打败 英 to get control of (a violent or dangerous person or group) by using force, punishment, etc.
fatal /'feɪtl/	中 adj. 致命的 英 causing death
dwell /dwel/	中 v. 居住 英 to live in a particular place 中 v. 持续地谈论 英 to speak or write insistently
comprise /kəm'praɪz/	中 v. 构成 英 to be made up of (something) *compromise 妥协?* 中 v. 包含 英 to include; contain
vicinity /və'sɪnəti/	中 n. 周边环境 英 the area around or near a particular place 中 n. （距离）近 英 the quality or sate of being near
tentative /'tentətɪv/	中 adj. 试探性的，临时的 英 not fully worked out, concluded, or agreed on; provisional 中 adj. 犹豫的，不确定的 英 hesitant and uncertain
pillage /'pɪlɪdʒ/	中 v. 掠夺 英 to plunder ruthlessly
pinnacle /'pɪnəkl/	中 n. 顶点 英 the highest point of development or achievement
ailment /'eɪlmənt/	中 n. 疾病 英 a sickness or illness

apprentice /ə'prentɪs/	中 *n.* 新手
	英 an inexperienced person
	中 *n.* 学徒
	英 a person who learns a job or skill by working for a fixed period of time for someone who is very good at that job or skill
preoccupied /pri'ɑːkjupaɪd/	中 *adj.* 专注的
	英 thinking about something a lot or too much
exhale /eks'heɪl/	中 *v.* 呼出
	英 to breathe out
rebuke /rɪ'bjuːk/	中 *v.* 指责，非难
	英 to speak in an angry and critical way to (someone)
cavalier /ˌkævə'lɪr/	中 *adj.* 随意的，轻蔑的
	英 marked by or given to offhand and often disdainful dismissal of important matters
hereditary /hə'redɪteri/	中 *adj.* 遗传的
	英 passing from a person who has died to that person's child or younger relative
shallow /'ʃæloʊ/	中 *adj.* 肤浅的
	英 lacking depth of intellect, emotion, or knowledge
deflect /dɪ'flekt/	中 *v.* 使…偏离，改变方向
	英 to cause (something that is moving) to change direction
	中 *v.* 使不受到…的影响
	英 to keep (something, such as a question) from affecting or being directed at a person or thing

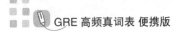

finesse /fɪˈnes/	中 *n.* 技巧高超
	英 skillful handling of a situation
	中 *v.* 躲避
	英 evade or skirt
	中 *v.* 巧妙地处理
	英 to handle, deal with or do (something) in an indirect and skillful or clever way
belated /bɪˈleɪtɪd/	中 *adj.* 晚的，迟的
	英 happening or coming very late or too late

158

Word List 15

音 频

sheer /ʃɪr/	中 *adj.* 完全的 英 complete and total 中 *adj.* 陡峭的，几乎垂直的 英 marked by great and continuous steepness
levity /ˈlevəti/	中 *n.* 不严肃，轻浮 英 a lack of seriousness
insidious /ɪnˈsɪdiəs/	中 *adj.* 阴险的，暗中为害的 英 causing harm in a way that is gradual or not easily noticed
amass /əˈmæs/	中 *v.* 积聚，积累 英 to come together
ostensible /ɑːˈstensəbl/	中 *adj.* 表面的，虚假的 英 seeming or said to be true or real but very possibly not true or real
somber /ˈsɑːmbər/	中 *adj.* 严肃的，悲伤的 英 very sad and serious 中 *adj.* 昏暗的 英 having a dull or dark color
profound /prəˈfaʊnd/	中 *adj.* 深刻的 英 having or showing great knowledge or understanding 中 *adj.* 强烈的 英 very strongly felt
contour /ˈkɑːntʊr/	中 *n.* 轮廓 英 the outline or outer edge of something

| chaos /ˈkeɪɑːs/ | 中 n. 混乱 |
| | 英 complete confusion and disorder |

| voluminous /vəˈluːmɪnəs/ | 中 adj. 巨大的，大量的 |
| | 英 very large |

| revile /rɪˈvaɪl/ | 中 v. 辱骂，斥责 |
| | 英 to speak about (someone or something) in a very critical or insulting way |

| corporeal /kɔːrˈpɔːriəl/ | 中 adj. 肉体的，有实体存在的 |
| | 英 having or consisting of a physical body or form |

oscillate /ˈɑːsɪleɪt/	中 v. 犹豫不决
	英 to vary between opposing beliefs, feelings or theories
	中 v. 摇摆
	英 to swing backward and forward like a pendulum

| monarchy /ˈmɑːnərki/ | 中 n. 君主政体 |
| | 英 a form of government in which a country is ruled by a monarch |

inoculate /ɪˈnɑːkjuleɪt/	中 v.（给某人）灌输，注入（想法）
	英 to introduce something into the mind of
	中 v. 注射疫苗
	英 to inject a material (as a vaccine) into to protect against or treat a disease

| subsist /səbˈsɪst/ | 中 v. 维持生存，生存下去 |
| | 英 to exist or continue to exist |

| suffrage /ˈsʌfrɪdʒ/ | 中 n. 选举权 |
| | 英 the right to vote in an election |

| patron /ˈpeɪtrən/ | 中 n. 赞助人 |
| | 英 a person who gives money and support to an artist, organization, etc. |

exile
/'eksaɪl/

中 n. 流放，放逐
英 a situation in which you are forced to leave your country or home and go to live in a foreign country
中 v. 流放，放逐
英 to banish or expel from one's own country or home

inhospitable
/ˌɪnhɑːˈspɪtəbl/

中 adj. 不友好的
英 not generous and friendly to guests or visitors
中 adj. 贫瘠的，荒凉的
英 having an environment where plants, animals or people cannot live or grow easily

oblique
/əˈbliːk/

中 adj. 间接的
英 not straightforward
中 adj. 倾斜的
英 having no right angle

bequeath
/bɪˈkwiːð/

中 v. 遗赠
英 to give or leave by will (used especially of personal property)
中 v. 留下，传下
英 to hand down

retention
/rɪˈtenʃn/

中 n. 保留
英 the act of keeping someone or something

ramify
/ˈræməˌfaɪ/

中 v. 使分叉
英 to split up into branches or constituent parts

prescribe
/prɪˈskraɪb/

中 v. 规定
英 to lay down as a rule or guide; enjoin

ramification?

~~deprive~~ /dɪ'praɪv/	中 v. 使丧失，剥夺 英 to take something away from
necessitate /nə'sesɪteɪt/	中 v. 使成为必要 英 to make (something) necessary
~~inhale~~ /ɪn'heɪl/	中 v. 吸入 英 to breathe in
~~dexterity~~ /dek'sterəti/	中 n. 聪明，伶俐 英 mental skill or adroitness; cleverness 中 n. 灵巧，敏捷 英 skill and grace in physical movement, especially in the use of the hands; adroitness
ooze /u:z/	中 v. 渗出 英 to flow out slowly 中 v. 表现，显示 英 to show (a quality, emotion, etc.) very clearly or strongly
~~patronize~~ /'peɪtrənaɪz/	中 v. 赞助 英 to give money or support to (someone or something) 中 v. 摆出高人一等的态度对待 英 to talk to (someone) in a way that shows that you believe you are more intelligent or better than other people 中 v. 经常光顾 英 to be a frequent or regular customer or user of
eject /i'dʒekt/	中 v. 驱逐，逐出 英 to force (someone) to leave 中 v. 喷出，发出 英 to push out
overdue /,oʊvər'du:/	中 adj. 延误的，拖延的 英 not appearing or presented by a stated, expected or required time

brusque
/brʌsk/

中 *adj.* 唐突的，无礼的
英 talking or behaving in a very direct, brief and unfriendly way

prose
/proʊz/

中 *adj.* 平凡的，乏味的（与 prosaic 相同）
英 dull or ordinary
中 *n.* 散文
英 writing that is not poetry

uprising
/'ʌpraɪzɪŋ/

中 *n.* 起义，叛乱
英 a usually violent effort by many people to change the government or leader of a country

touchstone
/'tʌtʃstoʊn/

中 *n.* 检验标准
英 something that is used to make judgments about the quality of other things

purveyor
/pər'veɪər/

中 *n.* 供应商
英 a person or business that sells or provides something

parody
/'pærədi/

中 *n.* 拙劣的模仿
英 a literary or musical work in which the style of an author or work is closely imitated for comic effect or in ridicule

decimate
/'desɪmeɪt/

中 *v.*（严重地）破坏
英 to destroy a large number of (plants, animals, people, etc.)

decipher
/dɪ'saɪfər/

中 *v.* 解释，破译
英 to find the meaning of (something that is difficult to read or understand)

amenable
/ə'miːnəbl/

中 *adj.* 愿意的，服从的
英 willing to agree or to accept something that is wanted or asked for

siphon /'saɪfn/	中 v. 抽走（资金，资源）
	英 to take and use (something, such as money) for your own purpose
annotate /'ænəteɪt/	中 v. 注释
	英 to add notes or comments to (a text, book, drawing, etc.)
procure /prə'kjʊr/	中 v. 获得
	英 to get (something) by some action or effort
hiatus /haɪ'eɪtəs/	中 n. 间歇
	英 a period of time when something (such as an activity or program) is stopped
cantankerous /kæn'tæŋkərəs/	中 adj. 易怒的
	英 often angry and annoyed
escalate /'eskəleɪt/	中 v. 加剧，恶化
	英 to become worse or to make (something) worse or more severe
	中 v. 升高，提升
	英 to become greater or higher or to make (something) greater or higher
bombard /baːm'baːrd/	中 v.（如炸弹般）攻击（人或事物）
	英 to hit or attack (something or someone) constantly or repeatedly
vernacular /vər'nækjələr/	中 adj. 口头语的，俗语的
	英 of, relating to or using the language of ordinary speech rather than formal writing
prevail /prɪ'veɪl/	中 v. 流行
	英 to be usual, common or popular
scenario /sə'næriou/	中 n. 情形
	英 a description of what could possibly happen

hitherto /ˌhɪðər'tuː/	中 *adv.* 至今 英 until now
vertiginous /vɜːr'tɪdʒɪnəs/	中 *adj.* 令人眩晕的 英 causing or likely to cause a feeling of dizziness especially because of great height
bravado /brə'vɑːdoʊ/	中 *n.* 装作勇敢 英 a pretense of bravery 中 *n.* 莽撞 英 the quality or state of being foolhardy
steadfast /'stedfæst/	中 *adj.* 坚定不移的 英 firm in belief, determination or adherence
oblivious /ə'blɪviəs/	中 *adj.* 无意识的，遗忘的 英 not conscious or aware of someone or something
refractory /rɪ'fræktəri/	中 *adj.* 不服管的，难处理的 英 resisting control or authority 中 *adj.* 难治愈的 英 resistant to treatment
resign /rɪ'zaɪn/	中 *v.* 接受 英 to accept something as inevitable 中 *v.* 辞职 英 to give up one's office or position
abiding /ə'baɪdɪŋ/	中 *adj.* 长期的 英 continuing for a long time
dull /dʌl/	中 *adj.* 无聊的 英 not exciting or interesting 中 *adj.* 笨的 英 mentally slow
debonair /ˌdebə'ner/	中 *adj.* 无忧无虑的，漠不关心的 英 lighthearted or nonchalant

165

| infuriate /ɪnˈfjʊrieɪt/ | 中 v. 使…愤怒 |
| | 英 to make (someone) very angry |

| crestfallen /ˈkrestfɔːlən/ | 中 adj. 沮丧的 |
| | 英 very sad and disappointed |

| wistful /ˈwɪstfl/ | 中 adj. 渴望的，思念过去的 |
| | 英 full of yearning or desire tinged with melancholy |

concur /kənˈkɜːr/	中 v. 同意
	英 to express agreement
	中 v. 同时发生
	英 to happen together

boast /boʊst/	中 v. 吹嘘
	英 speak vaingloriously
	中 v. 拥有
	英 have or contain

| extrapolate /ɪkˈstræpəleɪt/ | 中 v.（依据已知信息）推测 |
| | 英 to form an opinion or to make an estimate about something from known facts |

| resemble /rɪˈzembl/ | 中 v. 与…相似 |
| | 英 to be like or similar to |

ordain /ɔːrˈdeɪn/	中 v. 命令
	英 to order by virtue of superior authority; decree or enact
	中 v. 注定
	英 to prearrange unalterably; predestine

| mirth /mɜːrθ/ | 中 n. 欢乐 |
| | 英 happiness and laughter |

| jovial /ˈdʒoʊviəl/ | 中 adj. 高兴的 |
| | 英 full of happiness and joy |

cajole /kə'dʒoʊl/	中 *v.* 哄骗 英 to persuade with flattery or gentle urging especially in the face of reluctance
~~baneful~~ /'beɪnfl/	中 *adj.* 有害的 英 seriously harmful
~~identical~~ /aɪ'dentɪkl/	中 *adj.* 完全一样的 英 exactly the same
proscribe /proʊ'skraɪb/	中 *v.* 禁止 英 to not allow
~~arguably~~ /'ɑːrgjuəbli/	中 *adv.* 可以这样说地 英 it can be argued
obstreperous /əb'strepərəs/	中 *adj.* 不服管的，桀骜不驯的 英 difficult to control and often noisy
~~volition~~ /və'lɪʃn/	中 *n.* 自愿选择，自行决定 英 the power to make your own choices or decisions
~~hectic~~ /'hektɪk/	中 *adj.* 非常忙碌的 英 very busy and filled with activity
sumptuous /'sʌmptʃuəs/	中 *adj.* 奢侈的，华丽的 英 extremely costly, rich, luxurious or magnificent
gravitate /'grævɪteɪt/	中 *v.* 被吸引到，倾向 英 to be attracted to or toward something
~~particularize~~ /pər'tɪkjələraɪz/	中 *v.* 详细阐述 英 to give specific details or examples of
~~albeit~~ /ˌɔːl'biːɪt/	中 *conj.* 即使 英 although

~~abet~~ /əˈbet/	中 v. 怂恿，支持，教唆（犯罪） 英 to help, encourage or support someone in a criminal act
anodyne /ˈænədaɪn/	中 adj. 不惹人厌烦的 英 not likely to offend or upset anyone 中 adj. 缓解疼痛的 英 serving to alleviate pain
credulous /ˈkredʒələs/	中 adj. 易受欺骗的 英 too ready to believe things
~~asunder~~ /əˈsʌndər/	中 adj. 分裂的 英 into parts
petulant /ˈpetʃələnt/	中 adj.（说话，行为）粗鲁无礼的 英 insolent or rude in speech or behavior 中 adj. 易怒的，脾气坏的 英 having or showing the attitude of people who become angry and annoyed when they do not get what they want
~~winnow~~ /ˈwɪnoʊ/	中 v. 筛选 英 to narrow or reduce
yearn /jɜːrn/	中 v. 强烈渴望 英 to feel a strong desire or wish for something or to do something
~~indulgent~~ /ɪnˈdʌldʒənt/	中 adj. 纵容的 英 willing to allow someone to have or enjoy something even though it may not be proper, healthy, appropriate, etc. 中 adj. 享乐的 英 done or enjoyed as a special pleasure
preside /prɪˈzaɪd/	中 v. 主持，负责 英 to be in charge of something (such as a trial)

~~meretricious~~ /ˌmerəˈtrɪʃəs/	中 *adj.* 俗里俗气的 英 attractive in a cheap or false way
~~burgeon~~ /ˈbɜːrdʒən/	中 *v.* 繁荣，快速增长 英 to grow or develop quickly
~~flourish~~ /ˈflɜːrɪʃ/	中 *v.* 繁荣 英 to be very successful
~~gigantic~~ /dʒaɪˈɡæntɪk/	中 *adj.* 极大的 英 extremely large
~~snub~~ /snʌb/	中 *v.* 怠慢，不理睬 英 to ignore (someone) in a deliberate and insulting way
~~underplay~~ /ˌʌndərˈpleɪ/	中 *v.* 轻描淡写，低估 英 to make (something) seem less important than it actually is
~~obliterate~~ /əˈblɪtəreɪt/	中 *v.* 抹去，使…消失 英 to destroy (something) completely so that nothing is left

Word List 16

音频

seethe /siːð/	中 v. 强压怒火，生闷气
	英 to suffer violent internal excitement
	中 v. 攒动
	英 to move constantly and without order

| morph /mɔːrf/ | 中 v. 变形 |
| | 英 to change the form or character of |

| ~~subservient~~ /səbˈsɜːrviənt/ | 中 adj. 服服帖帖的，奉承的 |
| | 英 very willing or too willing to obey someone else |

obtuse /əbˈtuːs/	中 adj. 愚钝的，笨的
	英 stupid or unintelligent
	中 adj. 难懂的
	英 difficult to comprehend

~~trenchant~~ /ˈtrentʃənt/	中 adj. 尖酸刻薄的
	英 caustic
	中 adj. 犀利的，一针见血的
	英 sharply perceptive

| instigate /ˈɪnstɪɡeɪt/ | 中 v. 激起，挑起 |
| | 英 to cause (something) to happen or begin |

~~fusty~~ /ˈfʌsti/	中 adj. 过时的
	英 very old-fashioned
	中 adj. 腐臭的
	英 full of dust and unpleasant smells

| ~~cease~~ /siːs/ | 中 v. 停止 |
| | 英 to stop doing |

| implicate /ˈɪmplɪkeɪt/ | 中 v. 牵涉 |
| | 英 to show to be connected or involved |

vituperate
/vaɪ'tuːpə,reɪt/
中 v. 辱骂
英 to abuse or censure severely or abusively

rattle
/'rætl/
中 v. 扰乱
英 to upset (someone) especially to the point of loss of poise and composure

molder
/'moʊldər/
中 v. 腐烂，退化
英 to decay slowly

transmogrify
/,trænz'mɑːgrɪfaɪ/
中 v. 使…变形
英 to change or alter greatly and often with grotesque or humorous effect

choreograph
/'kɔːriəgræf/
中 v. 精心安排
英 to arrange or direct the movements, progress or details of
中 v. 编舞
英 to decide how a dancer or group of dancers will move during a performance

incipient
/ɪn'sɪpiənt/
中 adj. 开始的
英 beginning to develop or exist

antiquarian
/,æntɪ'kweriən/
中 adj. 古文物研究的
英 relating to the collection and study of valuable old things (such as old books)

boisterous
/'bɔɪstərəs/
中 adj. 吵闹的
英 very noisy and active in a lively way

renounce
/rɪ'naʊns/
中 v. 拒绝，否认
英 to give up, refuse or resign usually by formal declaration

compartmentalize
/kəm,pɑːrt'mentəlaɪz/
中 v. 分门别类，划分
英 to separate (something) into sections or categories

maelstrom
/'meɪlstrɑːm/

中 n. 混乱，动乱
英 a powerful often violent whirlpool sucking in objects within a given radius

captious
/'kæpʃəs/

中 adj. 挑刺的，吹毛求疵的
英 marked by an often ill-natured inclination to stress faults and raise objections

vulgar
/'vʌlgər/

中 adj. 粗俗的
英 not having or showing good manners, good taste or politeness
中 adj. 普通大众的
英 relating to the common people or the speech of common people

fealty
/'fiːəlti/

中 n. 忠诚
英 loyalty to a person, group, etc.

bristle
/'brɪsl/

中 v. 生气，愤怒
英 to become angry

await
/ə'weɪt/

中 v. 等待
英 to wait for (someone or something)

languish
/'læŋgwɪʃ/

中 v. 衰落，不活跃
英 to continue for a long time without activity or progress in an unpleasant or unwanted situation

nugatory
/'nuːgətɔːri/

中 adj. 不重要的
英 of little or no consequence

inept
/ɪ'nept/

中 adj. 无能的
英 generally incompetent
中 adj. 不恰当的，不合适的
英 not suited to the occasion

~~spartan~~ /'spɑːrtn/	中 *adj.* 简朴的 英 marked by simplicity, frugality or avoidance of luxury and comfort
ancillary /'ænsəleri/	中 *adj.* 辅助的 英 providing something additional to a main part or function
sequester /sɪ'kwestər/	中 *v.* 分离，隔离 英 to keep (a person or group) apart from other people
~~hasty~~ /'heɪsti/	中 *adj.* 快速的，仓促的 英 done or made very quickly or too quickly 中 *adj.* 易怒的 英 prone to anger
budding /'bʌdɪŋ/	中 *adj.* 新出现的 英 being in an early stage of development
vainglory /ˌveɪn'ɡlɔːri/	中 *n.* 极度夸耀，虚荣 英 excessive or ostentatious pride especially in one's achievements
consummate /'kɑːnsəmət/	中 *adj.* 完满的，圆满的 英 complete in every detail 中 *v.* 圆满完成 英 to make (something) perfect or complete
~~like-minded~~ /'laɪkˌmaɪndɪd/	中 *adj.* 思维相似的，想法一致的 英 having similar opinions and interests
ecumenical /ˌiːkjuː'menɪkl/	中 *adj.* 多元的，普遍的 英 involving people or things from different kind; of worldwide scope or applicability
ardent /'ɑːrdnt/	中 *adj.* 热衷的，热情的 英 characterized by warmth of feeling typically expressed in eager zealous support or activity

rescind /rɪ'sɪnd/	中 v. 废除（法律） 英 to end (a law, contract, agreement, etc.) officially
distend /dɪ'stend/	中 v. 膨胀 英 to become larger and rounder because of pressure from inside
self-regard /'selfrɪ'gɑːrd/	中 n. 自私自利 英 regard for or consideration of oneself or one's own interests
subterfuge /'sʌbtərfjuːdʒ/	中 n. 诡计 英 the use of tricks especially to hide, avoid or get something
agglomerate /ə'glɑːməreɪt/	中 v. 使成团，使结块 英 to gather into a ball, mass or cluster
goad /goʊd/	中 v. 刺激 英 to urge or force (someone) to do something
surfeit /'sɜːrfɪt/	中 n. 过量 英 an amount that is too much or more than you need
transitory /'trænsətɔːri/	中 adj. 短暂的 英 lasting only for a short time
prolix /'proʊlɪks/	中 adj. 冗长的 英 using too many words
exactitude /ɪg'zæktɪtuːd/	中 n. 准确 英 the quality or state of being accurate and correct
chastise /tʃæ'staɪz/	中 v. 谴责 英 to criticize (someone) harshly for doing something wrong

protract /prou'trækt/	中 v. 延长
	英 to prolong in time or space
stymie /'staɪmi/	中 v. 阻碍
	英 to present an obstacle to
seminal /'semɪnl/	中 adj. 非常有影响力的
	英 very important and influential
authoritarian /ə,θɔːrə'teriən/	中 adj. 专制的
	英 expecting or requiring people to obey rules or laws
leap /liːp/	中 v.（话题、言论）跳跃
	英 to pass abruptly from one state or topic to another
	中 v. 跳跃
	英 to jump from a surface
tepid /'tepɪd/	中 adj. 冷淡的，不热情的
	英 not energetic or excited
malodor /mæl'oʊdər/	中 n. 恶臭
	英 an offensive odor
senescence /sɪ'nesns/	中 n. 衰老
	英 the state of being old or the process of becoming old
decrepitude /dɪ'krepɪtuːd/	中 n. 衰老
	英 the state of being old and in bad condition or poor health
self-styled /'self'staɪld/	中 adj. 自称的
	英 called a particular thing by yourself
cognizant /'kɑːgnɪzənt/	中 adj. 知道的，有意识的
	英 aware of something

~~conversant~~ /kən'vɜːrsnt/	中 *adj.* 熟悉的 英 having knowledge or experience
tribulation /ˌtrɪbjuˈleɪʃn/	中 *n.* 痛苦（的经历） 英 unhappiness, pain or suffering or an experience that causes someone to suffer
~~open-ended~~ /ˈoʊpənˈendɪd/	中 *adj.* 开放的 英 allowing people to talk in a way that is not planned or controlled
falsify /ˈfɔːlsɪfaɪ/	中 *v.* 篡改，伪造 英 to change (something) in order to make people believe something that is not true
~~panorama~~ /ˌpænəˈræmə/	中 *n.* 全面展示 英 a comprehensive presentation of a subject 中 *n.* 全景 英 a full and wide view of something
~~beleaguer~~ /bɪˈliːgər/	中 *v.* 困扰，骚扰 英 to harass; beset 中 *v.* 围攻 英 to surround with troops; besiege
~~incumbent~~ /ɪnˈkʌmbənt/	中 *n.* 在职者 英 one that occupies a particular position or place 中 *adj.* 义不容辞，有责任的 英 obligatory
~~hermetic~~ /hɜːrˈmetɪk/	中 *adj.* 密闭的 英 closed tightly so that no air can go in or out 中 *adj.* 难懂的 英 relating to or characterized by occultism or abstruseness 中 *adj.* 退隐的，孤寂的 英 recluse or solitary

encapsulate
/ɪnˈkæpsjuleɪt/

中 v. 简要概括
英 to show or express the main idea or quality of (something) in a brief way
中 v. （如胶囊一样）封装
英 to enclose in or as if in a capsule

interdisciplinary
/ˌɪntərˈdɪsəplɪneri/

中 adj. 交叉学科的
英 involving two or more disciplines

impunity
/ɪmˈpjuːnəti/

中 v. 免于处罚，免罪
英 freedom from punishment, harm or loss

reprisal
/rɪˈpraɪzl/

中 n. 报复
英 a retaliatory act

myopic
/maɪˈɑːpɪk/

中 adj. 缺乏远见的
英 a lack of foresight or discernment

tarnish
/ˈtɑːrnɪʃ/

中 v. 玷污
英 to damage or ruin the good quality of

sublime
/səˈblaɪm/

中 adj. 令人崇敬的
英 characterized by nobility; majestic
中 adj. 卓越的，出众的
英 not to be excelled; supreme
中 n. 崇高
英 something sublime
中 v. 超群出众
英 to render sublime

remonstrate
/rɪˈmɑːnstreɪt/

中 v. 反对，抗议
英 to present and urge reasons in opposition

commiserate
/kəˈmɪzəreɪt/

中 v. 哀悼，同情
英 to express sadness or sympathy for someone who has experienced something unpleasant

expostulate
/ɪk'spɑːstʃuleɪt/
- 中 v. 争论，反驳
- 英 to disagree with something or argue against it

anneal
/ə'niːl/
- 中 v. 加固
- 英 strengthen or toughen

vicissitude
/vɪ'sɪsɪtuːd/
- 中 n. 变迁，变化
- 英 the quality or state of being changeable

piecemeal
/'piːsmiːl/
- 中 adv. 一次少量地，一件一件地
- 英 by a small amount at a time; in stages
- 中 adj. 逐个完成的
- 英 accomplished or made in stages

verbose
/vɜːr'boʊs/
- 中 adj. 冗长的
- 英 using more words than are needed

polyglot
/'pɑːliglɑːt/
- 中 adj. 多种语言的
- 英 knowing or using several languages
- 中 adj. 混杂的
- 英 made up of people or things from different cultures, countries, etc.

machination
/ˌmæʃɪ'neɪʃn/
- 中 n. 诡计
- 英 a scheming or crafty action or artful design intended to accomplish some usually evil end

flee
/fliː/
- 中 v. 逃脱，逃跑
- 英 to run away from danger

nefarious
/nɪ'feriəs/
- 中 adj. 邪恶的
- 英 evil or immoral

lachrymose
/'lækrɪmoʊs/
- 中 adj. 催泪的，悲伤的
- 英 tending to cause tears
- 中 adj. 爱哭的
- 英 tending to cry often

enmity /ˈenməti/	中 n. 恶意，憎恶
	英 a very deep unfriendly feeling

indignant /ɪnˈdɪgnənt/	中 adj. 非常愤怒的
	英 very angry

indigance? 本地后？

confront /kənˈfrʌnt/	中 v. 反抗
	英 to oppose or challenge (someone) especially in a direct and forceful way
	中 v. 面对
	英 to meet face-to-face

minutia /mɪˈnuʃiə/	中 n. 细节，小事
	英 a minute or minor detail

commensurable /kəˈmenʃərəbl/	中 adj. 相称的，成比例的
	英 commensurate; proportionate
	中 adj. 可用共同标准测量的
	英 measurable by a common standard

discriminatory /dɪˈskrɪmɪnətɔːri/	中 adj. 不公平的，歧视的
	英 not fair

sabotage /ˈsæbətɑːʒ/	中 v. 故意破坏
	英 to cause the failure of something deliberately

commend /kəˈmend/	中 v. 赞美
	英 to praise (someone or something) in a serious and often public way

command

gossamer /ˈgɑːsəmər/	中 adj. 轻而薄的，虚无缥缈的
	英 extremely light, delicate or tenuous

lenient /ˈliːniənt/	中 adj. 宽容的
	英 allowing a lot of freedom and not punishing bad behavior in a strong way

rectitude /'rektɪtuːd/	中 *n.* 正直 英 the quality of being honest and morally correct
~~**enamor**~~ /ɪ'næmər/	中 *v.* 使…喜爱 英 to cause (someone) to be loved or admired
immure /ɪ'mjʊr/	中 *v.* 囚禁 英 imprison 中 *v.*（像嵌在墙上一样）封闭 英 to enclose within or as if within walls
impudent /'ɪmpjədənt/	中 *adj.* 无礼的 英 very rude

immune 免疫

Word List 17

音 频

~~insolent~~ /'ɪnsələnt/	中 *adj.* 无礼的 英 rude or impolite
~~irenic~~ /aɪ'renɪk/	中 *adj.* 和平的 英 favoring, conducive to or operating toward peace, moderation or conciliation
shear /ʃɪr/	中 *v.* 剪（动物）毛 英 to cut the hair from 中 *v.* 剥夺 英 to deprive of something as if by cutting
coruscate /'kɔːrəskeɪt/	中 *v.* 闪烁，闪光 英 sparkle 中 *v.* 焕发魅力 英 to be brilliant or showy in technique or style
~~hideous~~ /'hɪdiəs/	中 *adj.* 丑陋吓人的 英 very ugly or disgusting 中 *adj.* 可恶的，令人难以忍受的 英 morally offensive

hideous? *tedious* 单调

~~trumpet~~ /'trʌmpɪt/	中 *v.* 鼓吹 英 to praise (something) loudly and publicly especially in a way that is annoying
~~strident~~ /'straɪdnt/	中 *adj.* 尖锐的，刺耳的 英 sounding harsh and unpleasant 中 *adj.* （表达意见）令人不悦的 英 expressing opinions or criticism in a very forceful and often annoying or unpleasant way

muckrake /'mʌk͵reɪk/	中 *v.* 揭露丑闻 英 to search out and publicly expose real or apparent misconduct of a prominent individual or business
proffer /'prɑːfər/	中 *v.* 提供 英 to offer or give (something) to someone
revel /'revl/	中 *v.* 陶醉 英 to take intense pleasure or satisfaction 中 *n.* 吵闹的狂欢 英 a noisy and wild celebration
predicate /'predɪkət/	中 *v.* 基于，取决于 英 to found or base something on 中 *v.* 断言，断定 英 to declare or affirm (something) as true or existing
prophylactic /͵proʊfə'læktɪk/	中 *adj.* 预防性的 英 acting to defend against or prevent something, especially disease; protective 中 *n.* 预防类物品 英 a prophylactic agent, device, or measure, such as a vaccine or drug
pilfer /'pɪlfər/	中 *v.* 盗用 英 to steal things that are not very valuable or to steal a small amount of something
constrict /kən'strɪkt/	中 *v.* 限制 英 to prevent or keep (something or someone) from developing freely 中 *v.* 压缩 英 to become narrower, smaller or tighter
imbibe /ɪm'baɪb/	中 *v.* 喝 英 to drink (something)

quaff /kwɑːf/	中 v. 大口喝，痛饮 英 to drink a large amount of (something) quickly
crumble /ˈkrʌmbl/	中 v. 崩溃，瓦解 英 to break down completely; to stop functioning
disintegrate /dɪsˈɪntɪɡreɪt/	中 v. 瓦解 英 to break apart into many small parts or pieces
brook /brʊk/	中 v. 容忍，忍受 英 to stand for; tolerate
muddle /ˈmʌdl/	中 v. 使困惑 英 to cause confusion in (someone or someone's mind)
unerring /ʌnˈɜːrɪŋ/	中 adj. 一贯准确的 英 committing no mistakes; consistently accurate
provenance /ˈprɑːvənəns/	中 n. 出处，起源 英 the origin or source of something
inscrutable /ɪnˈskruːtəbl/	中 adj. 难以理解的 英 difficult to understand; causing people to feel curious or confused
genial /ˈdʒiːniəl/	中 adj. 友好的 英 marked by or diffusing sympathy or friendliness
reluctant /rɪˈlʌktənt/	中 adj. 不情愿的 英 feeling or showing doubt about doing something; not willing or eager to do something

183

supple /'sʌpl/	中 adj. 灵活的
	英 readily adaptable or responsive to new situations
contravene /ˌkɑːntrə'viːn/	中 v. 违反
	英 to fail to do what is required by (a law or rule)
ungainly /ʌn'geɪnli/	中 adj. 笨拙的
	英 moving in an awkward or clumsy way;not graceful
ludicrous /'luːdɪkrəs/	中 adj. 滑稽可笑的
	英 amusing or laughable through obvious absurdity, incongruity, exaggeration or eccentricity
dispatch /dɪ'spætʃ/	中 n. 迅速
	英 promptness and efficiency in performance or transmission
handicap /'hændikæp/	中 n. 障碍
	英 a disadvantage that makes achievement unusually difficult
chimera /kaɪ'mɪrə/	中 n. 幻想
	英 something that exists only in the imagination and is not possible in reality
ominous /'ɑːmɪnəs/	中 adj. 不吉利的
	英 suggesting that something bad is going to happen in the future
limpid /'lɪmpɪd/	中 adj. 清澈透明的
	英 marked by transparency; pellucid
forsake /fər'seɪk/	中 v. 放弃
	英 to give up or leave (someone or something) entirely

(handwritten annotations: "in grain 根深蒂固", "handicapped 残疾人", "omnipresent", "limp 跛子 无力放松的")

exonerate
/ɪɡˈzɑːnəreɪt/

中 v. 免罪，免责
英 to prove that someone is not guilty of a crime or responsible for a problem, bad situation, etc.

annihilate
/əˈnaɪəleɪt/

中 v. 毁灭，毁坏
英 to destroy (something or someone) completely

surmise
/sərˈmaɪz/

中 v. 猜测
英 a thought or idea based on scanty evidence; conjecture

submerge

rapprochement
/ˌræproʊʃˈmɑːn/

中 n. 友好，和谐
英 the development of friendlier relations between countries or groups of people who have been enemies

exert
/ɪɡˈzɜːrt/

中 v. 使用
英 to use (strength, ability, etc.)

wield
/wiːld/

中 v. 使用
英 to have and use (power, influence, etc.)

Wild 野的

guzzle
/ˈɡʌzl/

中 v. 狂饮
英 to drink (something, such as beer or liquor) quickly or in large amounts

kinfolk
/ˈkɪnfoʊk/

中 n. 亲戚
英 a person's relatives

divergent
/daɪˈvɜːrdʒənt/

中 adj. 不同的
英 differing from each other or from a standard

vestige
/ˈvestɪdʒ/

中 n. 遗迹，遗留
英 the last small part that remains of something that existed before

| profusion /prə'fjuːʒn/ | 中 n. 大量 |
| | 英 a large amount of something |

forebode /fɔːr'boʊd/	中 v. 担忧
	英 to have an inward conviction of (as coming ill or misfortune)
	中 v. 预示
	英 foretell, portend

| calamity /kə'læməti/ | 中 n. 大灾难 |
| | 英 an event that causes great harm and suffering |

| beget /bɪ'get/ | 中 v. 导致 |
| | 英 to cause (something) to happen or exist |

| reprehensible /ˌreprɪ'hensəbl/ | 中 adj. 应受指责的 |
| | 英 very bad, deserving very strong criticism |

| divest /daɪ'vest/ | 中 v. 剥夺 |
| | 英 to deprive or dispossess especially of property, authority or title |

| wondrous /'wʌndrəs/ | 中 adj. 奇异的 |
| | 英 causing wonder or amazement, very beautiful or impressive |

| recalcitrant /rɪ'kælsɪtrənt/ | 中 adj. 顽固的 |
| | 英 stubbornly refusing to obey rules or orders |

| succinct /sək'sɪŋkt/ | 中 adj. 简洁的 |
| | 英 using few words to state or express an idea |

| recrudescent /ˌriːkruː'desnt/ | 中 adj. 复发的 |
| | 英 breaking out again, renewing |

~~frugal~~ /'fru:gl/	中 *adj.* 节俭的 英 careful about spending money or using things when you do not need to, using money or supplies in a very careful way
unseemly /ʌn'si:mli/	中 *adj.* 不得体的 英 not proper or appropriate for the situation, not seemly
preternatural /,pri:tər'nætʃrəl/	中 *adj.* 异乎寻常的 英 surpassing the normal or usual; extraordinary 中 *adj.* 超自然的 英 transcending the natural or material order; supernatural
provident /'prɑ:vɪdənt/	中 *adj.* 有远见的 英 making provision for the future: prudent 中 *adj.* 节俭的 英 frugal; economical
interlope /ɪn'tɜːr'loʊp/	中 *v.* 入侵，干涉 英 to intrude or interfere
coterie /'koʊtəri/	中 *n.* 小团体 英 an intimate and often exclusive group of persons with a unifying common interest or purpose
aplomb /ə'plɑ:m/	中 *n.* 自信沉着，泰然自若 英 complete and confident composure or self-assurance, poise
bemoan /bɪ'moʊn/	中 *v.* 哀悼，悲伤 英 to express deep grief or distress 中 *v.* 抱怨，不满 英 to regard with displeasure, disapproval or regret

mediate /ˈmiːdieɪt/	中 v. 调解
	英 to interpose between parties in order to reconcile them
	中 v. 影响
	英 to have an effect or influence in causing (something) to happen

exposé /ɪkˈspoʊz/	中 n. 揭露黑暗的报道
	英 a news report or broadcast that reveals something illegal or dishonest to the public

reticent /ˈretɪsnt/	中 adj. 沉默寡言的
	英 inclined to be silent or uncommunicative in speech, reserved
	中 adj. 有保留的
	英 restrained in expression, presentation or appearance

myriad /ˈmɪriəd/	中 adj. 大量丰富的
	英 both numerous and diverse

expurgate /ˈekspərgeɪt/	中 v. 删除（令人反感的内容）
	英 to change (a written work) by removing parts that might offend people

triumvirate /traɪˈʌmvərət/	中 n. 三头执政
	英 government by three persons or by a coalition of three parties

indefatigable /ˌɪndɪˈfætɪɡəbl/	中 adj. 不知疲倦的
	英 incapable of being fatigued, untiring

paean /ˈpiːən/	中 n. 赞歌
	英 a work that praises or honors its subject

hallmark /ˈhɔːlmɑːrk/	中 n. 特征
	英 a distinguishing characteristic, trait or feature

potent /'poʊtnt/	中 *adj.* 强有力的 英 possessing inner or physical strength; powerful 中 *adj.* 有权势的，有权力的 英 having great control or authority
lopsided /ˌlɑːpˈsaɪdɪd/	中 *adj.* 不均衡的 英 uneven or unequal
subtle /'sʌtl/	中 *adj.* 难以理解的 英 difficult to understand or perceive 中 *adj.* 灵巧的，精湛的 英 highly skillful, expert 中 *adj.* 聪明的 英 clever and indirect; not showing your real purpose
adamant /'ædəmənt/	中 *adj.* 固执的 英 not willing to change an opinion or decision; very determined
melancholy /'melənkɑːli/	中 *n.* 忧伤 英 a sad mood or feeling
unalloyed /ˌʌnəˈlɔɪd/	中 *adj.* 纯粹的，完全的 英 complete; unqualified
spew /spjuː/	中 *v.* 喷出，涌出 英 to send or cast forth with vigor or violence or in great quantity
maze /meɪz/	中 *n.* 迷宫 英 a complicated and confusing system of connected passages
misfeasance /mɪsˈfizəns/	中 *n.* 过失，不法行为 英 trespass; specifically the performance of a lawful action in an illegal or improper manner

rebellious
/rɪ'beljəs/

中 *adj.* 反抗的，难控制的
英 refusing to obey rules or authority or to accept normal standards of behavior, dress, etc.; having or showing a tendency to rebel

durable
/'dʊrəbl/

中 *adj.* 持久的，耐用的
英 staying strong and in good condition over a long period of time

varnish
/'vɑːrnɪʃ/

中 *v.* 装饰
英 adorn, embellish

labyrinthine
/ˌlæbə'rɪnθaɪn/

中 *adj.* 复杂的
英 of, relating to or resembling a labyrinth; intricate, involved

mar
/mɑːr/

中 *v.* 损毁，损伤
英 to ruin the beauty or perfection of (something); to hurt or damage the good condition of (something)

platitude
/'plætɪtuːd/

中 *n.* 陈词滥调
英 a banal, trite or stale remark

exclusive
/ɪk'skluːsɪv/

中 *adj.* 独有的，排外的
英 not shared; available to only one person or group

acclaim
/ə'kleɪm/

中 *v.* 欢呼，喝彩
英 to praise (someone or something) in a very strong and enthusiastic way

meld
/meld/

中 *v.* 混合
英 merge, blend

tremendous
/trə'mendəs/

中 *adj.* 巨大的
英 very large or great

scatter /ˈskætər/	中 *v.* 分散 英 to separate and go in different directions
concise /kənˈsaɪs/	中 *adj.* 简洁的 英 using few word; not including extra or unnecessary information
oracle /ˈɔːrəkl/	中 *n.* 先知 英 a person considered to be a source of wise counsel or prophetic opinions 中 *n.* 预言 英 an authoritative or wise statement or prediction
extenuate /ɪkˈstenjuˌeɪt/	中 *v.* 减轻 英 to lessen or to try to lessen the seriousness or extent of by making partial excuses; mitigate
viable /ˈvaɪəbl/	中 *adj.* 可行的 英 capable of being done or used 中 *adj.* 可以存活的 英 capable of living or of developing into a living thing
midst /mɪdst/	中 *n.* 当中 英 the interior or central part or point; middle
abuse /əˈbjuːs/	中 *v.* 滥用 英 to use (something) wrongly
cliché /kliːˈʃeɪ/	中 *n.* 陈词滥调 英 a hackneyed theme, characterization or situation

Word List 18

音频

contiguous /kən'tɪgjuəs/	中 *adj.* 临近的 英 used to describe things that touch each other or are immediately next to each other
~~endanger~~ /ɪn'deɪndʒər/	中 *v.* 危害 英 to cause (someone or something) to be in a dangerous place or situation
~~boorish~~ /'bʊrɪʃ/	中 *adj.* 粗鲁的，粗野的 英 resembling or befitting a boor (as in crude insensitivity)
~~high-minded~~ /haɪ'maɪndɪd/	中 *adj.* 高尚的 英 having or showing intelligence and a strong moral character
~~de-emphasize~~ /di'emfəsaɪz/	中 *v.* 降低…的重要性 英 to reduce in relative importance
poise /pɔɪz/	中 *v.* 使平衡 英 to hold (something) in a balanced and steady position
~~quandary~~ /'kwɑːndəri/	中 *n.* 困境 英 a situation in which you are confused about what to do
~~ploy~~ /plɔɪ/	中 *n.* 策略 英 a clever trick or plan that is used to get someone to do something or to gain an advantage over someone

temptation /temp'teɪʃn/	中 *n.* 诱惑 英 a strong urge or desire to have or do something
oppressive /ə'presɪv/	中 *adj.* 压迫的 英 unreasonably burdensome or severe
hyperbole /haɪ'pɜːrbəli/	中 *n.* 夸张 英 language that describes something as better or worse than it really is
~~**trickster**~~ /'trɪkstər/	中 *n.* 骗子 英 someone who tricks or deceives people especially in order to get something
~~**genteel**~~ /dʒen'tiːl/	中 *adj.* 有教养的，彬彬有礼的 英 having a quietly appealing or polite quality
impassioned /ɪm'pæʃnd/	中 *adj.* 充满激情的 英 showing or feeling very strong emotions
deduce /dɪ'duːs/	中 *v.* 推断 英 to use logic or reason to form (a conclusion or opinion about something) ; to decide (something) after thinking about the known facts
~~**flip**~~ /flɪp/	中 *v.* 翻动 英 to cause (something) to turn or turn over quickly
~~**infinite**~~ /'ɪnfɪnət/	中 *adj.* 无限的 英 having no limits 中 *adj.* 极大的 英 extremely large or great

| diffident /'dɪfədənt/ | 中 adj. 缺乏自信的，胆怯的 |
| | 英 lacking confidence; not feeling comfortable around people |

| neutralize /'nuːtrəlaɪz/ | 中 v. 抵消，使无效 |
| | 英 to stop (someone or something) from being effective or harmful |

| controvert /'kɑːntrəvɜːrt/ | 中 v. 争论，辩论 |
| | 英 to dispute or oppose by reasoning |

| succumb /sə'kʌm/ | 中 v. 屈服 |
| | 英 to stop trying to resist something |

| fury /'fjʊri/ | 中 n. 狂怒，暴怒 |
| | 英 violent anger |

| severe /sə'vɪr/ | 中 adj. 严厉的 |
| | 英 very harsh |

| conspire /kən'spaɪər/ | 中 v. 共谋，协力 |
| | 英 to secretly plan with someone to do something that is harmful or illegal |

| gleam /gliːm/ | 中 n. 微光 |
| | 英 a small, bright light |

| imperial /ɪm'pɪriəl/ | 中 adj. 帝国的 |
| | 英 of or relating to an empire or an emperor |

| paraphernalia /ˌpærəfə'neɪliə/ | 中 n. 行头，装饰品 |
| | 英 objects that are used to do a particular activity; objects of a particular kind |

| cast-iron /'kæst'aɪərn/ | 中 adj. 坚固的，顽强的 |
| | 英 very strong or tough |

| detritus /dɪ'traɪtəs/ | 中 n. 碎石，残余物 |
| | 英 the pieces that are left when something breaks, falls apart, is destroyed, etc. |

~~rivalry~~ /'raɪvlri/	中 *n.* 竞争，对抗 英 a state or situation in which people or groups are competing with each other
~~halt~~ /hɔːlt/	中 *v.* 停止 英 stop 中 *v.* 踌躇 英 to stand in perplexity or doubt between alternate courses; waver
~~avant-garde~~ /ˌævãː ˈɡɑːrd/	中 *n.* 先锋派，前卫派 英 a group of people who develop new and often very surprising ideas in art, literature, etc. 中 *adj.* 前卫的，先锋的 英 of or relating to an avant-garde
stipulate /'stɪpjuleɪt/	中 *v.* 规定 英 to specify as a condition or requirement (as of an agreement or offer) 中 *v.* 保证 英 to give a guarantee of
~~dispense~~ /dɪ'spens/	中 *v.* 分配，分发 英 to give or provide (something)
leach /liːtʃ/	中 *v.* 被冲走，滤去 英 to remove (nutritive or harmful elements) from soil by percolation
brackish /'brækɪʃ/	中 *adj.* 令人恶心的 英 distasteful; unpalatable
~~malodorous~~ /ˌmæl'oʊdərəs/	中 *adj.* 难闻的，恶臭的 英 having a bad smell
~~redolent~~ /'redələnt/	中 *adj.* 芬芳的 英 having a strong smell; full of fragrance or odor

~~noisome~~ /'nɔɪsəm/	中 *adj.* 有害的，恶臭的 英 very unpleasant or disgusting
adjudicate /ə'dʒuːdɪkeɪt/	中 *v.* 裁定，宣判 英 to make an official decision about who is right in a dispute
~~eschew~~ /ɪs'tʃuː/	中 *v.* 避免 英 to avoid (something) especially because you do not think it is right, proper, etc.
~~abbreviate~~ /ə'briːvieɪt/	中 *v.* 缩短 英 to make (something) shorter, especially to reduce (a word or name) to a shorter form
contingent /kən'tɪndʒənt/	中 *adj.* 偶然的，依赖（某些不确定性事情）的 英 depending on something else that might or might not happen
auspicious /ɔː'spɪʃəs/	中 *adj.* 吉兆的，幸运的 英 showing or suggesting that future success is likely
~~essential~~ /ɪ'senʃl/	中 *adj.* 重要的，必要的 英 extremely important and necessary
~~bootless~~ /'buːtlɪs/	中 *adj.* 无用的 英 useless, unprofitable
posit /'pɑːzɪt/	中 *v.* 假定，假设 英 to suggest (something, such as an idea or theory) especially in order to start a discussion
accrete /ə'kriːt/	中 *v.* 逐渐增长 英 to cause to adhere or become attached; accumulate

adjunct /'ædʒʌŋkt/	中 n. 附属物 英 something that is joined or added to another thing but is not an essential part of it
abound /ə'baʊnd/	中 v. 富于，充满 英 to be present in large numbers or in great quantity
subsequent /'sʌbsɪkwənt/	中 adj. 后来的，随后的 英 happening or coming after something else
heretofore /ˌhɪrtu'fɔːr/	中 adv. 迄今为止 英 until this time; before now
preponderance /prɪ'pɑːndərəns/	中 n.（数量上的）优势 英 a superiority or excess in number or quantity
uncompromising /ʌn'kɑːmprəmaɪzɪŋ/	中 adj. 不妥协的，坚定的 英 not willing to change a decision, opinion, method, etc.; not willing to make or accept a compromise
moralistic /ˌmɔːrə'lɪstɪk/	中 adj. 说教的 英 having or showing strong opinions about what is right behavior and what is wrong behavior
benevolent /bə'nevələnt/	中 adj. 仁慈的，慈善的 英 kind and generous
impose /ɪm'poʊz/	中 v. 把…强加于 英 to force someone to accept (something or yourself)

~~resume~~ /rɪˈzuːm/	中 v. 恢复 英 to begin again or go on with again after interruption
stalemate /ˈsteɪlmeɪt/	中 n. 僵局 英 a drawn contest; deadlock
~~insatiable~~ /ɪnˈseɪʃəbl/	中 adj. 无法满足的 英 always wanting more and not able to be satisfied
snappish /ˈsnæpɪʃ/	中 adj. 厉声说话的，暴躁的 英 feeling or showing irritation
peccadillo /ˌpekəˈdɪloʊ/	中 n. 小过失 英 a small mistake or fault that is not regarded as very bad or serious
reparation /ˌrepəˈreɪʃn/	中 n. 修理 英 something that is done or given as a way of correcting a mistake that you have made or a bad situation that you have caused 中 n. 赔偿 英 money that a country or group that loses a war pays because of the damage, injury, deaths, etc., it has caused
inextricable /ˌɪnɪkˈstrɪkəbl/	中 adj. 纠缠不清的，无法解脱的 英 impossible to separate; closely joined or related
impregnable /ɪmˈpregnəbl/	中 adj. 坚固的 英 not able to be captured by attack; very strong
impotent /ˈɪmpətənt/	中 adj. 无力的，无效的 英 lacking power or strength

~~precede~~ /prɪˈsiːd/	中 v. 领先，在…之前 英 to happen, go or come before (something or someone)
supplant /səˈplænt/	中 v. 取代 英 to take the place of (someone or something that is old or no longer used or accepted)
~~encounter~~ /ɪnˈkaʊntər/	中 v. 遭遇，遇到 英 to have or experience (problems, difficulties, etc.)
~~beset~~ /bɪˈset/	中 v. 困扰 英 to cause problems or difficulties for (someone or something)
~~fatigue~~ /fəˈtiːg/	中 n. 疲劳 英 the state of being very tired; extreme weariness
offish /ˈɔːfɪʃ/	中 adj. 冷漠的 英 somewhat cold and reserved
~~jockey~~ /ˈdʒɑːki/	中 ~~v. 不择手段地谋取有利地位~~ 英 to do something in an effort to get an advantage
~~perceptive~~ /pərˈseptɪv/	中 adj. 有洞察力的，敏锐的 英 having or showing an ability to understand or notice something easily or quickly
~~shortcut~~ /ˈʃɔːrtkʌt/	中 n. 捷径 英 a quicker or easier way to do something
~~jubilant~~ /ˈdʒuːbɪlənt/	中 adj. 喜悦的 英 feeling or expressing great joy; very happy

sensuous /'senʃuəs/	中 *adj.* 赏心悦目的 英 highly appreciative of the pleasures of sensation
~~controversial~~ /ˌkɑːntrə'vɜːrʃl/	中 *adj.* 有争议的 英 relating to or causing much discussion, disagreement or argument; likely to produce controversy
seamy /'siːmi/	中 *adj.* 丑恶的 英 of or relating to unpleasant and usually illegal things (such as crime, drugs, etc.)
pledge /pledʒ/	中 *v.* 保证，许诺 英 to formally promise to give or do (something)
retain /rɪ'teɪn/	中 *v.* 保持 英 to keep (someone) in a position, job, etc.
~~disproportionate~~ /ˌdɪsprə'pɔːrʃənət/	中 *adj.* 不成比例的 英 having or showing a difference that is not fair, reasonable or expected; too large or too small in relation to something
temper /'tempər/	中 *v.* 调和，使缓和 英 to make (something) less severe or extreme
outdo /ˌaʊt'duː/	中 *v.* 超过，胜过 英 to do better than (someone or something); to be more successful than (someone or something)
~~abash~~ /ə'bæʃ/	中 *v.* 使羞愧，使困窘 英 to destroy the self-possession or self-confidence of ; disconcert

unexceptional /ˌʌnɪkˈsepʃənl/	中 *adj.* 普通的 英 not unusually good, interesting, etc.; not exceptional
obtrusive /əbˈtruːsɪv/	中 *adj.* 显著的，突兀的 英 undesirably noticeable
impasse /ˈɪmpæs/	中 *n.* 僵局 英 a situation in which no progress seems possible
superficial /ˌsuːpərˈfɪʃl/	中 *adj.* 表面的 英 presenting only an appearance without substance or significance 中 *adj.* 肤浅的 英 concerned only with the obvious or apparent; shallow
moderate /ˈmɑːdərət/	中 *adj.* 有节制的，适度的 英 being within reasonable limits; not excessive or extreme 中 *v.* 使缓和 英 to lessen the violence, severity, or extremeness of
decode /ˌdiːˈkoʊd/	中 *v.* 破译，解码 英 to find or understand the true or hidden meaning of (something)
vagary /ˈveɪgəri/	中 *n.* 反复无常 英 an extravagant or erratic notion or action; caprice

evangelist /ɪˈvændʒəlɪst/	中 *n.* 狂热支持者 英 an enthusiastic advocate 中 *v.* 福音传教士 英 one who practices evangelism
pedigree /ˈpedɪɡriː/	中 *n.* 血统，门第 英 the origin and history of something especially when it is good or impressive
prominent /ˈprɑːmɪnənt/	中 *adj.* 显著的 英 immediately noticeable; conspicuous 中 *adj.* 著名的 英 widely known; eminent
enforce /ɪnˈfɔːrs/	中 *v.* 实施，强制 英 to make (a law, rule, etc.) active or effective; to make sure that people do what is required by (a law, rule, etc.)
amid /əˈmɪd/	中 *prep.* 在…之中 英 in or into the middle of (something)
boost /buːst/	中 *v.* 增加，促进 英 to increase the force, power or amount of (something)
stagger /ˈstæɡər/	中 *v.* 使…震惊 英 to shock or surprise (someone) very much 中 *v.* 跌跌撞撞地走 英 to move on unsteadily
imperil /ɪmˈperəl/	中 *v.* 使处于危险 英 to put (something or someone) in a dangerous situation

Word List 19

音 频

piety /'paɪəti/	中 *n.* 虔诚 = *pious* 英 devotion to God; the quality or state of being pious
flair /fler/	中 *n.* 天资，天分 英 an unusual and appealing quality or style
braggadocio /ˌbræɡə'doʊtʃioʊ/	中 *n.* 自夸，吹牛大王 英 the annoying or exaggerated talk of someone who is trying to sound very proud or brave
hurtle /'hɜːrtl/	中 *v.* 猛冲，猛烈碰撞 英 to cause (something or someone) to move or go with great speed and force
savor /'seɪvər/	中 *v.* 享受 英 to enjoy (something) for a long time
eviscerate /ɪ'vɪsəreɪt/	中 *v.* 使…失去力量 英 to deprive of vital content or force
mince /mɪns/	中 *v.* 装腔作势 英 to utter or pronounce with affectation 中 *v.* 委婉表达 英 to restrain (words) within the bounds of decorum
exterminate /ɪk'stɜːrmɪneɪt/	中 *v.* 使灭绝，消除 英 to destroy or kill (a group of animals, people, etc.) completely
intact /ɪn'tækt/	中 *adj.* 完整的 英 not broken or damaged; having every part

belittle /bɪˈlɪtl/	中 v. 轻视，贬低 英 to describe (someone or something) as little or unimportant
obstruct /əbˈstrʌkt/	中 v. 阻碍，妨碍 英 to slow or block the movement, progress or action of (something or someone)
proximity /prɑːkˈsɪməti/	中 n. 距离近 英 the state of being near
harness /ˈhɑːrnɪs/	中 v. 利用 英 to use (something) for a particular purpose
spurious /ˈspjʊriəs/	中 adj. 假的 英 not genuine, sincere or authentic
apocryphal /əˈpɑːkrɪfl/	中 adj. 被人们普遍接受却不正确的，假的 英 well-known but probably not true
applaud /əˈplɔːd/	中 v. 赞美，支持 英 to express approval of or support for (something or someone)
bifurcate /ˈbaɪfərkeɪt/	中 v. 一分为二 英 to cause to divide into two branches or parts
cacophony /kəˈkɑːfəni/	中 n. 刺耳的声音，不和谐的声音 英 harsh or discordant sound
catastrophe /kəˈtæstrəfi/	中 n. 大灾难 英 a terrible disaster
circumlocution /ˌsɜːrkəmləˈkjuːʃn/	中 n. 拐弯抹角的话语 英 the use of an unnecessarily large number of words to express an idea

clairvoyance
/kleɪr'vɔɪəns/

中 *n.* 异常的洞察力
英 ability to perceive matters beyond the range of ordinary perception

cloying
/'klɔɪɪŋ/

中 *adj.* 令人腻烦的
英 disgusting or distasteful by reason of excess

collude
/kə'luːd/

中 *v.* 同谋
英 to work with others secretly especially in order to do something illegal or dishonest

concord
/'kɑːŋkɔːrd/

中 *n.* 意见一致
英 a state of agreement

cosset
/'kɑːsɪt/

中 *v.* 溺爱
英 to give (someone) a lot of care and attention or too much care and attention

counterbalance
/ˌkaʊntər'bæləns/

中 *n.* 平衡，抵消
英 any force or influence that balances or offsets another
中 *v.* 平衡，抵消
英 to offset

covet
/'kʌvət/

中 *v.* 渴求
英 to feel immoderate desire for that which is another's

cursory
/'kɜːrsəri/

中 *adj.* 草率的，仓促的
英 performed rapidly with little attention to detail

weary
/'wɪri/

中 *adj.* 令人厌烦的
英 having one's patience, tolerance or pleasure exhausted
中 *adj.* 疲劳的
英 lacking strength, energy or freshness because of a need for rest or sleep

allegory /ˈæləgɔːri/	中 n. 象征
	英 a symbolic representation
	中 n. 寓言
	英 a story in which the characters and events are symbols that stand for ideas about human life or for a political or historical situation
peripheral /pəˈrɪfərəl/	中 adj. 不重要的
	英 not relating to the main or most important part
perspicacious /ˌpɜːrspɪˈkeɪʃəs/	中 adj. 有洞察力的
	英 of acute mental vision or discernment
perspicuous /ˌpɜːrspɪkjuəs/	中 adj. 清晰的，易懂的
	英 plain to the understanding especially because of clarity and precision of presentation
sleazy /ˈsliːzi/	中 adj. 低俗的，龌龊的
	英 dishonest or immoral
indemnify /ɪnˈdemnɪfaɪ/	中 v. 赔偿
	英 to make compensation to for incurred hurt, loss or damage
eyesore /ˈaɪsɔːr/	中 n. 碍眼的事物
	英 something offensive to view
archive /ˈɑːrkaɪv/	中 v. 存档，保存
	英 to file or collect in or as if in an archive
xenophobic /ˌzenəˈfoʊbɪk/	中 adj. 排外的，仇视外国的
	英 marked by unduly fearful of what is foreign and especially of people of foreign origin

ineffable
/ɪnˈefəbl/

中 adj. 难以言表的
英 too great, powerful, beautiful, etc., to be described or expressed

fluid
/ˈfluːɪd/

中 adj. 流动的
英 characterized by or employing a smooth easy style
中 adj. 多变的，不固定的
英 available for various uses

despotic
/dɪˈspɑːtɪk/

中 adj. 独裁的，专制的
英 marked by absolute power and authority

capitulate
/kəˈpɪtʃuleɪt/

中 v. 投降
英 to stop fighting an enemy or opponent

abominate
/əˈbɑːmɪneɪt/

中 v. 憎恶，憎恨
英 to feel great hatred for (someone or something)

accommodate
/əˈkɑːmədeɪt/

中 v. 调解
英 to bring into agreement or concord
中 v. 帮助
英 to provide what is needed or wanted for (someone or something)
中 v. 提供住处
英 to make room for

mandate
/ˈmændeɪt/

中 v. 命令
英 to officially demand or require (something)

saturate
/ˈsætʃəreɪt/

中 v. 填满
英 to fill (something) completely with something
中 v. 浸泡
英 to make (something) very wet

untoward /ʌn'tɔːrd/	中 *adj.* 不利的
	英 adverse or inauspicious
	中 *adj.* 不得体的
	英 not proper or appropriate
	中 *adj.* 不服管理的
	英 difficult to guide, manage or work with
peruse /pə'ruːz/	中 *v.* 仔细读
	英 to examine or read (something) in a very careful way
enthrall /ɪn'θrɔːl/	中 *v.* 吸引
	英 to hold the attention of (someone) by being very exciting, interesting or beautiful
emphatic /ɪm'fætɪk/	中 *adj.* 着重强调的
	英 said or done in a forceful or definite way
~~nonplus~~ /ˌnɑːn'plʌs/	中 *v.* 使困惑，使不知所措
	英 to perplex
phlegmatic /fleg'mætɪk/	中 *adj.* 性格冷淡的
	英 not easily upset, excited or angered
~~antidote~~ /'æntidoʊt/	中 *n.* 解药
	英 something that corrects or improves the bad effects of something
impersonal /ɪm'pɜːrsənl/	中 *adj.* 没有人情味的
	英 not engaging the human personality or emotions
	中 *adj.* 客观的
	英 having no personal reference or connection
ensue /ɪn'suː/	中 *v.* 紧随其后
	英 to come afterward

gore /gɔːr/	中 n. 血，血块
	英 blood, especially clotted blood
	中 n. 毛骨悚然
	英 gruesomeness depicted in vivid detail

| **fallow** /'fæloʊ/ | 中 adj. 休耕的 |
| | 英 left uncultivated or unplanted |

| ~~**unruly**~~ /ʌn'ruːli/ | 中 adj. 不服管理的，难以控制的 |
| | 英 not readily ruled, disciplined or managed |

| **synoptic** /sɪ'nɑːptɪk/ | 中 adj. 摘要的 |
| | 英 presenting a general view or summary |

conviction /kən'vɪkʃn/	中 n. 信念
	英 a strong belief
	中 n. 定罪
	英 a convicting or being convicted

| **patrimony** /'pætrɪmoʊni/ | 中 n. 继承，世袭 |
| | 英 property that is given to somebody when their father dies |

| **vicarious** /vaɪ'keriəs/ | 中 adj. 身临其境的 |
| | 英 felt or experienced by watching or reading about somebody else doing something, rather than by doing it yourself |

| ~~**ductile**~~ /'dʌktaɪl/ | 中 adj. 可延展的，易受影响的 |
| | 英 capable of being bent or pulled into different shapes |

| **dolorous** /'doʊlərəs/ | 中 adj. 悲伤的 |
| | 英 very sorrowful or sad |

| **antiquated** /'æntɪkweɪtɪd/ | 中 adj. 老旧的，过时的 |
| | 英 old-fashioned and no longer suitable for modern conditions |

wayward
/ˈweɪwərd/

中 *adj.* 任性的
英 following one's own capricious, wanton or depraved inclinations
中 *adj.* 无法预料的
英 following no clear principle or law

errant
/ˈerənt/

中 *adj.* 偏离目标的
英 moving about aimlessly or irregularly
中 *adj.* 错误的
英 behaving wrongly

cannibalize
/ˈkænɪbəlaɪz/

中 *v.* 采用…作为主要来源
英 to draw on as a major source
中 *v.* 剥夺（关键成分用于别处）
英 to deprive of vital elements or resources, such as personnel, equipment or funding, for use elsewhere

discordant
/dɪsˈkɔːrdənt/

中 *adj.* 不一致
英 being at variance; disagreeing
中 *adj.* 不和谐的
英 disagreeable in sound; harsh or dissonant

insinuate
/ɪnˈsɪnjueɪt/

中 *v.* 暗示（表不满）
英 to introduce (as an idea) gradually or in a subtle, indirect or covert
中 *v.* 巧妙地介入（表不满）
英 to introduce (as oneself) by stealthy, smooth or artful means

slinky
/ˈslɪŋki/

中 *adj.* 鬼鬼祟祟的
英 stealthy, furtive and sneaking

attune
/əˈtuːn/

中 *v.* 使协调一致
英 to bring into harmony

bluster	中 v.（虚张声势地）恐吓
/ˈblʌstər/	英 to talk or act with noisy swaggering threats
	中 n. 咆哮
	英 loud, arrogant speech, often full of empty threats

nonsensical	中 adj. 无意义的
/nɑːnˈsensɪkl/	英 lacking intelligible meaning
	中 adj. 愚蠢的
	英 foolish; absurd

| **villainous** | 中 adj. 极坏的，恶劣的 |
| /ˈvɪlənəs/ | 英 appropriate to a villain, as in wickedness or depravity |

| **drudgery** | 中 n. 苦工 |
| /ˈdrʌdʒəri/ | 英 tedious, menial or unpleasant work |

| **millstone** | 中 n. 重担 |
| /ˈmɪlstoʊn/ | 英 a heavy weight; a burden |

| **canard** | 中 n. 谣言 |
| /kəˈnɑːrd/ | 英 an unfounded or false, deliberately misleading story |

accolade	中 n. 赞美
/ˈækəleɪd/	英 an expression of approval; praise
	中 v. 赞扬
	英 to praise or honor

laurel	中 n. 荣誉
/ˈlɔːrəl/	英 honor and glory won for great achievement
	中 v. 授予荣誉
	英 to honor, especially with an award or a prize

| ~~**intimidate**~~ | 中 v. 恐吓 |
| /ɪnˈtɪmɪdeɪt/ | 英 to make (someone) afraid |

| temerity /tə'merəti/ | 中 v. 鲁莽 |
| | 英 the quality of being confident and unafraid of danger or punishment especially in a way that seems rude or foolish |

| assemblage /ə'semblɪdʒ/ | 中 v.（人、物的）集聚 |
| | 英 a group of people or things |

embattle /ɪm'bætl/	中 v. 整甲备战
	英 to prepare for battle
	中 v. 设防于，加强巩固
	英 to fortify

desultory /'desəltɔːri/	中 adj. 漫无目的的
	英 marked by lack of definite plan, regularity or purpose
	中 adj. 散漫的
	英 done without serious effort

| expunge /ɪk'spʌndʒ/ | 中 v. 去除 |
| | 英 to remove (something) completely |

| jaundice /'dʒɔːndɪs/ | 中 n. 嫉妒 |
| | 英 a state or feeling of negativity or bitterness arising especially from envy or world |

| dainty /'deɪnti/ | 中 adj. 小巧精致的 |
| | 英 delicately beautiful or charming and usually small |

| obloquy /'ɑːbləkwi/ | 中 n. 诋毁，谩骂 |
| | 英 abusively detractive language or utterance |

| remiss /rɪ'mɪs/ | 中 adj. 粗心的，疏忽大意的 |
| | 英 not showing enough care and attention |

balkanize
/ˈbɔːlkənaɪz/
中 v. 肢解，分裂
英 to divide or compartmentalize

oxymoron
/ˌɑːksɪˈmɔːrɑːn/
中 n. 矛盾修饰法
英 a combination of words that have opposite or very different meanings

gaiety
/ˈɡeɪəti/
中 n. 欢快
英 a happy and lively quality

altercate
/ˈɔːltəkeit/
中 v. 争吵
英 to dispute angrily or noisily

coerce
/koʊˈɜːrs/
中 v. 强制
英 to make (someone) do something by using force or threats

gregarious
/ɡrɪˈɡeriəs/
中 v. 群居的，好交际的
英 enjoying the company of other people

squander
/ˈskwɑːndər/
中 v. 浪费，挥霍
英 to use (something) in a foolish or wasteful way

congruent
/ˈkɑːŋɡruənt/
中 adj. 相一致的
英 matching or in agreement with something

wallow
/ˈwɑːloʊ/
中 v. 沉溺于
英 to spend time experiencing or enjoying something without making any effort to change your situation, feelings, etc.

derelict
/ˈderəlɪkt/
中 adj. 被遗弃的
英 abandoned especially by the owner or occupant
中 adj. 不负责任的，玩忽职守的
英 lacking a sense of duty

dilapidate /dɪ'læpɪdeɪt/	中 *v.* 使…破败 英 to bring into a condition of decay or partial ruin
invert /ɪn'vɜːrt/	中 *v.* 颠倒，倒置 英 to change the position, order or relationship of things so that they are the opposite of what they had been
introspect /ˌɪntrə'spekt/	中 *v.* 自省 英 to examine and analyse one's own thoughts and feelings
~~**repertoire**~~ /'repərtwɑːr/	中 *n.* 全部节目 英 all the plays, songs, dances, etc., that a performer or group of performers knows and can perform 中 *n.* 全部才能，全部本领 英 all the things that a person is able to do
solace /'sɑːləs/	中 *v.* 安慰 英 to give comfort to in grief or misfortune; console 中 *n.* 安慰，慰藉 英 someone or something that gives a feeling of comfort to a person who is sad, depressed, etc.; a source of comfort
inquisitive /ɪn'kwɪzətɪv/	中 *adj.* 好奇的 英 tending to ask questions; having a desire to know or learn more
figment /'fɪgmənt/	中 *n.* 虚构的事物 英 something produced by the imagination; something that does not really exist

intermittent /ˌɪntərˈmɪtənt/	中 *adj.* 间歇的，断断续续的 英 starting, stopping and starting again; not constant or steady
impervious /ɪmˈpɜːrviəs/	中 *adj.* 不能渗透的 英 not allowing something (such as water or light) to enter or pass through 中 *adj.* 不受影响的 英 not bothered or affected by something
inappropriate /ˌɪnəˈproʊpriət/	中 *adj.* 不适当的，不合适的 英 not right or suited for some purpose or situation; not appropriate or suitable
indiscernible /ˌɪndɪˈsɜːrnəbl/	中 *adj.* 不明显的 英 impossible to see, hear or know clearly
disreputable /dɪsˈrepjətəbl/	中 *adj.* 声明狼藉的 英 not respected or trusted by most people; having a bad reputation
plebeian /pləˈbiːən/	中 *n.* 平民，粗俗的人 英 a common person 中 *adj.* 普通的 英 crude or coarse in manner or style: common
clairvoyant /klerˈvɔɪənt/	中 *adj.* 有洞察力的 英 having clairvoyance; able to see beyond the range of ordinary perception
hallucinogen /həˈluːsɪnədʒən/	中 *n.* 迷幻剂 英 a substance (such as a drug) that causes people to see or sense things that are not real; a substance that causes hallucinations

voyeur /vwaɪˈɜːr/	中 n. 好刺探他人隐私者 英 a person who likes seeing and talking or writing about something that is considered to be private
boredom /ˈbɔːrdəm/	中 n. 厌倦 英 the state of being weary and restless through lack of interest
apogee /ˈæpədʒiː/	中 n. 最高点 英 the highest point of something
~~**acme**~~ /ˈækmi/	中 n. 最高点 英 the highest point of something
~~**precursor**~~ /priːˈkɜːrsər/	中 n. 先驱 英 something that comes before something else and that often leads to or influences its development
~~**civil**~~ /ˈsɪvl/	中 adj. 公民的 英 of or relating to the people who live in a country 中 adj. 有礼貌的 英 polite but not friendly; only as polite as a person needs to be in order to not be rude
peaceable /ˈpiːsəbl/	中 adj. 和平的，温顺的 英 not liking or wanting to fight or argue
unfaltering /ʌnˈfɔːltərɪŋ/	中 adj. 坚定的 英 not wavering or weakening; firm
~~**superfluous**~~ /suːˈpɜːrfluəs/	中 adj. 多余的 英 beyond what is needed; not necessary

uncertainty
/ʌnˈsɜːrtnti/

中 n. 不确定，不可靠

英 something that is doubtful or unknown; something that is uncertain

cautious
/ˈkɔːʃəs/

中 adj. 小心谨慎的

英 careful about avoiding danger or risk

Word List 20

音 频

cater /'keɪtər/	中 v. 迎合 英 to supply what is required or desired
~~clot~~ /klɑːt/	中 v. 凝固结块 英 to become thick and partly solid
elate /i'leɪt/	中 v. 使兴奋，使高兴 英 to make (someone) very happy and excited
avert /ə'vɜrt/	中 v. 阻止 英 to prevent (something bad) from happening
fad /fæd/	中 n. 一时流行的风尚 英 a fashion that is taken up with great enthusiasm for a brief period of time; a craze
ape /eɪp/	中 v.（笨拙的）模仿 英 to imitate or mimic in an inept way
~~irk~~ /ɜːrk/	中 v. 使…厌烦 英 to annoy
~~ebb~~ /eb/	中 v. 衰落 英 to get worse 中 v. 退潮 英 to fall back from the flood stage
yen /jen/	中 n.（强烈的）渴望 英 a strong desire or propensity
opt /ɑːpt/	中 v. 选择 英 to make a choice

curb /kɜːrb/	中 v. 限制，控制
	英 to check, restrain or control
	中 n. 限制
	英 something that checks or restrains

curt /kɜːrt/	中 adj. 语言简练的
	英 sparing of words
	中 adj. 说话简短而粗鲁的
	英 rudely brief or abrupt in speech

| snag /snæg/ | 中 n. 故障，问题 |
| | 英 an unexpected problem or difficulty |

glut /glʌt/	中 n. 过量
	英 an excessive quantity
	中 v. 暴饮暴食
	英 to fill especially with food to satiety

| woo /wuː/ | 中 v. 吸引 |
| | 英 to try to attract |

| coax /koʊks/ | 中 v. 诱骗 |
| | 英 to influence or gently urge by caressing or flattering |

bent /bent/	中 adj. 有倾向的
	英 strongly inclined
	中 n. 才能，爱好
	英 a special inclination or capacity

| balk /bɔːk/ | 中 v.（突然地）拒绝 |
| | 英 to refuse abruptly |

| avid /ˈævɪd/ | 中 adj. 非常渴望的，贪婪的 |
| | 英 desirous to the point of greed |

| agog /əˈɡɑːɡ/ | 中 adj. 急切渴望的 |
| | 英 full of intense interest or excitement |

tout /taʊt/	中 *v.* 兜售
	英 to promote or praise energetically

choke /tʃoʊk/	中 *v.* 抑制
	英 to check or hinder the growth, development or activity of

erect /i'rekt/	中 *adj.* 笔直的
	英 straight up and down

awry /ə'raɪ/	中 *adj.* 错误的
	英 away from the correct course

quip /kwɪp/	中 *n.* 机智幽默的评论
	英 a clever, witty remark

aver /ə'vɜːr/	中 *v.* 断言
	英 to say (something) in a very strong and definite way

quash /kwɑːʃ/	中 *v.* 废止，使无效
	英 to annul or put an end to
	中 *v.* 镇压，平息
	英 to suppress or extinguish completely

glib /glɪb/	中 *adj.* 即兴的
	英 performed with a natural, offhand ease
	中 *adj.* 油嘴滑舌的
	英 marked by ease and fluency in speaking or writing often to the point of being insincere or deceitful

roil /rɔɪl/	中 *v.* 使…混乱
	英 to cause to be in a state of agitation or disorder

rant /rænt/	中 *v.* 辱骂
	英 to speak or write in an angry or emotionally charged manner

lull /lʌl/	中 v. 使平静
	英 to cause to sleep or rest
	中 n. 暂时的平静，间歇
	英 a relatively calm interval

| avow /əˈvaʊ/ | 中 v. 承认 |
| | 英 to acknowledge or declare openly and unashamedly |

| trio /ˈtriːoʊ/ | 中 n. 三个一组 |
| | 英 a group of three |

sage /seɪdʒ/	中 adj. 智慧的
	英 very wise
	中 n. 智者
	英 one distinguished for wisdom

lurk /lɜːrk/	中 v. 潜藏
	英 to exist unobserved or unsuspected
	中 v. 暗中行动
	英 to move furtively

| hoax /hoʊks/ | 中 v. 欺骗 |
| | 英 to deceive or cheat |

| flit /flɪt/ | 中 v. 快速移动 |
| | 英 to move quickly from one condition or location to another |

| apex /ˈeɪpeks/ | 中 n. 最高点，顶峰 |
| | 英 the highest point or the highest level |

| spur /spɜːr/ | 中 v. 刺激 |
| | 英 to incite or stimulate |

| scant /skænt/ | 中 adj. 稀缺的 |
| | 英 inadequately supplied |

| abhor /əbˈhɔːr/ | 中 v. 厌恶 |
| | 英 to dislike very much |

| prone /proʊn/ | 中 adj. 有…倾向的 |
| | 英 having a tendency or inclination |

| usurp /juːˈzɜːrp/ | 中 v. 篡夺 |
| | 英 to seize and hold in possession by force without right |

| pithy /ˈpɪθi/ | 中 adj. 简洁有力的 |
| | 英 forceful and brief |

| tonic /ˈtɑːnɪk/ | 中 adj. 有益健康的 |
| | 英 restorative or stimulating to health or well-being |

niche /niːʃ/	中 n. 小众市场
	英 a special area of demand for a product or service
	中 n. 称心如意的活动、工作等
	英 a situation or activity specially suited to a person's interests, abilities or nature

| trite /traɪt/ | 中 adj. 陈词滥调的 |
| | 英 not evoking interest because of overuse or repetition |

| stoic /ˈstoʊɪkl/ | 中 adj. 不以苦乐为意的，淡泊的 |
| | 英 seemingly indifferent to or unaffected by pleasure or pain; impassive |

murky /ˈmɜːrki/	中 adj. 昏暗的
	英 dark or dim
	中 adj. 难懂的，不清晰的
	英 not clearly known, understood or expressed

blunt /blʌnt/	中 adj. 直率的
	英 abrupt and often disconcertingly frank in speech
	中 adj. 钝的，不锋利的
	英 having a dull edge or end; not sharp
	中 adj. 反应迟钝的
	英 obtuse in understanding or discernment
flout /flaʊt/	中 v. 蔑视，鄙视
	英 to treat with contemptuous disregard
rue /ruː/	中 n. 后悔
	英 regret, sorrow
rote /roʊt/	中 n. 死记硬背
	英 the use of memory usually with little intelligence
dire /'daɪər/	中 adj. 可怕的，严重的
	英 very bad; causing great fear or worry
snob /snɑːb/	中 n. 势利小人
	英 someone who tends to criticize, reject or ignore people who come from a lower social class, have less education, etc.
shun /ʃʌn/	中 v. 躲避
	英 to avoid
idle /'aɪdl/	中 adj. 空闲的
	英 not working, active or being used
	中 adj. 没有价值的
	英 having no value, use or significance

crass /kræs/	中 *adj.* 粗鲁的
	英 so crude and unrefined as to be lacking in discrimination and sensibility
	中 *adj.*（用于贬义词加强语气的）非常的
	英 used as a pejorative intensifier
apt /æpt/	中 *adj.* 合适的
	英 exactly suitable
	中 *adj.* 有…倾向的
	英 having a natural tendency
	中 *adj.* 聪明的，灵巧的
	英 quick to learn or understand
hone /hoʊn/	中 *v.* 磨炼（技能）
	英 to perfect or make more intense or effective
veto /ˈviːtoʊ/	中 *v.* 否决
	英 to reject (a proposed law) officially
blur /blɜːr/	中 *v.* 使…模糊不清
	英 to make (something) unclear or difficult to see or remember
verge /vɜːrdʒ/	中 *n.* 边缘
	英 an area along the edge of a road, path, etc.
	中 *n.* 临界点
	英 brink or threshold
swift /swɪft/	中 *adj.* 快速的
	英 happening or done quickly or immediately
	中 *adj.* 反应灵敏的
	英 smart or intelligent
sever /ˈsevər/	中 *v.* 打碎，分裂
	英 to divide into parts
	中 *v.* 割断
	英 to cut off (a part) from a whole

extol /ɪk'stoʊl/	中 *v.* 赞美 英 to praise highly
exalt /ɪg'zɔːlt/	中 *v.* 赞美 英 to praise or honor 中 *v.* 提升 英 to raise in rank, character or status
tweak /twiːk/	中 *v.* 拧 英 to twist sharply 中 *v.* 略微调整 英 to make usually small adjustments in
verve /vɜːrv/	中 *n.* 热情，活力 英 great energy and enthusiasm
coy /kɔɪ/	中 *adj.* 腼腆的 英 having a shy or sweetly innocent quality 中 *adj.* 含糊其辞的 英 showing reluctance to make a definite commitment
whit /wɪt/	中 *n.* 少量 英 a very small amount
pine /paɪn/	中 *v.* 渴望 英 to yearn intensely and persistently especially for something unattainable 中 *v.* 憔悴 英 to become thin and weak because of sadness or loss
demur /dɪ'mɜːr/	中 *v.* 反对 英 to voice opposition; object

belie /bɪˈlaɪ/	中 *v.* 掩盖 英 to give a false impression of 中 *v.* 与…相矛盾 英 to run counter to 中 *v.* 证明…为假 英 to show (something) to be false or wrong
spike /spaɪk/	中 *v.*（短期大幅）上升 英 to increase greatly in a short period of time
quell /kwel/	中 *v.* 压制，镇压 英 to end or stop (something) usually by using force
vapid /ˈvæpɪd/	中 *adj.* 无聊的 英 lacking liveliness
venal /ˈviːnl/	中 *adj.* 贪污的 英 open to bribery
hitch /hɪtʃ/	中 *n.*（隐形的）问题，难题 英 a hidden problem that makes something more complicated or difficult to do
rebut /rɪˈbʌt/	中 *v.* 驳斥 英 to refute by offering opposing evidence or arguments
delve /delv/	中 *v.* 搜寻，挖掘 英 to search deeply and laboriously 中 *v.* 深入探讨 英 to discuss or explain a subject in detail
totem /ˈtoʊtəm/	中 *n.* 标志，象征 英 a venerated emblem or symbol
edify /ˈedɪfaɪ/	中 *v.* 启迪 英 to instruct especially so as to encourage intellectual, moral or spiritual improvement

grip /grɪp/	中 *v.* 吸引 英 to get and hold the interest or attention of (someone)
crave /kreɪv/	中 *v.* 极度渴望 英 to have a very strong desire for (something)
~~**mimic**~~ /'mɪmɪk/	中 *v.* 模仿 英 to imitate or copy
gauge /geɪdʒ/	中 *v.* 评估，判断，衡量 英 to evaluate or estimate
deter /dɪ'tɜːr/	中 *v.* 阻止 英 to prevent (something) from happening
bogus /'boʊgəs/	中 *adj.* 假的 英 not real or genuine
cloak /kloʊk/	中 *v.* 伪装，掩盖 英 to hide or disguise
~~**aloof**~~ /ə'luːf/	中 *adj.* 冷漠的，疏远的 英 removed or distant either physically or emotionally
akin /ə'kɪn/	中 *adj.* 相似的，相关的 英 essentially similar, related or compatible
croon /kruːn/	中 *v.* 低吟浅唱 英 to sing in a low soft voice
bland /blænd/	中 *adj.* 无聊的 英 dull or insipid 中 *adj.* 温和的 英 pleasant in manner
surly /'sɜːrli/	中 *adj.* 傲慢的，粗暴的 英 sullenly ill-humored; gruff

| probe /proʊb/ | 中 v. 仔细调查 |
| | 英 to search into and explore very thoroughly |

| hoard /hɔːrd/ | 中 n. / v. 贮藏 |
| | 英 v. to collect and hide a large amount of |

sap /sæp/	中 n. 活力
	英 vitality
	中 v. 使…失去活力
	英 to deplete or weaken gradually

| rive /raɪv/ | 中 v. 劈开 |
| | 英 to divide into pieces |

| riot /'raɪət/ | 中 n. 暴乱 |
| | 英 a situation in which a large group of people behave in a violent and uncontrolled way |

| glum /glʌm/ | 中 adj. 悲伤的 |
| | 英 sad or depressed |

whet /wet/	中 v. 削尖
	英 to make sharper or stronger
	中 v. 使…更灵敏
	英 to make keen or more acute

plod /plɑːd/	中 v.（勤奋而单调地）工作
	英 to work laboriously and monotonously
	中 v.（缓慢或无聊地）进行
	英 to proceed slowly or tediously

| gloat /gloʊt/ | 中 v. 洋洋自得，幸灾乐祸 |
| | 英 to show in an improper or selfish way that you are happy with your own success or another person's failure |

| loath /loʊθ/ | 中 adj. 不情愿的 |
| | 英 unwilling to do something |

chic /ʃiːk/	中 *adj.* 时尚的 英 fashionable style
sham /ʃæm/	中 *adj.* 虚假的 英 not genuine
don /dɑːn/	中 *v.* 穿上 英 to put on
oust /aʊst/	中 *v.* 驱逐 英 to cause or force to leave a position 中 *v.* 取代 英 to take the place of
sift /sɪft/	中 *v.* 分离，筛选 英 to separate or remove
expel /ɪkˈspel/	中 *v.* 驱逐 英 to officially force (someone) to leave a place or organization
~~loose~~ /luːs/	中 *adj.* 松弛的 英 not tightly fastened, attached or held
adept /ˈædept/	中 *adj.* 精通的 英 very good at doing something hard
~~lapse~~ /læps/	中 *v.* 停止 英 to go out of existence 中 *n.* 疏忽大意 英 a slight error usually caused by lack of attention or forgetfulness
guile /gaɪl/	中 *n.* 欺骗 英 deceitful cunning
~~decay~~ /dɪˈkeɪ/	中 *v.* 衰退 英 to decline in health, strength or vigor

sloth /sloʊθ/	中 n. 懒惰
	英 the quality of being lazy
~~**dwarf**~~ /dwɔːrf/	中 v. 使…变得矮小或不重要
	英 to cause to appear smaller or to seem inferior
deify /'deɪɪfaɪ/	中 v. 奉…为神，尊敬
	英 to treat (someone or something) like a god or goddess
hoary /'hɔːri/	中 adj. 老掉牙的
	英 extremely old
pique /piːk/	中 v. 激怒，惹怒
	英 to make someone annoyed or angry
~~**hubris**~~ /'hjuːbrɪs/	中 n. 自大，傲慢
	英 exaggerated pride or self-confidence
hew /hjuː/	中 v. 遵守
	英 to confirm or adhere
	中 v. 砍树
	英 to cut down (a tree)
tilt /tɪlt/	中 v. / n. 倾斜
	英 n. slant or bias
feat /fiːt/	中 n.（彰显技艺等的）成就
	英 an act or achievement that shows courage, strength or skill
~~**marvel**~~ /'mɑːrvl/	中 v. 震惊，惊讶
	英 to feel great surprise, wonder or admiration
	中 n. 令人惊异的人（或事）
	英 one that causes wonder or astonishment
~~**leak**~~ /liːk/	中 v. 泄漏信息
	英 to give out (information) surreptitiously

guild /ɡɪld/	中 *n.* 协会 英 an organized group of people who have joined together because they share the same job or interest
slur /slɜːr/	中 *n.* 诽谤 英 an insulting or disparaging remark or innuendo 中 *v.* 含糊不清地说 英 to slide or slip over without due mention, consideration or emphasis
cede /siːd/	中 *v.* 割让 英 to give control of (something) to another person, group, government, etc.
shrill /ʃrɪl/	中 *v.* 尖叫 英 to utter in a shrill manner; scream
skim /skɪm/	中 *v.* 浏览 英 to read or glance through (a book, for example) quickly or superficially
wilt /wɪlt/	中 *v.* 萎蔫，衰弱 英 to lose energy, confidence, effectiveness, etc.
mete /miːt/	中 *v.* 分配 英 to distribute as deserved
spunk /spʌŋk/	中 *n.* 勇气 英 spirit, courage and determination
cinch /sɪntʃ/	中 *n.* 容易做的事 英 something that is very easy to do

Word List 21

音 频

backwater /'bækwɔːtər/	中 n. 停滞，落后的地方 英 a place or situation regarded as isolated, stagnant or backward
moonshine /'muːnʃaɪn/	中 n. 空话，假话 英 empty talk; foolish or untrue words
brainchild /'breɪntʃaɪld/	中 n.（辛苦劳动的）成果，结晶 英 a product of one's creative effort
deadpan /'dedpæn/	中 adj. 表情、行为严肃冷淡的 英 impassively matter-of-fact, as in style, behavior or expression 中 n. 一种以面无表情而产生幽默的喜剧
sidestep /'saɪdstep/	中 v. 回避，绕过 英 bypass, evade
upshot /'ʌpʃɑːt/	中 n. 结局 英 the final result
upbeat /'ʌpbiːt/	中 adj. 积极乐观的，愉快的 英 positive and cheerful
downsize /'daʊnsaɪz/	中 v. 缩小 英 to reduce in size 中 v. 裁员 英 to fire (employees) for the purpose of downsizing a business
impressionable /ɪm'preʃənəbl/	中 adj. 易受影响的 英 easy to influence
personable /'pɜːrsənəbl/	中 adj. 品貌兼优的 英 pleasant or amiable in person

inviting /ɪnˈvaɪtɪŋ/	中 *adj.* 吸引人的 英 attractive
liken /ˈlaɪkən/	中 *v.* 比较 英 compare
~~**wholesale**~~ /ˈhoʊlseɪl/	中 *adj.* 大规模的 英 affecting large numbers of people or things
~~**wholesome**~~ /ˈhoʊlsəm/	中 *adj.* 有益健康的 英 promoting health of body
~~**romanticize**~~ /roʊˈmæntɪsaɪz/	中 *v.* 浪漫化 英 to think about or describe something as being better or more attractive or interesting than it really is
defining /dɪˈfaɪnɪŋ/	中 *adj.* 最典型的，起决定性作用的 英 critically important
telling /ˈtelɪŋ/	中 *adj.* 有明显效果的，显著的 英 carrying great weight and producing a marked effect
dour /ˈdaʊər/	中 *adj.* 严肃的，阴郁的 英 gloomy, sullen
teem /tiːm/	中 *v.* 充满 英 to become filled to overflowing
backbone /ˈbækboʊn/	中 *n.* 支柱，支撑 英 the main support or major sustaining factor
pronounced /prəˈnaʊnst/	中 *adj.* 显著的，明显的 英 strongly marked
~~**calculated**~~ /ˈkælkjuleɪtɪd/	中 *adj.* 故意的，精打细算的 英 carefully planned for a particular and often improper purpose

backfire
/ˌbækˈfaɪər/
中 v. 事与愿违，起反作用
英 to have the reverse of the desired or expected effect

redoubtable
/rɪˈdaʊtəbl/
中 adj. 令人肃然起敬的
英 causing or deserving great fear or respect

gridlock
/ˈɡrɪdlɑːk/
中 n. 交通堵塞
英 a situation in which streets are so full that vehicles cannot move
中 n. 僵局
英 a situation in which no progress can be made

bookish
/ˈbʊkɪʃ/
中 adj. 书呆子气的
英 more interested in reading books and studying than doing more physical activities (such as sports)

wanting
/ˈwɑːntɪŋ/
中 adj. 未达到要求的
英 not being up to standards or expectations

airtight
/ˈertaɪt/
中 adj. 密封的，不透气的
英 impermeable to air or nearly so
中 adj. 无懈可击的
英 having no noticeable weakness, flaw or loophole

lest
/lest/
中 conj. 唯恐
英 for fear that

streamline
/ˈstriːmlaɪn/
中 v. 简化
英 to make simpler or more efficient
中 v. 使现代化
英 to bring up to date

grandstand
/ˈɡrænstænd/
中 adj. 博眼球的
英 done for show or to impress on lookers
中 v. 赚取眼球
英 to play or act so as to impress on lookers

foreboding /fɔːrˈboʊdɪŋ/	中 *n.* 不祥的预感
	英 a feeling that something bad is going to happen
smother /ˈsmʌðər/	中 *v.* 使…窒息
	英 to kill someone by covering the face so that breathing is not possible
	中 *v.* 遏制，阻止
	英 to try to keep from happening
effortless /ˈefərtləs/	中 *adj.* 不费力的
	英 showing or requiring little or no effort
discerning /dɪˈsɜːrnɪŋ/	中 *adj.* 有洞察力的
	英 showing insight and understanding
rife /raɪf/	中 *adj.* 非常普遍的
	英 prevalent especially to an increasing degree
girth /ɡɜːrθ/	中 *n.* 尺寸
	英 size
	中 *n.* 围长
	英 a measure around a body
hard-boiled /hɑːrdˈbɔɪld/	中 *adj.* 强硬的，不动感情的
	英 devoid of sentimentality; tough
spiteful /ˈspaɪtfl/	中 *adj.* 恶毒的
	英 having or showing a desire to harm, anger or defeat someone
forbear /fɔːrˈber/	中 *v.* 克制，忍耐
	英 to control oneself when provoked
wont /wɔːnt/	中 *adj.* 有…倾向的
	英 inclined, apt

enjoin /ɪnˈdʒɔɪn/	中 v. 禁止
	英 to prevent someone from doing something
glean /gliːn/	中 v. 慢慢收集
	英 to gather or collect in a gradual way
glisten /ˈglɪsn/	中 v. 表面闪烁光芒
	英 to shine with light reflected off a wet surface
cleave /kliːv/	中 v. 忠诚于…
	英 to adhere firmly and closely or loyally and unwaveringly
	中 v. 劈开
	英 to split with sharp instrument
undue /ˌʌnˈduː/	中 adj. 过量的
	英 exceeding what is appropriate or normal
qualm /kwaːm/	中 n. 不安
	英 an uneasy feeling about the propriety or rightness of a course of action
inestimable /ɪnˈestɪməbl/	中 adj. 无法估量的
	英 impossible to estimate or compute
	中 adj. 无价的
	英 invaluable
mishap /ˈmɪshæp/	中 n. 不幸
	英 an unfortunate accident
brink /brɪŋk/	中 n. （事情发生的）边缘
	英 the point at which something is likely to begin
	中 n. （悬崖峭壁的）边缘
	英 the upper edge of a steep or vertical slope

underpin /ˌʌndər'pɪn/	中 v. 支持，支撑 英 to strengthen or support (something) from below
bleak /bliːk/	中 adj. 阴暗的，阴郁的 英 gloomy and somber 中 adj. 寒冷的 英 cold and cutting 中 adj. 荒凉的，光秃秃的 英 unsheltered and barren
whisk /wɪsk/	中 v. 迅速送走（人或事物） 英 to move something or someone to another place nimbly and quickly
savvy /'sævi/	中 adj. 有见识的 英 well informed and perceptive 中 n. 知识和见识 英 practical understanding or knowledge of something
buoy /bɔɪ/	中 v. 使浮起来 英 to keep afloat or aloft 中 v. 鼓励 英 to hearten or inspire
makeshift /'meɪkʃɪft/	中 n. 权宜之计 英 a temporary or expedient substitute for something else 中 adj. 权宜的，临时代用的 英 suitable as a temporary or expedient substitute
forthwith /ˌfɔːrθ'wɪθ/	中 adj. 马上，立刻 英 without delay
cornerstone /'kɔːrnərstoʊn/	中 n. 最重要部分，基石 英 an indispensable and fundamental basis

~~bedrock~~ /'bedrɑːk/	中 *n.* 根基 英 the very basis
~~resourceful~~ /rɪ'sɔːrsfl/	中 *adj.* 足智多谋的 英 able to act effectively or imaginatively, especially in difficult situations
~~appreciable~~ /ə'priːʃəbl/	中 *adj.* 可感知的，可衡量的 英 capable of being perceived or measured
sate /seɪt/	中 *v.* 使…厌倦，使…腻烦 英 to cloy with overabundance 中 *v.* 使…满足 英 to appease by indulging to the full
stonewall /'stoʊnwɔːl/	中 *v.* 拒绝合作 英 to refuse to comply or cooperate with 中 *v.* 采用拖延的战术 英 to engage in delaying tactics
involuntary /ɪn'vɑːlənteri/	中 *adj.* 无意识的 英 not done or made consciously
~~astronomical~~ /ˌæstrə'nɑːmɪkl/	中 *adj.* 巨大的 英 immense 中 *adj.* 天文的 英 of or relating to astronomy
misgiving /ˌmɪs'ɡɪvɪŋ/	中 *n.* 不安 英 doubt, distrust or apprehension
testy /'testi/	中 *adj.* 易怒的 英 irritated, impatient or exasperated
categorical /ˌkætə'ɡɔːrɪkl/	中 *adj.* 绝对的，坚定的 英 being without exception or qualification; absolute

recollect
/ˌrekə'lekt/
中 v. 记忆
英 to remember something

peerless
/'pɪrləs/
中 adj. 无与伦比的
英 being such as to have no match

proofread
/'pruːfriːd/
中 v. 校对
英 to read in order to find errors and mark corrections

heartfelt
/'hɑːrtfelt/
中 adj. 真诚的
英 deeply or sincerely felt

vainglorious
/ˌveɪn'glɔːriəs/
中 adj. 自负的，自命不凡的
英 excessively proud of oneself

override
/ˌoʊvər'raɪd/
中 v. 否决，推翻
英 to make (something) no longer valid
中 v. 凌驾于，比…更重要
英 to have more importance or influence than (something)

hereabouts
/ˌhɪrə'baʊts/
中 adv. 在附近
英 in this vicinity

groundless
/'graʊndləs/
中 adj. 毫无根据的
英 not based on facts

uneventful
/ˌʌnɪ'ventfl/
中 adj. 平凡的，没有大事发生的
英 lacking in significant events

daredevil
/'derdevl/
中 adj. 鲁莽的
英 recklessly and often ostentatiously daring

incomparable
/ɪn'kɑːmprəbl/
中 adj. 无与伦比的
英 better than any other

tower 塔?

towering /ˈtaʊərɪŋ/	中 adj. 高大的 英 impressively high or great 中 adj. 强烈的 英 reaching a high point of intensity 中 adj. 过度的 英 going beyond proper bounds
slapdash /ˈslæpdæʃ/	中 adj. 草率的，粗心大意的 英 quick and careless
invaluable /ɪnˈvæljuəbl/	中 adj. 极具价值的 英 extremely valuable or useful
slipshod /ˈslɪpʃɑːd/	中 adj. 粗心大意的 英 very careless or poorly done or made
heartrending /ˈhɑːrtˌrendɪŋ/	中 adj. 令人心痛的 英 causing great sadness or sorrow
retiring /rɪˈtaɪərɪŋ/	中 adj. 羞涩的，不善交际的 英 quiet and shy
belabor /bɪˈleɪbər/	中 v. 批评 英 to attack or criticize
yardstick /ˈjɑːrdstɪk/	中 n. 准绳，标准 英 a standard for making a critical judgement
downcast /ˈdaʊnkæst/	中 adj. 不开心的，沮丧的 英 low in spirit
telltale /ˈtelteɪl/	中 adj. 泄露内情的 英 indicating or giving evidence of something 中 n. 告密者 英 informer
moody /ˈmuːdi/	中 adj. 喜怒无常的 英 given to frequent changes of mood 中 adj. 悲伤的 英 expressive of a mood, especially a sullen or gloomy mood

retire 退休

| discriminating /dɪˈskrɪmɪneɪtɪŋ/ | 中 adj. 有洞察力的，有鉴别能力的 |
| | 英 discerning, judicious |

collected /kəˈlektɪd/	中 adj. 冷静的
	英 self-possessed; composed
	中 adj. 收集在一起的
	英 brought or placed together from various sources

| taxing /ˈtæksɪŋ/ | 中 adj. 繁重的，劳累的 |
| | 英 burdensome and wearing |

demanding /dɪˈmændɪŋ/	中 adj. 费力的
	英 requiring much effort or attention
	中 adj.（对别人）高标准要求的
	英 requiring others to work hard or meet high expectations

| riveting /ˈrɪvɪtɪŋ/ | 中 adj. 吸引人的 |
| | 英 wholly absorbing or engrossing one's attention |

| celebrated /ˈselɪbreɪtɪd/ | 中 adj. 出名的 |
| | 英 known and praised widely |

| pressing /ˈpresɪŋ/ | 中 adj. 紧急的 |
| | 英 demanding immediate attention |

exacting /ɪgˈzæktɪŋ/	中 adj. 要求高的
	英 making severe demands
	中 adj. 费力的
	英 requiring great care and effort

| earnest /ˈɜːrnɪst/ | 中 adj. 严肃的，真诚的 |
| | 英 showing or expressing sincerity or seriousness |

| unfeeling /ʌnˈfiːlɪŋ/ | 中 adj. 冷血的，没有同情心的 |
| | 英 not sympathetic to others |

whereabouts /'werəbaʊts/	中 *n.* 行踪，下落 英 approximate location
uproot /ˌʌp'ruːt/	中 *v.* 连根拔起，消灭 英 to destroy or remove completely
~~**agreeable**~~ /ə'griːəbl/	中 *adj.* 适合的 英 suitable and conformable 中 *adj.* 宜人的，令人愉悦的 英 to one's liking
composed /kəm'poʊzd/	中 *adj.* 冷静的 英 calm
barring /'bɑːrɪŋ/	中 *prep.* 除了…以外 英 apart from the occurrence of; excepting
prohibitive /prə'hɪbətɪv/	中 *adj.* 昂贵的 英 so high or burdensome as to discourage purchase or use
phenomenal /fə'nɑːmɪnl/	中 *adj.* 出众的 英 extraordinary and outstanding
~~**incisive**~~ /ɪn'saɪsɪv/	中 *adj.* 一针见血的，深刻尖锐的 英 impressively direct and decisive
amiss /ə'mɪs/	中 *adj.* 错误的 英 in the wrong way
musty /'mʌsti/	中 *adj.* 霉臭的 英 having a bad smell because of wetness, old age or lack of fresh air
needy /'niːdi/	中 *adj.* 贫穷的 英 being in need; impoverished
canny /'kæni/	中 *adj.* 精明的，聪明的 英 very clever and able to make intelligent decisions

Word List

uncanny /ʌnˈkæni/	中 *adj.* 奇异的 英 strange or unusu... surprising or difficult ...
mighty /ˈmaɪti/	中 *adj.* 强大的 英 having or showing great strength or power
locale /loʊˈkæl/	中 *n.* 地点 英 the place where something happens
finale /fɪˈnæli/	中 *n.* 大结局 英 the last part of something (such as a musical performance, play, etc.)
rationale /ˌræʃəˈnæl/	中 *n.* 基本原理 英 the reason or explanation for something
halfhearted /hæfˌhɑːrtɪd/	中 *adj.* 不认真的，不热心的 英 feeling or showing a lack of interest or enthusiasm
morale /məˈræl/	中 *n.* 士气 英 the feelings of enthusiasm and loyalty that a person or group has about a task or job
proverbial /prəˈvɜːrbiəl/	中 *adj.* 家喻户晓的 英 commonly spoken of or widely known
shorthand /ˈʃɔːrthænd/	中 *n.* 速记 英 a method of writing quickly by using symbols or abbreviations for sounds, words or phrases

ap
/ædkæp/
- 中 *adj.* 鲁莽的，行为冲动的
- 英 behaving or acting impulsively or rashly; wild

leading
/'liːdɪŋ/
- 中 *adj.* 最重要的
- 英 most important
- 中 *adj.* 有影响力的
- 英 having great importance, influence or success

degenerate
/dɪ'dʒenəreɪt/
- 中 *adj.* 道德败坏的
- 英 having low moral standards
- 中 *v.* 退化
- 英 to change to a worse state or condition

testing
/'testɪŋ/
- 中 *adj.* 费力的
- 英 difficult to deal with

lengthy
/'leŋθi/
- 中 *adj.* 冗长的
- 英 protracted excessively

materialize
/mə'tɪriəlaɪz/
- 中 *v.* 实现
- 英 to begin to happen or exist
- 中 *v.* 使…具体化，使…物质化
- 英 to cause to appear in bodily form

calculable
/'kælkjələbl/
- 中 *adj.* 可计算的
- 英 subject to or ascertainable by calculation
- 中 *adj.* 可靠的
- 英 that may be counted on

gainsay
/ˌɡeɪn'seɪ/
- 中 *v.* 否认
- 英 to deny or disagree with (something)

officious
/ə'fɪʃəs/
- 中 *adj.* 爱掺和的，爱管闲事的
- 英 volunteering one's services where they are neither asked nor needed

增益拖? (handwritten)

appraise
/ə'preɪz/

中 v. 评估
英 to evaluate the worth, significance or status of

restless
/'restləs/

restive (handwritten)

中 adj. 不安的
英 not relaxed or calm
中 adj. 失眠的
英 having little or no rest or sleep

bighearted
/bɪg'hɑːrtɪd/

中 adj. 慷慨的，宽大的
英 generous, charitable

artless
/'ɑːrtləs/

中 adj. 朴实的，单纯的
英 sincerely simple
中 adj. 自然的
英 free from artificiality
中 adj. 拙劣的，粗糙的
英 made without skill

pitfall
/'pɪtfɔːl/

中 n. 陷阱
英 a danger or problem that is hidden or not obvious at first

hardy
/'hɑːrdi/

中 adj. 吃苦耐劳的
英 capable of withstanding adverse conditions
中 adj. 勇敢的，大胆的
英 audacious or brazen

aback
/ə'bæk/

中 adv. 大吃一惊，震惊
英 by surprise

weighty
/'weɪti/

中 adj. 重要的
英 very important and serious
中 adj. 有影响力的，有说服力的
英 powerful and telling
中 adj. 笨重的
英 having a lot of weight

disown /dɪsˈoʊn/	中 v. 否认
	英 to refuse to acknowledge as one's own

virtually /ˈvɜːrtʃuəli/	中 adv. 几乎
	英 almost

unearth /ʌnˈɜːrθ/	中 v. 揭露
	英 to find or discover (something) that was hidden or lost

uptake /ˈʌpteɪk/	中 n. 理解
	英 understanding or comprehension
	中 n. 吸收
	英 an act or instance of absorbing and incorporating especially into a living organism, tissue or cell

instrumental /ˌɪnstrəˈmentl/	中 adj. 重要的
	英 very important in helping or causing something to happen or be done

reserved /rɪˈzɜːrvd/	中 adj. 沉默寡言的
	英 not openly expressing feelings or opinions

pretext /ˈpriːtekst/	中 n. 借口
	英 a reason that you give to hide your real reason for doing something

subtext /ˈsʌbtekst/	中 n. 潜台词
	英 an underlying meaning, theme, etc.

setback /ˈsetbæk/	中 n. 挫折
	英 a difficulty or problem that delays or prevents something, or makes a situation worse

backlash /ˈbæklæʃ/	中 n. 激烈反对
	英 an antagonistic reaction to an earlier action

standstill /'stændstɪl/	中 *n.* 静止，停滞 英 a state characterized by absence of motion or of progress
level-headed /'levl,hedɪd/	中 *adj.* 头脑清晰冷静的 英 having or showing an ability to think clearly and to make good decisions
byword /'baɪwɜːrd/	中 *n.* 典型，代名词 英 someone or something that is closely connected with a particular quality
one-stop /wʌn,stɑːp/	中 *adj.* 一站式的，全方位的 英 providing or offering a comprehensive range of goods or services at one location; provided or offered at such a location
upright /'ʌpraɪt/	中 *adj.* 垂直的 英 perpendicular or vertical 中 *adj.* 正直的 英 marked by strong moral rectitude
acquired /ə'kwaɪərd/	中 *adj.* 后天习得的 英 of or relating to a disease, condition or characteristic that is not congenital but develops after birth
rosy /'roʊzi/	中 *adj.* 乐观的 英 having or producing hope for success or happiness in the future
becoming /bɪ'kʌmɪŋ/	中 *adj.* （尤指有吸引力的）得体的，合适的 英 attractively suitable
sententious /sen'tenʃəs/	中 *adj.* 简洁的；喜欢说教的 英 terse, aphoristic or moralistic in expression

artifice /'ɑːrtɪfɪs/	中 n. 诡计，欺骗
	英 dishonest or insincere behavior or speech that is meant to deceive someone
unrest /ʌn'rest/	中 n. 不安
	英 a disturbed or uneasy state
deadlock /'dedlɑːk/	中 n. 僵局
	英 a situation in which an agreement cannot be made
expendable /ɪk'spendəbl/	中 adj. 可消耗的
	英 not worth saving
porous /'pɔːrəs/	中 adj. 可渗透的
	英 easy to pass or get through
scuffle /'skʌfl/	中 v. 扭打
	英 to struggle at close quarters with disorder and confusion
unnerve /ˌʌn'nɜːrv/	中 v. 使…失去勇气
	英 to cause to lose courage or firmness of purpose
clueless /'kluːləs/	中 adj. 无知的
	英 not having knowledge about something
studied /'stʌdɪd/	中 adj. 深思熟虑的
	英 carefully considered or prepared
	中 adj. 博学的
	英 knowledgeable or learned
privation /praɪ'veɪʃn/	中 n. 贫穷，匮乏
	英 a lack or loss of the basic things that people need to live properly

distance
/'dɪstəns/
中 v. 超出，把…甩在后面
英 to leave far behind; outstrip
中 v. 使…远离
英 to place or keep at a distance

list
/lɪst/
中 n. 倾斜
英 an inclination to one side; a tilt

passage
/'pæsɪdʒ/
中 n. （事物从一个状态到另一个状态的）转变
英 the process of changing

sound
/saʊnd/
中 adj. 状态良好的
英 in good condition
中 adj. 明智的，合理的
英 showing good judgement

faculty
/'fæklti/
中 n. 才能，本领
英 a talent or natural ability for something

function
/'fʌŋkʃn/
中 n. 重大聚会
英 an official ceremony or a formal social occasion
中 v. 运转
英 to work or operate

avatar
/'ævətɑːr/
中 n. 化身，代表
英 someone who represents a type of person, an idea or a quality

liberal
/'lɪbərəl/
中 adj. 慷慨的
英 tending to give freely; generous
中 adj. 思想自由的
英 broad-minded and not bound by orthodoxy or traditional forms

license
/'laɪsns/
中 n. 自由
英 freedom to act however you want to

latitude /ˈlætɪtuːd/	中 *n.* 自由
	英 freedom to choose how to act or what to do
	中 *n.* 纬度
	英 distance north or south of the equator measured in degrees up to 90 degrees

court /kɔːrt/	中 *v.* 招致
	英 to behave so as to invite or incur
	中 *v.* 吸引
	英 to attempt to gain the favor of by attention or flattery

contract /ˈkɑːntrækt/	中 *v.* 招致
	英 to acquire or incur
	中 *v.* 患病
	英 to become ill with (disease)
	中 *v.* 收缩
	英 to become reduced in size

| betray /bɪˈtreɪ/ | 中 *v.* （无意中）显露 |
| | 英 to make known unintentionally |

| qualify /ˈkwɑːlɪfaɪ/ | 中 *v.* 限制 |
| | 英 to modify, limit or restrict, as by listing exceptions or reservations |

| stomach /ˈstʌmək/ | 中 *v.* 容忍 |
| | 英 to bear without overt reaction or resentment |

resolve /rɪˈzɑːlv/	中 *v.* 决定，决心要做
	英 to make a definite and serious decision to do something
	中 *v.* 解决
	英 to find an answer or solution to

arrest /ə'rest/	中 v. 阻止 英 to bring to a stop 中 v. 吸引 英 to attract and hold the attention of 中 v. 逮捕 英 to use the power of the law to take and keep
digest /dai'dʒest/	中 n. 文摘 英 a summation or condensation of a body of information 中 v.（对信息的）消化理解 英 to think over so as to understand (news, information, etc.)
nexus /'neksəs/	中 n. 连接 英 a means of connection 中 n. 核心，中心 英 the core or center
kindle /'kɪndl/	中 v. 点燃 英 to ignite 中 v. 激起情绪 英 to arouse (an emotion)
waffle /'wɑːfl/	中 v. 犹豫不决 英 to be unable to make a decision 中 v. 闪烁其词 英 to speak, write or act evasively about
off-key /'ɔːf'kiː/	中 adj. 出格的，不正常的 英 being out of accord with what is considered normal or appropriate 中 adj. 跑调的 英 pitched higher or lower than the correct notes of a melody

balloon /bə'lu:n/	中 v. 快速上升
	英 to increase or rise quickly
	中 n. 气球

fetch /fetʃ/	中 v. 卖得（某个价格）
	英 to bring in as a price
	中 v. 去拿来
	英 to go after and bring back

contain /kən'teɪn/	中 v. 限制
	英 to hold or keep with limits; restrain
	中 v. 容纳
	英 to have within; hold

stem /stem/	中 v. 阻止，限制
	英 to check or go counter to
	中 v. 源于，因为
	英 to develop as a consequence of

check /tʃek/	中 v. 阻止
	英 to hold in restraint
	中 v. 检测
	英 to inspect so as to determine accuracy, quality or other condition

still /stɪl/	中 adj. 静止的
	英 lacking motion or activity
	中 adj. 安静的
	英 uttering no sound

clinical /'klɪnɪkl/	中 adj. 不感情用事的，冷静的
	英 analytical or dolly dispassionate

novel /'nɑ:vl/	中 adj. 新颖的
	英 new and different from what has been known before
	中 adj. 原创的
	英 original or striking especially in conception or style

mighty 强大的

| **might** /maɪt/ | 中 n. 力量，权力 |
| | 英 power to do something |

grave /greɪv/	中 adj. 严肃的
	英 dignified and somber in conduct or character
	中 v. 雕刻，铭记
	英 to stamp or impress deeply

affect /əˈfekt/	中 v. 伪装，装腔作势
	英 to put on a false show of
	中 v. 喜欢
	英 to have or show a liking for
	中 v. 影响
	英 to have an influence on

| **flag** /flæg/ | 中 v. 衰弱 |
| | 英 to lose vigor or strength; weaken or diminish |

| **pan** /pæn/ | 中 v. 严厉批评 |
| | 英 to criticize or review harshly |

compromise /ˈkɑːmprəmaɪz/	中 n. / v. 妥协，让步
	英 v. to arrive at a settlement by making concessions
	中 v. 降低
	英 to reduce in quality, value or degree
	中 v. 破坏
	英 to impair, as by disease or injury

founder /ˈfaʊndər/	中 v. 彻底失败
	英 to fail utterly; collapse
	中 n. 创始人，奠基人
	英 one who establishes something or formulates the basis for something

| **august** /ɔːˈɡʌst/ | 中 adj. 庄严的，肃穆的 |
| | 英 respected and dignified |

~~assume~~ /əˈsuːm/	中 *v.* 假装 *假浮* 英 to pretend to have
~~pedestrian~~ /pəˈdestriən/	中 *adj.* 无聊的，普通的 英 not interesting or unusual 中 *n.* 行人 英 a person going on foot
~~champion~~ /ˈtʃæmpiən/	中 *n.* 支持者 英 an ardent defender or supporter of a cause or another person 中 *v.* 支持 英 to defend or support
coin /kɔɪn/	中 *v.* 发明（一个新词） 英 to devise (a new word or phrase)
weather /ˈweðər/	中 *v.* 渡过（危机） 英 to come through (something) safely
~~document~~ /ˈdɑːkjumənt/	中 *v.* 详细记录 英 to methodically record the details of 中 *v.* 证明，支持 英 to support with evidence or decisive information
~~contest~~ /ˈkɑːntest/	中 *v.* 质疑，否认 *辩* 英 to try to disprove or invalidate (something) as by argument or legal action
~~intrigue~~ /ɪnˈtriːg/	中 *n.* 密谋，诡计 英 the activity of making secret plans
occasion /əˈkeɪʒn/	中 *v.* 引起 英 to cause something

Word List 23

音 频

---

effect
/ɪ'fekt/

中 v. 引起
英 to bring about; make happen

---

spell
/spel/

中 n.（一段）时间
英 a short, indefinite period of time

---

husband
/'hʌzbənd/

中 v. 节省
英 to carefully use or manage, to use sparingly

---

industry
/'ɪndəstri/

中 n. 努力
英 the habit of working hard and steadily

---

demonstrative
/dɪ'maːnstrətɪv/

中 adj. 显露情感的
英 freely and openly showing emotion or feelings

---

pursuit
/pər'suːt/

中 n. 事业
英 an activity that one engages as a vocation, profession or avocation

---

emergent
/i'mɜːrdʒənt/

中 adj. 新兴的
英 newly formed or prominent
中 adj. 突然出现的
英 arising unexpectedly
中 adj. 紧急的
英 urgent, calling for prompt action

---

inform
/ɪn'fɔːrm/

中 v. 通知
英 to give information to
中 v. 影响
英 to be the characteristic quality of

---

appropriate /ə'proupriət/	中 *adj.* 合适的
	英 suitable or compatible
	中 *v.* 私自占有，私自挪用
	英 to take or make use of without authority or right
	中 *v.* 为…拨（款）
	英 to set apart for or assign to a particular purpose or use
circumstantial /ˌsɜːrkəm'stænʃl/	中 *adj.* 详细的
	英 complete and particular; full of detail
	中 *adj.* 视情况而定的
	英 of, relating to or depends on circumstances
	中 *adj.* 相关但不重要的
	英 pertinent but not essential
project /'prɑːdʒekt/	中 *v.* 投掷
	英 to throw forward
	中 *v.* 投影
	英 to cause to appear on a surface by the controlled direction of light
	中 *v.* 预算，预测
	英 to calculate, estimate or predict
subject /'sʌbdʒɪkt/	中 *v.* 屈服
	英 to subjugate; subdue
object /'ɑːbdʒekt/	中 *v.* 反对
	英 to present a dissenting or opposing argument
long /lɔːŋ/	中 *v.* 渴望
	英 to have an earnest, heartfelt desire
pacific /pə'sɪfɪk/	中 *adj.* 爱好和平的
	英 loving peace, not wanting war or conflict
involved /ɪn'vɑːlvd/	中 *adj.* 复杂的
	英 complicated and intricate

score /skɔːr/	中 v. 获得…成就 英 to achieve or accomplish
intimate /ˈɪntɪmət/	中 adj. 亲密无间的 英 characterized by close personal acquaintance or familiarity 中 v. 暗示 英 to say or suggest in an indirect way
portentous /pɔːrˈtentəs/	中 adj. 不吉利的 英 giving a sign or warning that something usually bad or unpleasant is going to happen 中 adj. 自命不凡的 英 self-consciously solemn or important
rail /reɪl/	中 v. 抨击，批评 英 to express objection or criticisms in bitter, harsh or abusive language
base /beɪs/	中 adj. 卑鄙的 英 having or showing a lack of decency
course /kɔːrs/	中 n. 过程 英 progression through a development or period or a series of acts or events
mount /maʊnt/	中 v. 上升 英 to increase in amount
count /kaʊnt/	中 v. 有重要性 英 to have importance 中 v. 指望，相信 英 to believe or consider to be
insulate /ˈɪnsəleɪt/	中 v. 绝热，绝缘，隔音 英 to prevent the passage of heat, electricity or sound into or out of 中 v.（从危险的事物中）隔离 英 to keep separate from something unpleasant or dangerous

row /roʊ/	中 *n.* （多人之间的）争吵 英 a lot of loud arguing or complaining usually involving many people
jade /dʒeɪd/	中 *v.* 使…厌烦 英 to become weary or dulled 中 *v.* 使…疲惫不堪 英 to wear out by overwork or abuse
trammel /ˈtræml/	中 *v.* 限制自由 英 to hinder the activity or free movement of 中 *n.* 束缚 英 something that restricts activity, expression, or progress; a restraint
comb /koʊm/	中 *v.* 仔细检查，仔细搜寻 英 to search or examine systematically 中 *n.* 梳子
jealous /ˈdʒeləs/	中 *adj.* 死守严防的，精心守护的 英 vigilant in guarding a possession 中 *adj.* 妒忌的 英 feeling a mean anger toward someone because he or she is more successful
usher /ˈʌʃər/	中 *v.* 引领…进入 英 to cause to enter; to introduce 中 *n.* 引导员 英 a person who leads people to their seats
~~**cow**~~ /kaʊ/	中 *v.* 恐吓 英 to make someone too afraid to do something

hedge /hedʒ/	中 *n.* 故意模棱两可、不绝对的言论
	英 a calculatedly noncommittal or evasive statement
	中 *v.* 避免（言论）过于绝对
	英 to avoid giving a promise or direct answer
obscure /əb'skjʊr/	中 *adj.* 不清晰的，不易辨别的
	英 not clearly seen or easily distinguished
	中 *adj. / v.* 难以理解的，使…难懂
	英 *adj.* not clearly understood or expressed
	中 *adj.* 不出名的
	英 not well-known
	中 *v.* 遮蔽
	英 to conceal or hide
yield /jiːld/	中 *v.* 投降，屈服
	英 to surrender or submit
	中 *v.* 产出
	英 to be productive of
skirt /skɜːrt/	中 *v.* 回避，避开（话题）
	英 to evade, as by circumlocution
asset /'æset/	中 *n.* 有价值的人或事
	英 a valuable person or thing
	中 *n.* 资产
	英 something that is owned by a person, company, etc.
dense /dens/	中 *adj.* 浓密的
	英 thick
	中 *adj.* 难以理解的
	英 difficult to understand because of complexity or obscurity
	中 *adj.* 笨的
	英 slow to apprehend

frown
/fraʊn/

中 v. 皱眉
英 to wrinkle the brow
中 v. 厌恶
英 to regard something with disapproval or distaste

content
/'kɑːntent/

中 adj. 满足的
英 desiring no more than what one has
中 n. 内容
英 the substance or significance of a written work

sanction
/'sæŋkʃn/

中 v. 支持
英 to give official authorization or approval to
中 n. 支持（做不可数名词）
英 official permission or approval
中 n. 制裁（做可数名词）
英 the penalty for noncompliance with a law or legal order

accent
/'æksent/

中 v. 发重音
英 to pronounce with accent
中 v. 着重强调，凸显
英 to give prominence to

perennial
/pə'reniəl/

中 adj. 多年生的（植物）
英 present at all seasons of the year
中 adj. 持续的，长期的
英 continuing without interruption

confound
/kən'faʊnd/

中 v. 使困惑
英 to cause to become confused or perplexed
中 v. 驳斥，证明…错误
英 to prove (someone or something) wrong; refute
中 v. 混淆
英 to fail to distinguish; mix up

promise
/'prɑːmɪs/

中 *n.* 前景光明
英 an indication of future success or improvement

中 *v.* 预示
英 to show signs of

acknowledge
/ək'nɑːlɪdʒ/

中 *v.* 感谢
英 to express gratitude or obligation for

中 *v.* 承认
英 to say that you accept or do not deny the truth or existence of (something)

volume
/'vɑːljuːm/

中 *n.* 音量
英 the degree of loudness or the intensity of a sound

中 *n.* 书卷
英 book

中 *n.* 体积
英 the amount of space occupied by a three-dimensional object as measured in cubic units

discharge
/dɪs'tʃɑːrdʒ/

中 *v.* 解雇
英 to tell (someone) officially that they can or must leave

中 *v.* 履行（责任，义务）
英 to do all that is required to perform or fulfill

中 *v.* 还清，偿还
英 to pay off (a debt)

apology
/ə'pɑːlədʒi/

中 *n.* 辩护
英 something that is said or written to defend something that other people criticize

中 *n.* 抱歉
英 a statement saying that you are sorry about something

patent
/'pætnt/

中 *adj.* 明显的
英 obvious or clear

~~fell~~ /fel/	中 *v.* 砍树 英 to cut down (a tree) 中 *v.* 打倒 英 to beat or knock down (someone or something)
appreciate /əˈpriːʃieɪt/	中 *v.* 升值 英 to increase the value of 中 *v.* 感谢 英 to be grateful for
~~reliable~~ /rɪˈlaɪəbl/	中 *adj.*（结论、模型等）可靠的 英 giving the same result on successive trials 中 *adj.* 可依赖的 英 able to be trusted to do or provide what is needed
~~abandon~~ /əˈbændən/	中 *n.* 放纵 英 a feeling or attitude of wild or complete freedom 中 *v.* 放弃 英 to leave and never return to
~~harry~~ /ˈhæri/	中 *v.* 打扰，骚扰 英 to disturb, distress or exhaust by repeated demands or criticism
~~experimental~~ /ɪkˌsperɪˈmentl/	中 *adj.* 新颖的，创新的 英 using a new way of doing or thinking about something
second /ˈsekənd/	中 *v.* 同意 英 to agree with (a suggestion or statement) 中 *v.* 帮助，支持 英 to give support or encouragement to

usage /ˈjuːsɪdʒ/	中 *n.* 对待方式 英 manner of treating
~~autumn~~ /ˈɔːtəm/ 不火天	中 *n.* 晚年，暮年 英 the later part of someone's life or of something's existence
~~measured~~ /ˈmeʒəd/	中 *adj.* 慎重的，缓慢谨慎的 英 done with thought and care
entrance /ˈentrəns/	中 *v.* 使…着迷 英 to fill (someone) with delight and wonder
color /ˈkʌlər/ colour	中 *v.* 扭曲，影响 英 to alter or influence to some degree, as by distortion or exaggeration
~~economy~~ /ɪˈkɑːnəmi/	中 *n.* 节省 英 thrifty and efficient use of material resources 中 *n.* 经济体系 英 the process or system by which goods and services are produced, sold and bought in a country or region
listless /ˈlɪstləs/	中 *adj.* 没精打采的 英 lacking energy or spirit
~~humor~~ /ˈhjuːmər/	中 *n.* 幽默 英 a funny or amusing quality 中 *n.* 脾气，秉性 英 characteristic or habitual disposition or bent
~~complaint~~ /kəmˈpleɪnt/	中 *n.* 抱怨 英 expression of grief, pain or dissatisfaction 中 *n.* 疾病，痛苦 英 a bodily ailment or disease

tender /'tendər/	中 v. 提供 英 to present for acceptance 中 adj. 温柔的 英 very loving and gentle 中 adj. 疼痛的 英 painful when touched
anchor /'æŋkər/	中 v. 使…稳定 英 to hold (something) firmly in place 中 v. 扮演重要角色 英 to be the strongest and most important part of (something) 中 n. 依靠，支柱 英 a reliable or principal support
bitter /'bɪtər/	中 adj. 怨恨的，气愤的 英 angry or unhappy because of unfair treatment 中 adj. 苦的 英 being the opposite of sweet
husbandry /'hʌzbəndri/	中 n. 农业，畜牧业，饲养业 英 the activity of raising plants or animals for food 中 n. 节省 英 the management or wise use of resources
anticipate /æn'tɪsɪpeɪt/	中 v. 期待 英 to look forward to (something) 中 v. （为防止…而）预先处理 英 to foresee and deal with in advance
hail /heɪl/	中 v. 欢呼，喝彩 英 to greet or acclaim enthusiastically 中 n. 欢呼，赞美 英 the act of greeting or acclaiming

anonymous /əˈnɑːnɪməs/	中 *adj.* 不出名的
	英 not distinct or noticeable
	中 *adj.* 匿名的
	英 made or done by someone unknown
tend /tend/	中 *v.* 照顾，养育
	英 to apply oneself to the care of
	中 *v.* 倾斜
	英 to move in a particular direction
dissipate /ˈdɪsɪpeɪt/	中 *v.* 使…消散
	英 to cause (something) to spread out and disappear
	中 *v.* 浪费，挥霍
	英 to use all or a lot of (something, such as money or time) in a foolish way
misuse /ˌmɪsˈjuːs/	中 *v.* 不公平地对待
	英 to treat (someone) unfairly
	中 *v.* 误用
	英 to use incorrectly
physical /ˈfɪzɪkl/	中 *adj.* 实体的
	英 existing in a form that you can touch or see
	中 *adj.* 自然科学的
	英 of or relating to natural science
	中 *adj.* 肉体的
	英 relating to the body of a person instead of the mind
embrace /ɪmˈbreɪs/	中 *v.* 接受
	英 to accept (something or someone) readily or gladly
	中 *v.* 拥抱
	英 to hold someone in your arms as a way of expressing love or friendship

descendant
/dɪ'sendənt/

中 *adj.* 下降的
英 moving or directed downward
中 *n.* 后代
英 someone who is related to a person or group of people who lived in the past

abstraction
/æb'strækʃən/

中 *n.* 抽象，概要
英 the state of being abstracted
中 *n.* 心不在焉
英 absence of mind or preoccupation

substantial
/səb'stænʃəl/

中 *adj.* 大量的
英 large in amount, size or number
中 *adj.* 坚固的
英 firmly constructed
中 *adj.* 重要的
英 important or essential

counterpart
/'kaʊntərpɑːrt/

中 *n.* 等价物
英 someone or something that has the same job or purpose as another
中 *n.* 补充
英 something that completes

mirror
/'mɪrər/

中 *v.* 与…相似
英 to be very similar to (something)

enterprise
/'entərpraɪz/

中 *n.* 活动
英 a systematic purposeful activity
中 *n.* 进取心
英 readiness to engage in daring or difficult action

shoulder
/'ʃoʊldər/

中 *v.* 承担
英 to assume the burden or responsibility of

recipe /ˈresəpi/	中 n. 秘诀，方法 英 a formula or procedure for doing or attaining something
cupidity /kjuːˈpɪdəti/	中 n. 贪心 英 a strong desire for money or possessions
square /skwer/	中 v. 符合，一致 英 to bring into conformity or agreement
slight /slaɪt/	中 v. 轻视 英 to treat (someone) with disrespect
finger /ˈfɪŋgər/	中 v. 指出 英 to point out
muddy /ˈmʌdi/	中 v. 使…模糊 英 to cause (something) to become unclear or confused
people /ˈpiːpl/	中 v. 充满 英 to supply or fill with people
immediate /ɪˈmiːdiət/	中 adj. 紧靠的，最接近的 英 directly touching or concerning a person or thing 中 adj. 当下的 英 of or relating to the here and now 中 adj. 直接的 英 acting or being without the intervention of another object, cause or agency
guesswork /ˈgeswɜːrk/	中 n. 猜测 英 work performed or results obtained by guess
untiring /ʌnˈtaɪərɪŋ/	中 adj. 不知疲倦的 英 working very hard with a lot of energy for a long time

take a grand ?

理解某事

grand /grænd/	中 adj. 富丽堂皇的 英 lavish or sumptuous 中 adj. 傲慢的 英 pretending to social superiority
~~corrosive~~ /kəˈrəʊsɪv/	中 adj.（言语）讽刺的，挖苦的 英 bitingly sarcastic
~~radical~~ /ˈrædɪkl/	中 adj. 极端的，激进的 英 advocating extreme measures to retain or restore a political state of affairs 中 adj. 颠覆性的 英 very different from the usual or traditional 中 adj. 根本的 英 very basic and important
~~fuel~~ /ˈfjuːəl/	中 v. 支撑，支持 英 to give support or strength to (something)
aside /əˈsaɪd/	中 n. 跑题 英 a straying from the theme

Word List 24

音 频

sequel
/'siːkwəl/
中 n. 后续，后果
英 something that follows; a continuation

factotum
/fæk'toʊtəm/
中 n. 杂工
英 a person whose job involves doing many different types of work

disputant
/'dɪspjutənt/
中 n. 争论者
英 a person who is involved in a dispute and especially in a legal dispute

novice
/'nɑːvɪs/
中 n. 新手
英 a person who has just started learning or doing something

tyro
/'taɪroʊ/
中 n. 新手
英 a person who has just started learning or doing something; a beginner or novice

neophyte
/'niːəfaɪt/
中 n. 新手
英 a person who has just started learning or doing something

maverick
/'mævərɪk/
中 n. 标新立异之人
英 a person who refuses to follow the customs or rules of group

martinet
/ˌmɑːrtn'et/
中 n. 要求严格纪律的人
英 a person who is very strict and demands obedience from others

sophist /'sɑːfɪst/	中 *n.* 哲学家 英 philosopher 中 *n.* 诡辩家 英 a captious or fallacious reasoner
quibbler /'kwɪblər/	中 *n.* 吹毛求疵的人 英 to argue or complain about small, unimportant things
pedant /'pednt/	中 *n.* 卖弄学问的人 英 a person who annoys other people by correcting small errors and giving too much attention to minor details
naysayer /'neɪˌseɪər/	中 *n.* 否定者，怀疑者 英 a person who says something will not work or is not possible; a person who denies, refuses or opposes something
acolyte /'ækəlaɪt/	中 *n.* 助手 英 someone who follows and admires a leader 中 *n.* 侍僧 英 someone who helps the person who leads a church service
associate /ə'souʃieɪt/	中 *n.* 同事，伙伴 英 a person who you work with or spend time with
canary /kə'neri/	中 *n.* 金丝雀 英 a small usually yellow or green tropical bird that is often kept in a cage
braggart /'brægərt/	中 *n.* 吹牛者 英 a person who brags a lot
dictator /'dɪkteɪtər/	中 *n.* 独裁者 英 a person who rules a country with total authority and often in a cruel or brutal way

tyrant
/'taɪrənt/

中 n. 暴君

英 a ruler who has complete power over a country and who is cruel and unfair

denizen
/'denɪzn/

中 n. 居民

英 a person, animal or plant that lives in or often is found in a particular place or region

bishop
/'bɪʃəp/

中 n. 主教

英 an official in some Christian religions who is ranked higher than a priest and who is usually in charge of church matters in a specific geographical area

clergy
/'klɜːrdʒi/

中 n. 神职人员，牧师

英 people (such as priests) who are the leaders of a religion and who perform religious services

prophet
/'praːfɪt/

中 n. 先知，预言者

英 a member of some religions (such as Christianity, Judaism and Islam) who delivers messages that are believed to have come from God

virtuoso
/ˌvɜːrtʃuˈoʊsoʊ/

中 n. 艺术品鉴赏家

英 one skilled in or having a taste for the fine arts

progeny
/'praːdʒəni/

中 n. 子孙，后裔

英 a person who comes from a particular parent or family; the child or descendant of someone

hardliner
/ˌhaːrd ˈlaɪnər/

中 n. 强硬分子

英 someone who advocates or involves a rigidly uncompromising course of action

dilettante /ˌdɪləˈtænti/	中 *n.* 半吊子，业余的人，一知半解的人
	英 a person having a superficial interest in an art or a branch of knowledge
spearhead /ˈspɪrhed/	中 *n.* 先锋部队
	英 a person, thing or group that organizes or leads something (such as a movement or attack)
vanguard /ˈvænɡɑːrd/	中 *n.* 先锋
	英 the group of people who are the leaders of an action or movement in society, politics, art, etc.
philistine /ˈfɪlɪstiːn/	中 *n.* 庸俗的人
	英 a person who is guided by materialism and is usually disdainful of intellectual or artistic values
polymath /ˈpɑːlimæθ/	中 *n.* 博学的人
	英 someone who knows a lot about many different things
prodigy /ˈprɑːdədʒi/	中 *n.* 神童
	英 a young person who is unusually talented in some way
interlocutor /ˌɪntərˈlɑːkjətər/	中 *n.* 对话者
	英 a person who is having a conversation with you
spendthrift /ˈspendθrɪft/	中 *n.* 挥霍的人
	英 a person who spends money in a careless or wasteful way
monger /ˈmʌŋɡər/	中 *n.* 商人，贩子
	英 broker, dealer—usually used in combination

culprit /ˈkʌlprɪt/	中 *n.* 罪犯，罪魁祸首 英 a person who has committed a crime or done something wrong
curator /kjʊˈreɪtər/	中 *n.* 管理者 英 a person who is in charge of the things in a museum, zoo, etc.
orator /ˈɔːrətər/	中 *n.* 演讲者 英 a person who makes speeches and is very good at making them
fledgling /ˈfledʒlɪŋ/	中 *n.* 无经验的人 英 someone or something that is getting started in a new activity
cynic /ˈsɪnɪk/	中 *n.* 认为人性自私的人 英 a person who has negative opinions about other people and about the things people do, especially a person who believes that people are selfish and are only interested in helping themselves
quixote /ˈkwiksət/	中 *n.* 爱空想的人 英 a quixotic person
expansionist /ɪkˈspænʃənɪst/	中 *n.* 扩张主义者 英 someone who holds the belief that a country should grow larger
electorate /ɪˈlektərət/	中 *n.* 选举人 英 the people who can vote in an election
preservationist /ˌprezərˈveɪʃənɪst/	中 *n.* 保护主义者 英 someone who works to preserve something (such as a building or an area of land)

zealot /'zelət/	中 *n.* 狂热者 英 a person who has very strong feelings about something (such as religion or politics) and who wants other people to have those feelings; a zealous person
extremist /ɪk'striːmɪst/	中 *n.* 极端主义者 英 someone who believes in and supports for ideas that are very far from what most people consider correct or reasonable
revisionist /rɪ'vɪʒənɪst/	中 *n.* 修正主义者 英 someone who supports ideas and beliefs that differ from and try to change accepted ideas and beliefs especially in a way that is seen as wrong or dishonest
mogul /'moʊɡl/	中 *n.* 有权势的人 英 a great personage, magnate
guru /'ɡuˌru/	中 *n.* 领袖 英 a teacher or guide that you trust 中 *n.* 专家 英 a person who has a lot of experience in or knowledge about a particular subject
tycoon /taɪ'kuːn/	中 *n.* 企业界大亨，巨头 英 a very wealthy and powerful business person
bellwether /'belweðər/	中 *n.* 领导者 英 someone or something that leads others or shows what will happen in the future
stickler /'stɪklər/	中 *n.* 坚持…的人 英 a person who believes that something is very important and should be done or followed all the time

sticker

diehard /'daɪhɑːrd/	中 adj. 顽固的 英 strongly or fanatically determined or devoted
nonentity /nɑ'nentəti/	中 n. 无足轻重的人 英 a person who is not famous or important
imposter /ɪm'pɑːstər/	中 n. 冒名顶替的人 英 a person who deceives others by pretending to be someone else
mastermind /'mæstərmaɪnd/	中 n. 策划者 英 a person who plans and organizes something
iconoclast /aɪ'kɑːnəklæst/	中 n. 提倡打破旧习的人 英 a person who criticizes or opposes beliefs and practices that are widely accepted
soothsayer /'suːθseɪər/	中 n. 预言家 英 a person who predicts the future by magical, intuitive or more rational means
connoisseur /ˌkɑːnə'sɜːr/	中 n. 鉴赏家，内行 英 a person who knows a lot about something (such as art, wine, food, etc.), an expert in a particular subject
boor /bʊr/	中 n. 粗人 英 a rude and rough person
playwright /'pleɪraɪt/	中 n. 剧作家 英 a person who writes plays
despot /'despɑːt/	中 n. 独裁者 英 a ruler who has total power and who often uses that power in cruel and unfair ways

apologist /ə'pɑːlədʒɪst/	中 *n.* 辩护人 英 one who speaks or writes in defense of someone or something
wastrel /'weɪstrəl/	中 *n.* 浪费的人 英 a person who wastes time, money, etc.
autocrat /'ɔːtəkræt/	中 *n.* 独裁者 英 a person who rules with total power
oddball /'ɑːdbɔːl/	中 *n.* 古怪的人 英 the use of tricks especially to hide, avoid or get something
bore /bɔːr/	中 *n.* 无聊的人 英 one that causes boredom
layperson /'leɪpɜːrsn/	中 *n.* 外行 英 a member of the laity
has-been /'hæz biːn/	中 *n.* 过时的人 英 a person who is no longer popular or successful
progenitor /proʊ'dʒenɪtər/	中 *n.* 先驱 英 precursor, originator
benefactor /'benɪfæktər/	中 *n.* 慈善家 英 someone who helps another person, group, etc., by giving money
gourmand /'ɡʊrmɑːnd/	中 *n.* 吃货 英 a person who loves to eat and drink
cronyism /'kroʊniːɪzəm/	中 *n.* 任用亲信 英 the unfair practice by a powerful person (such as a politician) of giving jobs and other favors to friends

nepotism
/ˈnepətɪzəm/
中 n. 任人唯亲
英 the unfair practice by a powerful person of giving jobs and other favors to relatives

totalitarianism
/touˌtælə'teriənɪzəm/
中 n. 极权主义
英 centralized control by an autocratic authority

utilitarianism
/ˌjuːtɪlɪ'teriənɪzəm/
中 n. 功利主义
英 the belief that a morally good action is one that helps the greatest number of people

cynicism
/ˈsɪnɪsɪzəm/
中 n. 认为人性自私
英 cynical beliefs; beliefs that people are generally selfish and dishonest

chauvinism
/ˈʃouvɪnɪzəm/
中 n. 盲目的爱国心
英 the belief that your country, race, etc., is better than any other

egalitarianism
/iˌgælɪ'teriənɪzəm/
中 n. 平等主义
英 a belief in human equality especially with respect to social, political and economic affairs

altruism
/ˈæltruɪzəm/
中 n. 无私，利他主义
英 feelings and behavior that show a desire to help other people and a lack of selfishness

anarchism
/ˈænərkɪzəm/
中 n. 无政府主义
英 a belief that government and laws are not necessary

anthropocentrism
/ˌænθrəpə'sentrɪzəm/
中 n. 人类中心说
英 a belief that considers human beings as the most significant entity of the universe

atheism
/'eɪθiɪzəm/
中 *n.* 无神论
英 a disbelief in the existence of deity

collectivism
/kə'lektɪvɪzəm/
中 *n.* 集体主义
英 a political or economic system in which the government owns businesses, land, etc.

dualism
/'duːəlɪzəm/
中 *n.* 二元论
英 the idea or belief that everything has two opposite parts or principles

feminism
/'femənɪzəm/
中 *n.* 女权主义
英 the belief that men and women should have equal rights and opportunities

hedonism
/'hiːdənɪzəm/
中 *n.* 享乐主义
英 the belief that pleasure or happiness is the most important goal in life

individualism
/ˌɪndɪ'vɪdʒuəlɪzəm/
中 *n.* 个人主义
英 the actions or attitudes of a person who does things without being concerned about what other people will think

nihilism
/'naɪɪlɪzəm/
中 *n.* 虚无主义
英 the belief that traditional morals, ideas, beliefs, etc., have no worth or value

teetotalism
/ˌtiː'toʊtəlɪzəm/
中 *n.* 禁酒主义
英 the principle or practice of complete abstinence from alcoholic drinks

renegade
/'renɪɡeɪd/
中 *n.* 叛徒
英 a deserter from one faith, cause, or allegiance to another

misanthrope
/'mɪsənθroʊp/
中 *n.* 厌恶人类的人，愤世嫉俗的人
英 one who hates or mistrusts humankind

| **leveling** /ˈlevl/ | 中 *n.* 使平等，使一致 |
| | 英 the act of making equal or uniform |

straddle /ˈstrædl/	中 *v.* 横跨
	英 to be on both sides of; extend over or across
	中 *v.* 观望
	英 to appear to favor both sides of an issue

baleful /ˈbeɪlfl/	中 *adj.* 邪恶的，不吉利的
	英 portending evil; ominous
	中 *adj.* （意图上）恶意的，险恶的
	英 harmful or malignant in intent or effect

| **shelve** /ʃelv/ | 中 *v.* 搁置 |
| | 英 If someone shelves a plan or project, they decide not to continue with it, either for a while or permanently |

| **scribble** /ˈskrɪbl/ | 中 *v.* 草率地写画 |
| | 英 to write or draw in a hurried, careless way |

| **abyss** /əˈbɪs/ | 中 *n.* 深渊（指危险的处境） |
| | 英 a very dangerous or frightening situation |

stunning /ˈstʌnɪŋ/	中 *adj.* 令人印象深刻的
	英 strikingly impressive especially in beauty or excellence
	中 *adj.* 令人吃惊的，出乎意料的
	英 causing astonishment or disbelief

bulwark /ˈbʊlwɜːrk/	中 *n.* 堡垒，壁垒
	英 a wall or embankment raised as a defensive fortification; a rampart
	中 *v.* 为…提供防御或保护
	英 to provide defense or protection for

showcase /'ʃoʊkeɪs/	中 v. 展示 英 to display prominently, especially to advantage
staunch /stɔːntʃ/	中 adj. 坚定的，忠诚的 英 steadfast in loyalty or principle
untrammeled /ʌn'træmld/	中 adj. 自由的，不受约束的 英 not limited or restricted; unrestrained
screed /skriːd/	中 n. 冗长，单调的说话或者文章 英 a long, monotonous harangue or piece of writing
stupefaction /ˌstuːpɪ'fækʃn/	中 n. 非常惊讶或惊慌失措 英 great astonishment or consternation
vitriolic /ˌvɪtri'ɑːlɪk/	中 adj. 尖酸刻薄的 英 bitterly scathing; caustic
bombastic /bɑːm'bæstɪk/	中 adj. 夸大的，言过其实的 英 (of somebody's words) sounding important but having little
waggish /'wægɪʃ/	中 adj. 诙谐的 英 characteristic of or resembling a wag; jocular or witty
retract /rɪ'trækt/	中 v. 收回，否认 英 to take back; disavow
etch /etʃ/	中 v. 铭记 英 to impress, delineate, or imprint clearly
exultant /ɪg'zʌltənt/	中 adj. 狂喜的 英 marked by great joy or jubilation; triumphant

六选二词表

hodgepodge	patchwork, welter, pastiche
impartial	disinterested, fair, detachment
endemic	native, domestic, indigenous
minuscule	diminutive
compensate	offset
discursive	aimless, digressional, rambling
overbearing	dominant
zealous	impassioned, fervent, fiery, passionate
extraneous	irrelevant
rehash	recycle
perfunctory	cursory, casual
envy	covet
unbounded	immoderate, expansive
specious	artificial, forged, fabricate, spurious
aimless	discursive
ingenuous	simple
intrinsic	inherent
inevitable	unavoidable, preordained, ineluctable
intransigent	resolute, obduracy
affable	easygoing, cordial, genteel
whimsy	capriciousness
tenacious	resolve, endurance
ridicule	deride

undermine	subvert, impair, undercut
capricious	impulsive, cavalier, fickle, versatile, volatile, flighty, erratic
unqualified	unalloyed
ameliorate	mitigate, extenuate
exemplar	model
extirpate	eliminate
parity	equality
utilitarian	functional
elicit	draw
construe	interpret
deteriorate	worsen, decline
truncate	shorten, foreshorten
haphazard	helter-skelter, random
provincial	insular
shackle	stifle
cumbersome	unwieldy
encomium	tribute
speculate	conjecture
vexation	chagrin
disdain	opprobrium, contempt
caterwaul	shriek
contemplate	ponder
dogmatic	doctrinaire, rigid
alleviate	mitigate
unwieldy	cumbersome

profess	proclaim
diffuse	disperse, spread; wordy
inhibit	hinder, bridle, suppress
censure	reprehend
peripatetic	itinerant
dwindle	contract
dishearten	depress, dismay
emulate	imitate
emblematic	totemic
indict	excoriate
opprobrium	vitriol, disdain
expedite	facilitate, accelerate
captivate	enamored
implacable	unyielding, inexorable
arduous	taxing, laborious
conciliatory	placatory
vindicate	defense, exculpate, exonerate
clandestine	covert, surreptitious
equivocal	ambiguous
conjecture	speculate; uncertain
tractable	compliant
warble	croon
knotty	complicated
dichotomy	contradictory
invigorate	refreshing

truculent	bellicose, combative, aggressive, pugnacious
insouciance	nonchalance
devastate	ruinous
keen	eager
flagrant	egregious
confine	limit, circumscribe
venerate	respect
upheaval	convulsion
unyielding	implacable
mendacious	prevarication, disingenuous
fertile	bountiful
decadent	disreputable
indispensable	essential, crucial
covert	clandestine
discern	detect, discover
orientation	bias
riddle	enigma, puzzle, conundrum
jejune	vapid
indifferent	apathy
lethargic	somnolent, indolent
fungible	interchangeable
conform	square with
acrimony	bitterness, rancor
ambiguous	equivocal
allure	charm

parsimony	stingy, illiberal
cunning	craft
highlight	accentuate
eclipse	outdo
impulsive	capricious, hasty
exculpate	vindicate
obfuscate	obscure, mystify
disperse	dissipate
exaggerate	overrate
inclusive	generic
diatribe	rant
promulgate	disseminate
bolster	buttress, prop up
nuance	subtlety
futile	fruitless, pointlessness, vain
unassuming	modest, humble
amicable	agreeable
unfounded	groundless, unwarranted, baseless
plastic	malleable
authoritative	definitive, cogent
placate	appease, conciliatory
disinterested	fair, impartial
lionize	eulogize
preachy	sanctimonious
spontaneous	intuitive

comprehensive	sweeping, generic, inclusive, exhaustive, thorough
sequential	successively
canned	formulaic
feign	false
daunting	formidable, sensational, forbidding
opulent	affluent
pervasive	rife
offset	compensate
omnipresent	ubiquitous, universal
dilatory	laggard
generic	inclusive
sensational	daunting, lurid
convoluted	intricate, tortuous
widespread	extensive, prevalent
compliant	tractable
trifling	minimal
tantamount to	synonymous with
espouse	advocate, defend, champion
fractious	skittish
figurative	symbolic
impeccable	flawless
stifle	shackle, smother
pragmatic	realistic
didactic	preachy
archaic	antediluvian, outdated

ubiquitous	omnipresent, universal
predilection	proclivity, preference
diminutive	minuscule
illustrious	distinguished, prominent
trivial	inconsequential, immaterial
sketchy	superficial, undeveloped; rudimentary
dovish	pacific
presage	portend
abstemious	austere, moderate
versatile	fickle, volatile, flighty, erratic, capricious, versatile
vacillate	fluctuate; irresolution
devious	indirect
astute	shrewd
consensus	accord
salient	prominent, obtrusive, conspicuous, visible
camaraderie	solidarity
cordial	easygoing, affable; conviviality
tribute	encomium
lambaste	denounce
undercut	subvert, impair, undermine
paradigm	model
robust	strong
betoken	signify
conceal	veil, hide

itinerant	peripatetic
sober	level-headed
affirmative	positive
emendation	revision
retrenchment	curtailment
commensurate	proportionate
long-winded	verbose, prolix
forbidding	daunting
diligent	industrious
engaging	winning
evanescent	momentary
rudimentary	elementary, sketchy, embryonic
circumscribe	confine, limit
elude	puzzle
detriment	deleterious
quixotic	idealistic
mockery	derision
numinous	occult
anomalous	aberrant
frank	forthright, candor
chicanery	subterfuge
verifiable	testable
scarce	deficient
lavish	sumptuous
sanguine	optimistic
waver	oscillate

engender	yield, inaugurate, induce
elusive	cryptic, evasive, slippery
ponder	contemplate
proliferate	abound
paucity	vacuousness, dearth
impertinent	presumptuous
momentary	evanescent, fleeting
acute	incisive; severe
monotonous	repetitive
manifest	obvious, self-evident; reveal
shriek	caterwaul
ephemeral	short-lived, transitory
erudite	learned
intriguing	fascinating
magnanimous	generous, benevolent
untether	divorce
formulaic	canned
stratify	hierarchical
exceptional	preternatural
palatable	appetizing
esoteric	arcane, recondite, abstruse
befuddle	perplex
deliberate	calculation
hamstring	impair
hinder	inhibit, block
formidable	daunting

compassionate	warmhearted
ignorant	unfamiliarity
loquacious	garrulous
marginal	peripheral, fringe
callous	heartless
discount	undervalue
thwart	frustrate
raillery	banter
exasperate	irascibility
enigmatic	perplexing, puzzle, riddle, conundrum
enervate	debilitate
extinguish	douse
excoriate	crab, indict
immutable	determinate
secretive	furtive
blatant	conspicuous
flamboyant	showy
lucid	clarity
opaque	inaccessible
divisive	controversial
transcend	overcome
resonate	ring true
impetuous	precipitate
disparate	heterogeneous, dissimilar; variant, diverse
respite	lull, relief, break

rankle	gall
acquiesce	accession
remedy	recipe
purposeful	designed
malleable	plastic
barbarity	cruelty, crudity
sanctimonious	preachy, didactic
inexorable	implacable
deference	respectful
lugubrious	gloomy
denounce	lambaste
parochial	provincial
primitive	ancient, rudimentary
encyclopedic	exhaustive
nondescript	unexceptional
adverse	unfavorable
dubious	suspect
serendipitous	fortuitous
mercurial	volatile, inconstant
fortuitous	accidental, serendipitous
luxuriant	rampant
recoil	shrink
fluctuate	vacillate; vary
contentious	controversial, fraught, polemical
patchwork	hodgepodge, welter
palpable	perceptible ,material

effusive	emotional, lyrical
sluggish	listless
ornamental	decorative
panacea	cure-all
inflammatory	provocative
ill-advised	misguided
malfeasance	fraudulence
egregious	flagrant
counterfeit	misrepresent
volatile	fickle, versatile, volatile, flighty, erratic, capricious
conundrum	enigma, puzzle, riddle
gratify	please,
deflate	soothe
animate	rouse, inspire, galvanize
contemporary	topical
banal	stale
paltry	insufficient, meager
miserly	stingy, parsimonious
renowned	celebrated
exhaustive	encyclopedic
polemical	contentious
unimpeachable	blameless
tortuous	convoluted
flighty	fickle, versatile, volatile, erratic, capricious

gall	rankle
compelling	interesting
fraudulent	malfeasance
perilous	precarious, dangerous
concede	acknowledge
placid	gentle
erratic	fickle, versatile, volatile, flighty, capricious
ingenious	clever
renaissance	revival
endorse	sanction, commend, authorize, support
harbinger	herald
illuminate	clarify
fickle	versatile, volatile, flighty, erratic, capricious
gloomy	lugubrious, cheerless
innate	inborn
tedious	boring; dreary
irascible	exasperation
impair	subvert, undercut, undermine, compromise, vitiate
prevalent	extensive, widespread
deprecate	detract
portend	predict, presage
proclaim	profess
overshadow	outlast; obscure

somnolent	lethargic
onerous	burdensome
comity	civility
douse	extinguish,
arbitrary	capricious
discretion	judicious
quiescent	calm
evasive	elusive, equivocal
innocuous	harmless, benign, inoffensive
arcane	esoteric; recondite; abstruse
unmistakable	decisive
antecedent	precursor
relish	delight
trepidation	apprehension
universal	omnipresent, ubiquitous
dampen	deaden
predate	antedate, precede
hypocrisy	insincerity
mitigate	abate; ameliorate; temper
wane	ebb, decline
reflective	pensive
recant	repudiate
mercenary	exploitative
negligible	insignificant, inconsequential, trifling
apathetic	passivity
blemish	defect

inertia	inactive
intelligible	readable
untenable	baseless
laconic	terse, curt, taciturn
paragon	model
outmoded	obsolete, fusty, unfashionable
fleeting	momentary
galvanize	animate, rouse
interchangeable	fungible
exiguous	scanty
valorize	exalt
meticulous	painstaking, exactitude, thorough, exacting
satire	mockery
obviate	displace; avert, preclude
audacious	brazen
antediluvian	archaic
detract	deprecate
chagrin	vexation
mordant	acerbic
pugnacious	belligerent, truculent
exacerbate	aggravate
furtive	secretive
archetypal	classic
adversarial	antagonistic
premature	precocious

jeopardize	endanger
conjure	imagine
enormous	magnitude
defy	disregard, flout
admonish	scolding
preclude	prevent, rule out
forswear	eschew
solidarity	camaraderie
conspicuous	prominent, salient, obtrusive, marked, noticeable, remarkable, noteworthy
disinformation	mendacity,
inexpressible	ineffable, unutterable
plethora	glut, surfeit
disregard	contempt, defy
antagonistic	adversarial, inimical
commonplace	pervasive
meager	insufficient, paltry
avaricious	rapacious
prefigure	anticipate
animus	hostility
justification	rationale
dearth	paucity, vacuousness
calumny	defamatory
pertinent	relevant
precocious	maturity
repudiate	recant

quirky	unconventional
proponent	defender, champion
conscientious	exacting
rapacious	avaricious
provisional	conditional
circumspect	prudent, chary, cautious
majestic	august
estrange	unlinked, disaffect
circuitous	indirect
propitious	auspicious
nullify	disprove
facilitate	speed up, expedite
appease	placate
deleterious	detrimental, devastating
rehabilitate	restore
bypass	circumvent, skirt
scathing	acerbic, sarcastic
block	hinder
profligate	extravagant, prodigal
nimble	dexterous, skillful, adroit
heterogeneous	disparate, dissimilar
verisimilitude	realism
sycophantic	obsequious, adulator
circumvent	bypass, skirt, sidestep
rigid	dogmatic
plaintive	elegiac

convulsion	upheaval
idiosyncrasy	distinct, atypical
pecuniary	economic
rancor	acrimony
pompous	bombastic
demarcate	line
adulation	sycophant
timely	opportune
obsequious	sycophantic
terse	curt, taciturn, laconic, succinct
abate	mitigate
flatter	fawn
accentuate	highlight
augment	extend, enhance
contrite	penitent, remorse
inimical	antagonistic, deleterious
hallow	respect
unexampled	novel
jubilation	enthusiasm
nonchalant	insouciant
prodigal	profligate, extravagant
diverse	varied, divergent
protean	versatile
pillory	vilify
conceive	imaginable
dismissive	ignorant

discrepancy	incongruity
acerbic	mordant, caustic, cutting, scathing
resurgence	recrudescent
analogous	comparable
castigate	chastise
static	invariable
forerunner	precursor
objective	fair
prophetic	prescient
condone	excuse
acumen	shrewdness
revere	venerate
belligerent	pugnacious
taciturn	terse, curt, laconic
penitential	contrite
eliminate	put to rest
predicament	dilemma, quandary
precarious	perilous
unrelenting	persistent
disseminate	transmit
banish	expel, oust
skittish	restive, fractious
tranquil	peaceful
decorous	seemly
disparage	slight
hackneyed	unoriginal

bucolic	pastoral
pastoral	bucolic
petty	small-minded
painstaking	meticulous
eminent	famous
safeguard	preserving
recondite	esoteric; arcane; abstruse
cure-all	panacea
scorn	deride
obsolete	outmoded, fusty
quotidian	workaday
veracious	truth
voracious	insatiable; prodigious
provocative	inflammatory, controversial; stimulating
impecunious	indigent
assiduous	industrious
abstruse	esoteric; arcane; recondite
render	reproduce, regurgitate
homogeneous	uniform, unvaried; resemblance
immense	colossal
kindred	affiliated
affiliate	kindred
refuge	oasis
mortify	embarrass
heterodox	iconoclastic
doctrinaire	dogmatic

sporadic	fitful; scanty
debacle	fiasco
boon	benefit
sullen	surly, grumpy
prudent	circumspect; provident
laborious	arduous
divert	entertain
obdurate	intransigence, fortitude
brandish	boast
erroneous	inaccurate
feasible	practicable
schism	factiousness
notorious	infamous
benign	innocuous, anodyne
abridge	synoptic
lurid	sensational
copious	abundant
negligent	lax, careless
supersede	preempt
relinquish	cede, abandon
fabricate	forge
bridle	inhibit
ecstatic	euphoric
euphoria	ecstasy
disgruntle	crestfallen
humdrum	dull

forge	fabricate
garrulous	loquacious
pristine	undisturbed
apposite	fitting, germane
germane	relevant, apposite
fitful	sporadic
imperturbable	unflappable
exigent	pressing
erstwhile	onetime
onetime	erstwhile
timorous	diffident
narcissism	self-flattery
forestall	avert, prevent
indebted	beholden
contemptuous	disdainful
nascent	budding, unformed
eloquent	rhetoric
adroit	dexterous; nimble; skillful; deft, acumen
bountiful	fertile
impolitic	tactless
fringe	marginal, peripheral
supplicate	entreat, solicit
entreaty	supplication
insipid	bland
nebulous	vague
aberrant	anomalous

requisite	essential
strenuous	vigorous
deviate	mislead
prodigious	preternatural
ailment	illness
cavalier	capricious
deflect	shrug off
amass	glean
somber	solemn
profound	trenchant
oscillate	waver
hiatus	break
vertiginous	dizzying
steadfast	unfaltering
abiding	stable
crestfallen	disgruntle
resemble	homogeneity
mirth	jovial
jovial	mirthful
cajole	coax
proscribe	forbid, enjoin
sumptuous	lavish
abet	instigate
anodyne	benign
credulous	trusting
burgeon	expansion, flourish

snub	slight
trenchant	profound, incisive
instigate	abet
fusty	obsolete, outmoded
boisterous	uproarious
ancillary	supplementary
hasty	impulsive, rapid
budding	nascent
rescind	abrogate
subterfuge	chicanery
surfeit	glut, plethora
transitory	ephemeral, evanescent
prolix	verbose, long-winded
chastise	castigate
malodor	noisome
senescence	decrepitude
decrepitude	senescence
commiserate	sympathize
expostulate	remonstrate
verbose	prolix, long-winded
enamor	favor, captivated, hooked on
prophylactic	preventive
pilfer	appropriation
constrict	constrain
imbibe	quaff
quaff	imbibe

crumble	disintegrate
disintegrate	crumble
brook	tolerate
muddle	confuse
unerring	settled
provenance	origin
inscrutable	uninformative, impenetrable, abstruse
genial	friendliness
reluctant	loath; unwillingly
supple	flexible
contravene	violate
ungainly	awkward
ludicrous	risible
dispatch	celerity
handicap	hindrance
chimera	illusion
ominous	inauspicious
limpid	pellucid
forsake	neglect
exonerate	absolve
annihilate	destroy
surmise	infer
rapprochement	reconciliation
exert	wield
wield	exert
guzzle	swill

kinfolk	relative
divergent	incongruous, disparate
vestige	relic
profusion	wealth
forebode	concern
calamity	disaster, catastrophic
beget	create
reprehensible	deplorable
divest	strip
wondrous	amazing
recalcitrant	headstrong
succinct	concision
recrudescent	resurgent
frugal	thrift
unseemly	indecorous
preternatural	prodigious
expurgate	censor
meld	combine
concise	brief
oracle	prophetic
quandary	dilemma, predicament
succumb	yield
auspicious	favorable
essential	indispensable
benevolent	magnanimous, altruistic
insatiable	quenchless

precede	predate, antedate
temper	moderate; mitigate; neutralize
superficial	shallow
moderate	temper
vagary	caprice, whim
prominent	salient
flair	virtuosity
eviscerate	gut
belittle	vilify
harness	utilize, exploit
spurious	implausible
counterbalance	offset
covet	envy
cursory	casual, perfunctory
sleazy	sordid
capitulate	submit
fallow	sterile
unruly	insubordinate, intractable, obstreperous
synoptic	abridged
conviction	certainty
antiquated	old-fashioned, outdated
wayward	errant; unpredictable
nonsensical	illogical
millstone	encumbrance
accolade	laurel
laurel	accolade

intimidate	scary
expunge	erase
altercate	quarrel
gregarious	social
congruent	consistent
introspect	self-analysis
elate	delight
avert	forestall
ebb	declining, waning
yen	craving, longing
curt	terse, taciturn, laconic
snag	hitch
glut	plethora, surfeit
tout	peddle
choke	strangle, suffocate
aver	assert
rant	diatribe
spur	foster
scant	limited
tonic	restorative
flout	disregard, defy
shun	eschew
hone	enhance
exalt	valorize
belie	contradict
vapid	jejune

hitch	snag
mimic	camouflage, replicate
gauge	reckon
deter	constrain
croon	warble
bland	insipid
surly	sullen
plod	slog
loath	reluctant, disinclined
chic	elegant
oust	expel, banish
expel	oust, banish
adept	proficient
guile	deviousness
decay	deterioration
hubris	arrogant
hew	conform
tilt	list
slur	aspersion
sidestep	circumvent
romanticize	idealized
wanting	flawed
discerning	perceptive, insightful
rife	pervasive
enjoin	proscribe
glean	obtain

undue	excessive
qualm	misgiving
bedrock	foundation
misgiving	trepidation, qualm
heartfelt	sincere
groundless	unwarranted
retiring	self-effacing
taxing	arduous
pressing	exigent, critical
exacting	proscriptive, rigorous; demanding
composed	unperturbed, collected, coolheaded
incisive	acuity, trenchant
musty	stale
canny	shrewd
halfhearted	tepid, lukewarm
unearth	extract
level-headed	sober
sententious	didactic, homiletic, preachy
unrest	anxiety
deadlock	impasse
expendable	superfluous
porous	permeable
stem	check
check	stem
novel	original, unexampled, unprecedented
compromise	concession; impair

pedestrian	uninspired, mundane, ordinary, prosaic
champion	defender, proponent, advocate; defend, espouse
coin	neologism
appropriate	borrow
pacific	dovish
trammel	restrain
obscure	unremarkable
yield	succumb; engender, output
skirt	bypass, circumvent
dense	concentrated; witless
content	gratification
sanction	endorse
perennial	long-standing
confound	perplex, obscure, flummox
abandon	desert; relinquish
experimental	innovative
economy	brevity
listless	sluggish
anticipate	foresee
hail	acclaim
anonymous	obscure
misuse	abuse
abstraction	generality; divorce
substantial	concrete, solid
counterpart	parallel, parallel

enterprise	diligence
cupidity	avarice
square	conform
guesswork	conjecture
aside	digression
tyro	neophyte
neophyte	tyro, novice
maverick	nonconformist
polymath	encyclopedic
extremist	zealot
layperson	nonspecialist
cronyism	nepotism
nepotism	cronyism
inappropriate	unacceptable
indiscernible	imperceptible
apogee	acme
acme	apogee
precursor	forerunner
unfaltering	steadfast
cautious	guarded

索 引

forestall / 147

foretell / 100

forge / 143

forgo / 64

formidable / 55

formulaic / 53

forsake / 184

forswear / 95

forthcoming / 106

forthwith / 237

fortuitous / 68

founder / 253

fractious / 34

frank / 47

fraudulent / 75

free-for-all / 44

fringe / 149

frivolous / 124

frown / 260

frugal / 187

fuel / 268

fulminate / 12

function / 249

fungible / 22

furtive / 93

fury / 194

fusty / 170

futile / 27

gadfly / 63

gaiety / 213

gainsay / 244

gall / 75

galvanize / 88

gambit / 53

garner / 151

garrulous / 143

gauge / 227

gawky / 139

generic / 32

genial / 183

genteel / 193

germane / 144

gigantic / 169

girth / 235

glamorous / 138

gleam / 194

glean / 236

glib / 220

glisten / 236

gloat / 228

gloomy / 78

glorify / 98

glum / 228

glut / 219

goad / 174

gore / 209

gossamer / 179

gourmand / 276

gracious / 142

grand / 268

grandiose / 8

grandstand / 234

grant / 141

grapple / 154

gratify / 72

grave / 253

gravitate / 167

gregarious / 213

gridlock / 234

grip / 227

grouchy / 97

groundless / 239

grudge / 6

guesswork / 267

guild / 231

guile / 229

guru / 274

gut / 110

guzzle / 185

habitable / 70

hackneyed / 128

hagiography / 118

hail / 264

halcyon / 114

half-formulated / 67

halfhearted / 243

hallmark / 188

hallow / 112

hallucinogen / 215

halt / 195

hamper / 66

hamstring / 54

handicap / 184

hand-wringing / 142

haphazard / 8

harbingern / 77

hard-boiled / 235

hardliner / 271

hard-nosed / 129

hardy / 245

harness / 204

harrow / 40

harry / 262

has-been / 276

hasty / 173

haughty / 143

hazardous / 47

heartfelt / 239

heartrending / 240

hectic / 167

hedge / 259

GRE 高频真词表 便携版

siphon / 164

sketchy / 36

skew / 121

skim / 231

skirt / 259

skittish / 127

skullduggery / 4

slapdash / 240

sleazy / 206

sleek / 6

slender / 151

slight / 267

slinky / 210

slippery / 43

slipshod / 240

sloth / 230

sluggish / 70

slump / 53

slur / 231

smother / 235

snag / 219

snappish / 198

snapshot / 110

snare / 147

snob / 223

snobbish / 41

snub / 169

sober / 41

soft-pedal / 30

solace / 214

solicitous / 22

solidarity / 95

solitary / 15

solitude / 19

somber / 159

somnolent / 81

sonorous / 20

soothsayer / 275

sophist / 270

sophisticated / 116

soporific / 126

sound / 249

spacious / 154

sparkling / 68

spartan / 173

spearhead / 272

specific / 91

specious / 3

speculate / 9

spell / 255

spendthrift / 272

spew / 189

spike / 226

spiteful / 235

splendor / 153

spontaneous / 29

sporadic / 135

spunk / 231

spur / 221

spurious / 204

squander / 213

square / 267

stagger / 202

stagnate / 54

stale / 28

stalemate / 198

stalwart / 35

stanch / 137

standstill / 247

staple / 130

static / 121

staunch / 280

steadfast / 165

stem / 252

sterling / 12

stickler / 274

stifle / 34

stigma / 58

still / 252

stilted / 76

stipulate / 195

stoic / 222

stomach / 250

stonewall / 238

straddle / 279

straggle / 121

stratify / 53

streamline / 234

strenuous / 154

strident / 181

stringent / 13

studied / 248

stunning / 279

stupefaction / 280

stymie / 175

subdue / 156

subject / 256

sublime / 177

subsequent / 197

subservient / 170

subsidize / 46

subsist / 160

substantial / 266

substantiate / 146

subterfuge / 174

subtext / 246

subtle / 189

succinct / 186

succumb / 194

suffice / 38

suffrage / 160

NEW GRE

ETS TOFEL